Turn Right
at the Fountain

**Fifty-three Walking Tours Through
Europe's Most Enchanting Cities**

George W. Oakes

with new and additional research material by
Alexandra Chapman

Turn Right at the Fountain

Fifth Edition

An Owl Book

Henry Holt and Company
New York

Henry Holt and Company, Inc.
Publishers since 1866
115 West 18th Street
New York, New York 10011

Henry Holt® is a registered trademark
of Henry Holt and Company, Inc.

Library of Congress Cataloging-in-Publication Data
Oakes, George W., 1909–1965.
    Turn right at the fountain: fifty-three walking tours through Europe's most
  enchanting cities / George W. Oakes; with new and additional research material by
  Alexandra Chapman—Rev. ed.
        p.   cm.
    Originally published: Holt, Rinehart and Winston, 1961.
    1. Europe—Tours.   2. Cities and towns—Europe—Tours.
  3. Walking—Europe—Guidebooks.   I. Title.
  D909.02   1996   95-11017
  914.04'55–dc20   CIP

ISBN 0-8050-2356-9

Henry Holt books are available for special promotions
and premiums. For details contact: Director, Special Markets.

First published in hardcover in 1961 by Holt, Rinehart and Winston.

Fifth Owl Book Edition—1996

DESIGNED BY BETTY LEW

Printed in the United States of America
All first editions are printed on acid-free paper. ∞

10   9   8   7   6   5   4   3   2   1

To Joanna, Diana, and James, who walked with me.

—G.W.O.

ACKNOWLEDGMENTS

My warmest thanks to:
Jiřina Rodolphe, for her invaluable comments on Prague since the "Velvet Revolution"; Olga Szalay, for reading the Budapest chapter and correcting all my spelling errors with a smile; Emmanuelle Klein and Catherine Rouyer for their practical help and moral support; and above all, to Dr. Robert Cartier, a seasoned traveler of the heart, for everything.

—A.C.

Contents

INTRODUCTION
to the 1996 Edition

Thirty years ago, in the first edition of *Turn Right at the Fountain*, George Oakes encouraged travelers to explore European cities on foot because "by strolling you'll absorb much more of the special appeal of each city you visit."

This, the fifth edition, is a travel guide covering all the monuments, museums, and major sites, yet featuring little-known havens of tranquility that European cities have managed to preserve: the little garden behind the Baroque church, a surprising island in the middle of the Danube, an archeological treasure lovingly restored in a modern luxury hotel.

The walks are planned so that you will appreciate the highlights of each city in a leisurely fashion, stopping for a *café au lait* in a chic bistro or sipping a glass of wine on a terrace overlooking the city. You will attend concerts in a cool Roman cloister, have your portrait painted in Montmartre, wander into a flower-filled courtyard, and pause to enjoy the harmony of stone and nature.

The great art treasures of Europe are waiting for you in their new settings: the Orsay Museum in Paris, formerly a train station, magnificently displays Impressionist art; the ultramodern Queen Sofia Art Center in Madrid is one of Europe's major modern art museums; and the lesser-known Zoubov collection in Geneva offers splendid samples of eighteenth-century furniture and oriental art. Museums are being restored and enlarged to best display the works that are an integral part of Europe's cultural legacy.

History springs to life as you saunter through the Forum in Rome, visit Kensington Palace in London with its fine historical exhibits, or admire the gravestones in Prague's Jewish Cemetery, the oldest in Europe. There's history in the making waiting for you: visiting the House of Commons or the French National Assembly is an early peek at tomorrow's headlines!

Mostly, there's the magic. The romantic spirit of Prague's Malà Strana, the reflection of Notre Dame in the glistening Seine, and the bustling markets in Barcelona will enchant you, whether you are a first-time visitor to Europe or a seasoned traveler. Some cities, like Cambridge or Toledo, are literally a walk into the past, for they have been miraculously preserved.

Despite every effort to indicate up-to-date opening and closing hours for museums and monuments, these are occasionally changed and some buildings may be closed for restoration or renovation when you visit them. It's best to check with the concierge in your hotel for the most current information.

This edition includes a new city, Budapest, "the Paris of the Danube." A vital, charming example of Mittel-Europa at its best, Hungary's capital offers architectural riches, unusual museums, and a peaceful floral paradise, Marguerite's Island, where the melody of a Mozart symphony lingers in the rose-scented air.

The past and the present, the glorious art and the imaginative contemporary architecture, merge in these twenty-one European cities, inviting you to walk straight into the twenty-first century.

—A.C.
Paris, February 1995

FOREWORD
to the 1965 Edition

In the course of many years of European travel I have discovered a secret—the only way to get to know a city is by walking through it. Whether you have a few hours or more than a week, you will discover that by strolling you'll absorb much more of the special appeal of each city you visit. You will have a chance to explore the hidden byways and unusual places which give every city its own character. You can set your own pace, spend as much time as you like in the spots that interest you, and altogether enjoy yourself more.

Unless you walk you are bound to miss much. You have to go on foot to find out-of-the-way corners, the hidden courtyards or tiny squares that often are so close to a great art gallery, for example, yet which so many tourists fail to see. To dash from a monumental cathedral to a famous museum is often too exhausting and concentrated to make for pleasant sight-seeing. You will appreciate what you see much more if you travel in leisure and experience variety along the way.

Aimless strolling—just wandering wherever your fancy suggests—can be a delight. But if you wish to visit the main places of interest, it will take weeks or even months to get to know a European city this way. The stroller who would see all that is great and beautiful and interesting in a reasonable length of time must follow a carefully planned route.

With this in mind, I decided to share my secret and wrote a series of "walking tour" articles for the travel section of *The New York Times*. This book came about as a result of the popularity of that series, which was started in the *Times* Travel Section in the spring of 1961. The response was so great and so many readers suggested that this series should be expanded into a book that I decided to rewrite the articles, add new walks, and include more cities to make the present volume.

In order that the information be as up-to-date as possible, I spent three months in Europe in the summer of 1962 and two months during the autumn of 1963 going over these walks. One experience on this trip made me realize how useful many visitors had found the articles in the *Times*. In London, the proprietor of The Grenadier, a pub located off Hyde Park Corner that I included in one walk, told me that during the previous summer several hundred people had stopped in, carrying the newspaper article describing this walk.

The countries chosen are those which more tourists visit, and the cities are the ones that visitors primarily interested in European history, art, and culture will want to see. In my view they represent the best of Europe.

The routes suggested do not include every important church, museum, art gallery, and historic building that you will want to visit. What I have done is to select routes that lead you to places of historic and artistic interest in the course of a walk through the more fascinating and delightful sections of each city. It so happens that these strolls do pass most of the places you'd want to see anyway. By following these walks, you will get a good overall impression of what's considered most worthwhile and unusual in each city.

No specific time schedule is given for the completion of each stroll; that's a matter each reader or walker will want to decide for himself. The time you take depends on how long you want to linger at any one spot. When you feel you have done enough, stop and resume another time. The idea is to offer enjoyable walks that the average sightseer will find convenient to take in a morning or afternoon. Some will want to do more, some less. Your European trip will be more enjoyable if you plan your daily program as you feel inclined.

There is no particular order in which the walks should be done. Just select those that appeal to you. Every walk is accompanied by a map that clarifies the route you will follow.

Each walk begins at a well-known place—often in the center of the city. The concierge at your hotel will tell you the best way to get there. As many of the walks are not circular, you should inquire for return directions at the same time. Most cities have either subways or buses that run to or from a point not far from the start and finish of each route. The London and Paris maps show the underground or Metro stations near each route.

All of the cities described in this book are gradually changing— some more than others—to keep pace with the needs of the day. So, here and there, some places may be slightly different from what they were in the summer of 1962 and autumn of 1963.

If this book helps you either to anticipate the pleasure you will have in these fourteen cities or to enjoy their attractions more while you are there, it will have served its purpose.

—G.W.O.
New York, January 1965

PART ONE

Britain

1.
London

"The City"—West
The Temple to Guildhall

The City of London, consisting of one square mile, is the oldest and original part of the present great metropolis. Because of its great age, you should approach it gradually, and with an awareness of due respect. You will get a better feel for this ancient community—believed to have been founded by the Romans shortly after they invaded Britain in A.D. 43—if you start your walk at the City's western limits.

Although small in area (677 acres) the City teems during the working week with over 400,000 office workers, who pour into this commercial, financial, and legal hub of Britain from all parts of London and its suburbs.

If the City has lost a good deal of its former worldwide influence on trade and finance, it is still very much an international business center. True to its tradition, it continues to be governed by the Lord Mayor and the Corporation. The City is in many ways a distinct

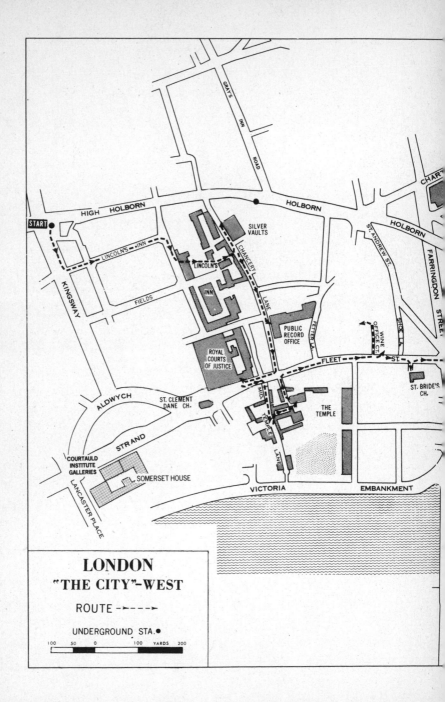

START

HIGH HOLBORN

HOLBORN

HOLBORN

GRAY'S INN ROAD

CHAR

ST. ANDREW ST.

FARRINGDON STREET

LINCOLNS — INN

SILVER VAULTS

LINCOLN'S

INN

CHANCERY LANE

KINGSWAY

FIELDS

PUBLIC
RECORD
OFFICE

FETTER LA.

SHOE LA.

WINE
OFFICE C.T.

ROYAL
COURTS
OF JUSTICE

FLEET

ST.

ST. BRIDE'S
CH.

ALDWYCH

ST. CLEMENT
DANE CH.

MIDL.

THE
TEMPLE

STRAND

INNER TEMPLE
LANE

COURTAULD
INSTITUTE
GALLERIES

SOMERSET HOUSE

LANCASTER PLACE

VICTORIA

EMBANKMENT

LONDON
"THE CITY"-WEST

ROUTE -----➤

UNDERGROUND STA. ●

100 50 0   100 YARDS 200

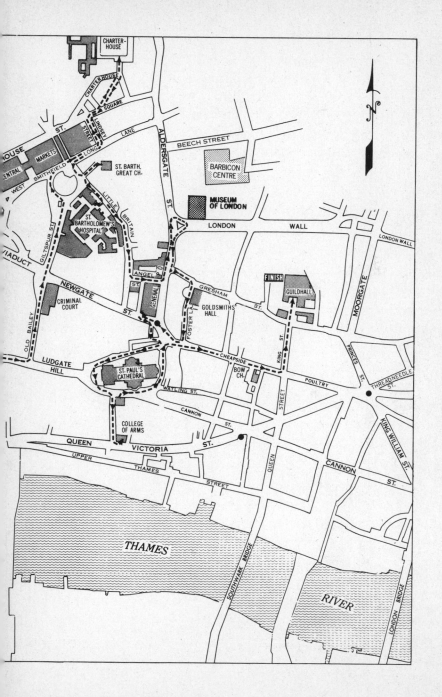

community, as you will observe during your stroll. Even its policemen wear a special badge to set them apart from ordinary "bobbies."

Begin your walk at **Lincoln's Inn Fields,** one of London's largest squares (a couple of blocks from Holborn Station on the Central and Piccadilly underground lines). Designed in 1618 by the great architect and landscape gardener, Inigo Jones, Lincoln's Inn Fields counts John Milton and Nell Gwyn among the famous historical figures who lived there. Today, most of the old houses are solicitors' offices. The attractive gardens and wide lawns under the lofty old plane trees, formerly frequented by office workers, have become a meeting place for the unemployed and the homeless.

On the north side of the square, at No. 13, is a little-known but intensely interesting house, the **Soane Museum** (open Tuesday–Saturday, 10:00–5:00, except April; lecture tour on Saturday at 2:30). Sir John Soane was the distinguished architect of the late eighteenth and early nineteenth century who designed the Bank of England. His house is unusual because he provided in his will that the building and its furniture, as well as his art collection, should remain forever exactly as they had been during his lifetime. It is fascinating to see how mirrors have been used to give the impression of greater space. Sir John also had an extraordinary method of hanging pictures on shutters—be sure to see the amusing Hogarth paintings, *The Rake's Progress* and *The Election.*

At the east end of the square stands Lincoln's Inn, one of the four **Inns of Court,** whose records date from 1424 (open Monday–Friday, 9:00–5:00). The Inns of Court—Lincoln's Inn, Gray's Inn, the Middle Temple, and the Inner Temple—dating from the reign of Edward I, make up a university of the law, exceeded only in age by the universities of Oxford and Cambridge, with which they have a centuries-old association. Go through the entrance into the delightful gardens with lawns as well manicured as putting greens, and ask at the old red-brick gatehouse for permission to see the fine Tudor Old Hall, built in 1492 and noted for its linenfold paneling and splendid roof. The vaulting under the Inigo Jones chapel nearby is most attractive.

Now return to the gatehouse and step through the archway into **Chancery Lane.** To the left, about fifty yards along on the opposite side of the street, are the fascinating **Silver Vaults,** which provide a unique experience for the tourist and shopper. Next to the Bank of England, the silver vaults and strong rooms in this safe-deposit building are considered the most secure in Britain. The entrance is on a street called Southampton Buildings, just to the right off Chancery Lane. You go down about thirty-five feet belowground to the building's subbasement, built in London blue rock under the **Holborn,** an ancient stream that ran from the village of Holborn to the Thames. Behind a three-ton steel door you will find thirty-five small shops along long corridors. Here you can browse for old silver, fine antiques, porcelain, and so forth. Londoners who are connoisseurs of old silver usually look here first for what they want. (Vaults are open Monday–Friday, 9:00–5:00.)

When you leave the silver vaults and return to Chancery Lane, turn left. A few hundred yards farther, beyond Lincoln's Inn, on the left side of the street you will come to the **Public Record Office** (open Monday–Friday, 1:00–5:00), the repository of Britain's historic documents. Among the outstanding exhibits here are two volumes of William the Conqueror's *Domesday Book,* an original copy of the Magna Carta, a letter from George Washington to his "great and good friend" George III (1795), and Nelson's logbook kept during the Battle of Trafalgar. If you enjoy looking at historic documents, you will find the Public Record Office a mine of information about Britain from its earliest days to the present.

At the end of Chancery Lane, turn right into Fleet Street, which used to be the heart of London's newspaper world. For economic reasons, London's daily papers have gone into "exile" to Canary Wharf, part of the Docklands urban renewal project. In a moment you will pass **Temple Bar,** which, since the twelfth century, has marked the western boundary of the City. Formerly, tolls were collected from all those passing the Bar.

Today, before entering the City, the Sovereign still goes through the formality of requesting permission to do so from the Lord Mayor, who signifies his approval by surrendering the City sword, point downward. When the sword is returned, the Lord Mayor bears it before Her Majesty as a symbol that he will protect her during her visit.

A few steps farther on are the **Law Courts** or, properly speaking, the Royal Courts of Justice. You can attend court to see the wigged judges and barristers in session Monday to Friday, 10:30 to 1:00 and 2:00 to 4:00.

Fleet Street, named for the stream that formerly flowed alongside (the water is now carried in a sewer), was at one time a Roman road. The spired church to the west, in the middle of the Strand, is Sir Christopher Wren's beautiful **St. Clement Danes.** Almost completely destroyed by bombing during World War II, the building has been extraordinarily well restored and is now the headquarters church of the RAF. In the section designated as a memorial to all airmen who lost their lives in the war, there is a special shrine consecrated to the U.S. Air Force. Take the Strand to the corner of Lancaster Place and to your right is Somerset House, built by William Chambers in the eighteenth century. On the first floor are the Courtauld Institute Galleries, housing an exceptional collection of Impressionist and Post-Impressionist art. (Open weekdays, 10:00–6:00; Sundays, 2:00–6:00; closed holidays.)

Return to the other side of Fleet Street and stop in for coffee and a bun at the tiny 250-year-old shop of **Twining Bros.,** the tea merchants. Inside, the walls are covered with prints of old London.

A few yards farther on is the Wren gatehouse to the **Middle Temple.** The Middle and Inner Temples are so named because they occupy property that once belonged to the order of Knights Templars, founded in 1118, during the Crusades. The Templars were a religious military order, dedicated to assisting pilgrims to the Holy Land. In Jerusalem, they made their headquarters near the church on the site of Solomon's Temple, from which they derived their name.

It is not clear just when during the Middle Ages the lawyers occupied the Temple as tenants of the Knights, but it was prior to 1381, the year Wat Tyler led his unsuccessful revolt against serfdom.

Walk under the archway into ancient **Middle Temple Lane.** The overhanging seventeenth-century building above the footway is one of the few surviving examples of London housing before the Great Fire of 1666. Just down the sloping lane on the right is **Middle Temple Hall,** one of England's magnificent Elizabethan halls, built about 1570 (open Monday–Friday, 10:00–12:00 and 3:00–4:30). Severely bombed during World War II, it has been remarkably restored with much of its original material. You will marvel at the famous double-hammerbeam, black-oak roof. The 29-foot-long table in the hall was made from a single oak tree from Windsor Forest. The tree was a gift of Queen Elizabeth I and was floated down the Thames. Below the dais is the "cupboard," a serving table made from timber of the *Golden Hind* and given to the inn by Sir Francis Drake, a member of the Templars. *Twelfth Night* was staged here in 1601 by the theatrical company in which Shakespeare was a partner. It is interesting to recall that five members of the Middle Temple signed the Declaration of Independence.

In the Temple buildings hereabout lived Dr. Johnson, Charles Lamb, Oliver Goldsmith, Sir William Blackstone, and William Makepeace Thackeray. Just below Middle Temple Hall are the delightful gardens where, during term time, barristers often stroll, wearing their traditional gowns. It was in these gardens, it is said, that the red and white roses which gave their names to the Wars of the Roses were plucked. As you wander along these old walks and through the ancient arches, you will sense the historic atmosphere of the Temple. There, during hundreds of years, the English legal system developed.

Go through the archway from Middle Temple Lane into the Inner Temple's Pump Court. On your right is **Inner Temple Hall,** recently rebuilt in Georgian style, and just beyond, toward the river, is Inner Temple Gardens.

Turn left to visit **Temple Church,** the finest of only four round churches that remain in England. It dates from the twelfth century and was built in the style of the Holy Sepulcher in Jerusalem (open daily, except Monday and Thursday, 10:00–1:00 and 2:00–5:00). Oliver Goldsmith is buried in the adjacent cemetery. Go through the archway from Temple Church to **King's Bench Walk** with its fine seventeenth-century houses.

Turn into Inner Temple Lane and you will come to Fleet Street through a gate below a timbered building with large bow windows. Look sharply for the entrance to No. 17 so you can visit **Prince Henry's Room.** This is an interesting example of a seventeenth-century, timber-constructed city house. The large paneled room on the first floor, with its Jacobean plastered ceiling, gives you a good idea of the ornate interior decoration of the period (open daily, 1:45–5:00.

As you return to Fleet Street, cross over at Fetter Lane and turn right a few yards to No. 145, the entrance to the well-known restaurant, **Ye Olde Cheshire Cheese,** established in 1667. It is pleasant to have lunch in this small old tavern with sawdust on the floor, which is believed to have been a favorite of Dr. Samuel Johnson's (a reservation is advisable). It still has a great deal of atmosphere, although frequented largely by tourists. Just down Wine Office Court (a few yards from the tavern) is **Dr. Johnson's house,** built in the seventeenth century, at 17 Gough Square, where you can visit the old garret in which he compiled his famous dictionary. Several mementos of the great lexicographer are on view, including two first editions of the dictionary, published in 1755. (The house is open daily, 11:00–5:30, except from October through April when it closes at 5:00.)

Cross Fleet Street again and just beyond Salisbury Court is the entrance to **St. Bride's Church,** one of Sir Christopher Wren's famous City churches, largely rebuilt after World War II. Fortunately, the lovely steeple, the City's tallest, survived the bombing attacks.

In a moment you will be at busy Ludgate Circus. Cross the circus, and a little farther along on Ludgate Hill, turn left and enter **Old Bailey.** Before you, on the right, you will find the noted Old Bailey Criminal Court, built on the site of **Newgate Gaol,** which was used as a prison as early as the eleventh century. Here, among countless others, William Penn and Daniel Defoe were jailed. You can attend sessions in the Public Gallery (open Monday–Friday, 10:00–1:00 and 2:00–4:00).

Cross Newgate Street and walk along Giltspur Street past "Bart's" (**St. Bartholomew's Hospital,** London's oldest) to West Smithfield, once the scene of medieval tournaments and now known for the adjacent **Smithfield Central Markets,** which cover ten acres and deal mainly in dressed meat, poultry, and dairy produce. It is the largest market of its kind in the world, where 350,000 tons of foodstuffs are sold yearly. The best time to visit the busy markets is between 5:00 and 9:00 A.M., so perhaps you will want to return on another occasion. Right now may be the moment to explore some of the colorful market pubs hereabout.

At the eastern end of the market, turn left on Lindsey Street, and walk through Charterhouse Square to visit **Charterhouse,** originally a fourteenth-century priory but later, in 1611, a hospital accommodated eighty poor brethren and forty poor students. From this foundation grew the well-known public school of the same name, but the school was moved, almost a hundred years ago, to Surrey, and now the old brick and timbered buildings are the residence of only a few elderly bachelors and widowers. Ask the porter at the gate to show you the original monastery gates and the outlines of the monks' cells, as well as the Great Hall dating from the sixteenth century and the splendid Elizabethan Great Chamber above the library. (Open Wednesday at 2:15, May–July.)

Return to West Smithfield, and at the beginning of Little Britain you will find on the left the Norman **Church of St. Bartholomew the Great,** London's oldest parish church. It is well worth visiting as an interesting example of a London church erected before the Great Fire of 1666. Also, you will enjoy its charming, although tiny, cloisters and shaded churchyard with ancient tombstones. Benjamin Franklin worked as a printer in what is now the **Lady Chapel,** a site that has had a checkered history through the centuries, being first a chapel, then a private house, a printing works, a public house, a dance hall, a factory, and in the 1890s restored to its original state.

Now walk to the corner of Aldergate Street and the Roman Wall to the **Museum of London,** which houses Saxon and Roman antiquities (from the former Guildhall Museum) as well as relics documenting the history of the City of London. (Open Tuesday–Saturday, 10:00–6:00; Sunday, 12:00–6:00; closed Mondays and holidays.)

Continue on Aldergate Street and turn right on Beech Street to visit the **Barbican Centre** (entrance on Silk Street). A modern cultural center, it includes a concert hall—home of the London Philharmonic—two theaters, and art exhibits. (Open 9:00 A.M.–11:00 P.M., Monday–Saturday; 12:00–11:00 P.M., Sunday and holidays.

Retrace your steps and stroll down Little Britain and King Edward Street, and turn left at Angel Street, opposite London's main post office. Turn left again and walk a half-block to Gresham Street. Turn right, and a block farther along will bring you to Foster Lane and the **Goldsmiths' Hall.** You can see this palatial hall—one of the leading City livery companies, where lovely gold plate and antique silver are exhibited on special occasions—if you write in advance to the Clerk of the Goldsmiths' Company, Cheapside, London E.C. 2 (the hall is closed in August and September).

These City livery companies, of which eighty-one still exist, have a membership of about ten thousand. Their members, who include leading professional men and businessmen in the City, maintain the age-old traditions and customs of the companies. Originally medieval craft guilds, the livery companies became closely associated with the municipal affairs of the City. The liverymen of the companies nominate the candidate for Lord Mayor. Aside from their role in the governing of the City, the companies are concerned with charitable and philanthropic activities and are associated with thirty famous schools. Several are responsible for important technical training schools and colleges. For example, the Goldsmiths, one of the wealthiest and oldest (founded in 1327), established a school at London University. The company also still conducts the London Assay Office for hallmarking gold and silver plate.

Leaving Goldsmiths' Hall, walk down Foster Lane to Cheapside.

Cross the busy thoroughfare and enter the churchyard of Wren's masterpiece, **St. Paul's Cathedral,** the architectural and spiritual glory of the City. Stroll around the gardens on your way to the front of the cathedral and look up at the huge dome outlined against the sky. This is a peaceful oasis in the City, with flower beds and birds singing in the shrubbery. St. Paul's was built between 1675 and 1710 and is the largest cathedral in Britain. You will want to make a leisurely visit, either now or at another time, to see the cathedral proper, the crypt with the tombs of Nelson and Wellington, and, if you are energetic, the whispering gallery and the stone gallery, which commands a superb view of London. (Open daily, 9:00–4:30.)

At this point you should take a slight diversion to visit the **College of Arms,** the official headquarters for the determination of armorial bearings and pedigrees. It was chartered in 1555. As you leave St. Paul's, cross the main road and stop in at the information center of the City of London before entering Godliman Street. At the corner of Queen Victoria Street you will find an old red-brick building where the College of Arms, or Heralds' Office, is located.

Here is the office of the Earl Marshal, the chief ceremonial officer of the Kingdom and the head of the college. The other officials of the college are the three kings of arms, the six heralds, and the four pursuivants. These functionaries have important and colorful duties to perform at the time of the coronation of the British Sovereign or at the annual opening of Parliament. The kings of arms have the legal right to trace, establish, and record pedigrees. The college library and collection maintain the most complete heraldic and genealogical records in the world. Visitors may inquire at the college for heraldic data. For a fee, and on submission of proper documentary evidence that your family has been authorized to display arms, you can be granted your armorial bearings. (The college is open Monday–Friday, 10:00–4:00.)

Now retrace your steps to the information center. Ahead of you is a large new building, the extension of the Bank of England. Cross over to **Watling Street,** one of the main roads built by the Romans. You can either go through the bank building to see the sunken gardens or turn left on Bread Street to reach Cheapside. After a few yards you will pass Wren's famous **Bow Church.** Tradition has it that anyone born within the sound of Bow Bells is a "cockney," a true Londoner. The proverbial bells of Dick Whittington's time were destroyed in 1666. Their replacements were ruined during the bombing of the church in World War II, but new bells were installed in 1962 and are rung on various occasions.

Turning left at King Street, you will see before you the ancient and impressive **Guildhall,** the Hall of the Corporation of the City of London, dating from the early fifteenth century.

As you enter the Great Hall, the seat of government of the City, you will note its coat of arms over the Gothic porch, bearing the words *Domine dirige nos* ("Lord, direct us"). The hall is often the scene of presentations of "the freedom of the City of London" to distinguished citizens of Britain and foreign countries. Here, too, are held the annual Lord Mayor's banquets as well as state dinners. You will be fascinated by the shields and embroidered banners of the city livery companies, as well as by the wooden figures of Gog and Magog, the famed giants of English mythology who are traditionally associated with the Guildhall. The originals of these famous statues were destroyed in the 1940 air-raid fire, and later replaced. An impressive statue of Sir Winston Churchill is probably the best work of art in the Hall. During your tour of the Guildhall, be sure to use the radio-tour instrument, available without cost, to listen to a twenty-minute talk on the Guildhall. Both the Queen's and Churchill's voices can be heard in excerpts from their Guildhall speeches.

You should stop in at the **Guildhall Library,** which contains many instructive exhibits about the City and its famous residents, as well as over 140,000 books. (Open Monday–Friday, 9:30–5:00.)

As you wander about Guildhall, so intimately bound up with past centuries of old London, you will share the feeling of long tradition that is characteristic of the City and which lives to some degree in the hearts of all Englishmen.

"The City"—East
Guildhall to the Tower

If you have taken the first walk in the City, you will have ended up at the **Guildhall.** To resume your tour of the square mile of London's financial and business center from the Guildhall, you return to Cheapside, which leads into **Poultry** (named for the poultry dealers located there in medieval times). After you turn left into Poultry you pass the street named **Old Jewry,** where the Jews lived prior to their expulsion from England in 1290. In another block you will reach the heart of the City, the busy square where the Bank of England, the Royal Exchange, and the Mansion House are located.

On the other hand, you may prefer to start this walk in the City at the **Mansion House,** the official residence of the Lord Mayor. The easiest way to get there from London's West End is to come by underground (Bank Station).

At the corner of Poultry and Queen Victoria Street you will see the Corinthian portico of the eighteenth-century Mansion House to your right. This is the Lord Mayor's residence during his year of office—the last great town house in the City.

To view the interior of the Mansion House (it is open to the public Saturday mornings only), you should write to the Lord Mayor's private secretary well in advance. The principal rooms are the Egyptian Hall, where large banquets and receptions are held; the salon, which displays a Waterford glass chandelier with eight thousand pieces; and the Court of Justice. The Lord Mayor presides over this court, which administers justice in the southern part of the City. Below the courtroom there are prison cells.

The classic building within the angle formed by Cornhill and Threadneedle Street is the **Royal Exchange.** (Open Monday–Friday, 10:00–4:00; Saturday, 10:00–12:00.) Queen Elizabeth I ordered that the first building on this site be given its royal designation because it was the great meeting place for the city merchants. Part of the pavement from Sir Thomas Gresham's original building on this same site can be seen in the central court below the glass dome. The present structure dates from the mid-nineteenth century.

The Royal Exchange chimes are run at 9:00, 12:00, and 6:00, and they play English, Scottish, Welsh, Canadian, and Australian airs to add notes of gaiety to the somber businesslike surroundings.

As you stand on the steps of the Royal Exchange surveying the traffic jam of big red buses, taxis, and cars that converge here from seven main streets, you will see to your right the massive and imposing **Bank of England.** In the interests of security, a forbidding stone wall surrounds the bank's four acres. If you look carefully, you will notice in the pediment facing you the statue of Britannia, referred to as "the Old Lady of Threadneedle Street."

The Bank of England, now a national institution, was chartered in 1694. Its best-known function today is the issuance of all paper money in the United Kingdom. As the government's banker, it establishes the official interest or bank rate, manages the national debt, handles exchange controls, and guards in its vaults the nation's gold reserves. It has been said of it that "no bank has played so large or so distinguished a part, not merely in the fortunes of a great nation, but in the general financial activities of the world."

Following a custom dating from 1780 when rioters threatened

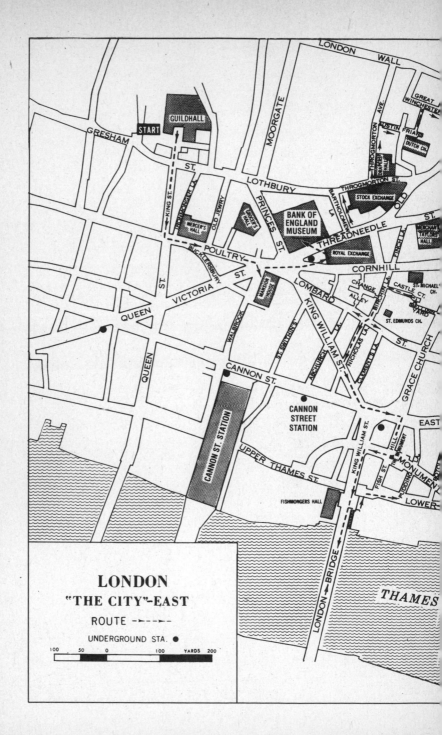

LONDON

"THE CITY"-EAST

ROUTE -->-->

UNDERGROUND STA. ●

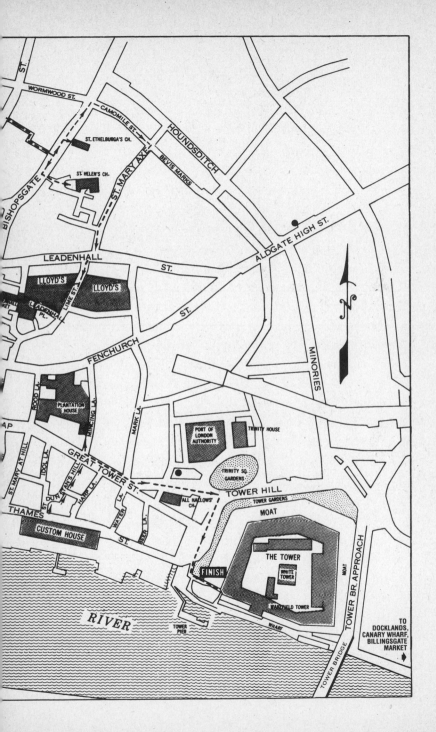

the Bank, each evening at 6:00 a detachment from the Brigade of Guards, consisting of one officer and sixteen rank and file, arrives to protect the famous edifice. You'll want to visit the **Bank of England Museum,** opened in 1988 and tracing the bank's colorful history, (Open Easter–September, Monday–Saturday, 10:00–6:00; Sunday, 2:00–6:00; October–Easter, Monday–Friday, 10:00–6:00.)

It's worth applying for admission to the entrance hall in advance. There the gatekeepers and bank messengers, dressed in red vests, pink tailcoats, long-tailed scarlet gowns, and tricorn hats after the fashion of the first governor's early-eighteenth-century gate porters, lend a historic air to the venerable institution. From the hall you have a glimpse of the charming courtyard with mulberry trees planted on its lawn.

Having set foot in the famous precincts of the bank, turn left along Threadneedle Street to the first cross street, Bartholomew Lane. Follow it a short block, and then make a right on Throgmorton Street and walk to No. 8, known as "The House," the entrance to the **London Stock Exchange.** Until 1801, the exchange operated in the Royal Exchange and in coffeehouses located in Change Alley and Threadneedle Street.

There is a special visitors' gallery where trading can be observed taking place in the large galleries Monday to Friday, between 9:30 and 3:30. Guides explain not only the intense activity of the 2,500 brokers on the huge floor below, but even their sartorial garb (some can still be seen wearing high silk hats). You can watch a special film explaining exactly how the Stock Exchange works. After watching the jobbers and brokers carrying out transactions by word of mouth, go downstairs to Throgmorton Street.

From here you wander around the byways of the City, crowded with black-coated workers. The hubbub in these tiny streets and alleys—many closed to motor traffic—gives the City its peculiar character and air of excitement. The buildings all around you are offices of banks, stock brokerages, insurance companies, accountant firms, and all those intimately involved in finance and commerce. Stop at any one of them and read the names inscribed on plaques at the entrance. You will get a feel for the City's international character by the number of foreign business houses listed on almost every building.

Opposite the Stock Exchange is Throgmorton Avenue. This takes you past **Drapers' Hall,** at No. 28, the home of the Draper's Company, the third-ranking livery company. Contact the City Information Centre for information on how to obtain permission to visit. (Located in St. Paul's cemetery, the center is open except in August on weekdays, 9:30–5:00; Saturday, 9:30–12:30; telephone, 606 30 30.) Turn right in Austin Friars to the modern **Dutch Church,** religious center of Dutch Protestants in London since 1550, except during the reign of Catholic Mary.

Opposite the church is Austin Friars passage, leading to Great Winchester Street. Turn right here and after a few yards you will be at Old Broad Street. The tall new stone building ahead is **Goodenough House,** home of Barclays Bank. Cross the street and to the right walk through Gresham House, which has a private lift right in the middle of the corridor that leads to Bishopsgate.

On the opposite side of this busy thoroughfare to the right, just beyond St. Helen's Place, you go through an archway to **St. Helen's Church,** one of the oldest in the City, dating from the early years of the thirteenth century (open daily, 10:00–4:00). The courtyard in front of the church, with trees and a tiny lawn, is a charming spot. St. Helen's Church is particularly interesting because it is one of the few City churches that escaped the Great Fire. It is often known as the "Westminster Abbey of the City" for its fine early English architecture and many ancient tombs of prominent city figures, like Sir Thomas Gresham, founder of the Royal Exchange.

Retrace your steps to Bishopsgate, turn right, and a hundred yards along on the right you will find the smallest church in the City, **St. Ethelburga's** (60 by 30 feet), founded about the beginning of the fifteenth century. Inside are three stained glass windows in memory of Henry Hudson, the discoverer of the Hudson River in New York.

Continue along Bishopsgate, turn right down Camomile Street, and right again into St. Mary Axe.

Stop in at No. 24, **Cayzer House.** There is a fascinating world map on the wall in the reception hall that shows the movements of all the ships operated by the Union Castle and associated lines.

From here return along St. Mary Axe into Leadenhall Street. On the opposite side, along Lime Street, is **Lloyd's,** the world-renowned corporation of insurance underwriters. Its present membership of more than four thousand has grown from a few merchants who met nearby in Edward Lloyd's coffeehouse about 1685, for whom Lloyd collected and posted shipping news. By 1769 the patrons of the coffeehouse set up their own establishment under the same name, and a few years later they obtained premises in the Royal Exchange. Lloyd's was incorporated by an Act of Parliament in 1871 and has been engaged in all kinds of insurance (except life) since 1911.

Ask the waiter wearing a red cloak and top hat (his title goes back to the coffeehouse days) for permission to look at "The Room," the huge Underwriting Room where the eighteenth-century **Lutine Bell** in the center is rung twice for good news and once for bad. During a busy period, three thousand people will be here. On exhibition in the Nelson Room is the admiral's logbook containing his original message signaled to the Fleet at the Battle of Trafalgar: "England expects every man to do his duty."

Just past Lloyd's, down Leadenhall Place and on the left, you will have an amusing time wandering around the meat and provision stalls of **Leadenhall Street Market** (open weekdays, 9:00–5:00). Fish, poultry, green vegetables, fruit, flowers, and cheese are sold in shops under the grass-covered arcade. Often well-dressed businessmen take a few minutes off from their work in August to dash in and purchase grouse flown down from Scottish moors as a special treat for their families.

You can leave the market on Gracechurch Street. Cross over and walk to the left under an arch, and turn right into Bell Inn Yard a bit down the street. This will lead you through archways and little passages into Castle Court and Birchin Lane. Here is a fascinating bit of the City; at times you think you are in a maze. If you feel like lunching in a well-known City chophouse, try **The George and Vulture** in St. Michael's Alley just before you reach Birchin Lane (open weekdays, 12:00–3:00). It is said to have been founded in 1715 as "The George," but is mainly known because Charles Dickens was an habitué (ask to see Mr. Pickwick's bedroom). It may be noisy but, if you can seclude yourself in a booth, you will be entertained by the general bustle and perhaps even by snatches of conversation you may have with your table companions. Upon leaving, you come out on Lombard Street by following Birchin Lane just a few yards to the left.

Lombard Street, London's banking center since the Middle Ages, was named for the Lombard merchants of Italy who became moneylenders in the city during the twelfth century. Be sure to notice the banking signs still hung out, following the custom of medieval days, by Britain's largest commercial bank, **Martin's,** at No. 68.

Cross Lombard Street and walk down Nicholas Lane to King William Street. After turning left you will shortly have a glimpse of the top of the **Monument,** which Sir Christopher Wren designed and erected between 1671 and 1677 as a memorial to the Great Fire. Its 202-foot height is said to be the exact distance from its base to the baker's shop in Pudding Lane where the Great Fire began. Keep to the left at the crossroads to the pedestrian island in Gracechurch Street. Then cross to Fish Street Hill and the column will be directly ahead of you. If you can face climbing 311 steps to the balcony below the golden ball, you will be rewarded by a fine view over the City, including the Tower and the Pool of London. (Open Monday–Friday, 10:00–6:00; Saturday and Sunday, 2:00–6:00.)

Many visitors will want to set foot on **London Bridge,** even though little now remains of the romance once attached to the bridge, which was built in 1831 and has now been removed, stone by stone, and reerected in Arizona. Approach the bridge by King William Street, a block from the Monument. Near the site of London Bridge, the highest navigable point for shipping, stood earlier bridges going back to the tenth century.

If you walk over London Bridge, you'll see the more publicized **Tower Bridge** downstream and the famous **Tower** along the embankment. You'll want to return here another time to explore a vast urban development program, still in progress, the **Docklands.** It begins at Tower Bridge, and offers a spectacular view of the Thames. A fascinating mixture of modern architecture and industrial history, the Docklands deserves a special visit, notably **Canary Wharf.** Call the London Docklands Visitors' Centre at 512 11 11 for more information. Be sure to visit the Billingsgate Market, which has recently moved to the Docklands. Beyond the far end of London Bridge, on the right, stands **Southwark Cathedral,** well worth a visit on another occasion. On the Southwark bank, cranes and hoists may be loading freighters. Upstream there is a fine view of the dome of St. Paul's.

Cross Lower Thames Street and, a few yards farther along, turn left into St. Dunstan's Hill, which leads to Great Tower Street. On the opposite side you will be in **Mincing Lane,** center of commodity markets in tea, sugar, cocoa, rubber, jute, tortoiseshell, and ivory ever since the Genoese landed many of these goods here in the sixteenth century. Tea, long associated with Mincing Lane, is still the most important item of trade in this fascinating street of exotic commerce that the spice trade made famous. **Plantation House,** the large building on the left along Mincing Lane, has an elephant, symbol of the tea trade, over the entrance. Wander into Hale & Son just inside, and you will see brokers handling such bizarre products as feathers or animal horns from India. There are also auction rooms for tea, coffee, sugar, and rubber in this building.

Returning to Great Tower Street, you walk along it a couple of short blocks to the open space of **Tower Hill.** Just before you get there, you will see **All Hallows' by-the-Tower Church** on your right. This old church, dating from A.D. 675, was reconstructed under Cromwell and boasts eleventh-century Roman pillars, which survived the Great Fire. Americans will be interested in the fact that President John Quincy Adams was married, and William Penn baptized, here. In front of you now stands the historic **Tower of London,** which has played a prominent role in British history since William the Conqueror.

The Tower, Britain's most famous fortress, has been a royal palace, first prison of the realm, execution site, repository of the Crown jewels, treasure vault, mint, court of justice, arsenal, munitions factory, naval station, and garrison. It covers eighteen acres. To see it properly requires at least an hour, and to learn its fascinating history you should buy a special guide to the Tower. (Open in summer: Monday–Saturday, 9:00–6:00; Sunday, 10:00–6:00. In winter: Monday–Saturday, 9:30–5:00; Sunday, 10:00–5:00.)

After crossing the moat, now filled in with grass and flowers, you may want to start at the Bell Tower, where Elizabeth I walked along the ramparts as a prisoner before becoming queen.

Next to the Wakefield Tower is the **Bloody Tower,** where the little princes were murdered in 1483 and where Sir Walter Raleigh was confined for thirteen years while he wrote *The History of the World.*

On Tower Green, you will see the famous ravens. It is said that when they no longer appear, the end of Britain will occur. Note the brass plate that commemorates the site of the royal scaffold where Anne Boleyn and the Earl of Essex were executed. Off Tower Green is the special Jewel House in the Waterloo Block, where the Crown jewels are on display. Here you will see St. Edward's Crown, the oldest in Britain. It was made for Charles II and last used in Queen Elizabeth II's coronation. Other royal regalia, including the Royal Sceptre, Orb, and Sword of State, are also on display.

The **White Tower,** dating from William the Conqueror, contains the oldest chapel in London and a large collection of armor and old weapons. Just nearby, sections of the old **Roman Wall** that surrounded London have been excavated.

While wandering around the Tower grounds you will encounter yeomen warders wearing their colorful blue uniforms of Tudor days. Contrary to popular impression, they are not the "beef-eaters," a term reserved for yeomen of the guard. To see the seven-hundred-year-old ceremony of the warders locking the gates at 10:00 in the evening and handing over the keys to the Governor, you must write the Governor for permission. The Governor commands the troops stationed in the Tower, which has been a military garrison for nine hundred years.

After touring the Tower, walk along **Tower Wharf** by the river, where ancient guns are on display and where today the Honourable Artillery Company of the City fires salutes on state occasions. As you turn back toward **Traitor's Gate** and contemplate the great personalities and events that have made the Tower probably the most storied spot in British history, you may be just in the mood for something out of the ordinary. After walking through the City and seeing it up close, why not view it from the water by taking one of the sight-seeing boats from here to the West End. During the summer season, they leave from the Tower for Westminster Bridge every twenty minutes from 11:00 to 5:30. En route you will hear a very informative talk on all the points of interest that you pass on both banks of the Thames.

Westminster
The Hub of Britain

Here is a walk in the heart of London that is particularly suited to visitors who wish to see some of the most interesting and accessible places but can spare only a couple of hours. In fact, if you have business or shopping to do in the West End, you can fit this pleasant stroll into those plans and visit some fascinating out-of-the-way spots.

Carrying a raincoat or umbrella, just in case the blue skies disappear all of a sudden (as they do too often in London) and a bit of rain descends, start at **Piccadilly Circus,** London's hub. Its name comes from "piccadill," a high collar with lace edges that was popular in the seventeenth century. You can pick up some gastronomic delights at Fortnum and Mason—patronized by the royal family—or buy an umbrella, always useful in London, at Brigg and Sons. In the center of the circus is the aluminum statue known as *Eros,* not intended by the sculptor to represent the God of Love, as generally believed, but rather the Angel of Christian Charity.

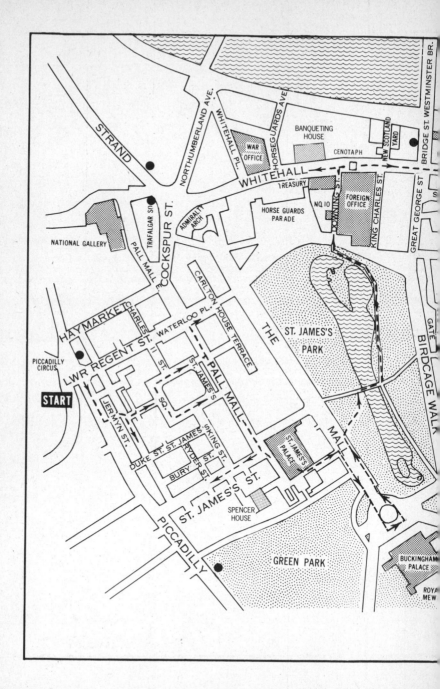

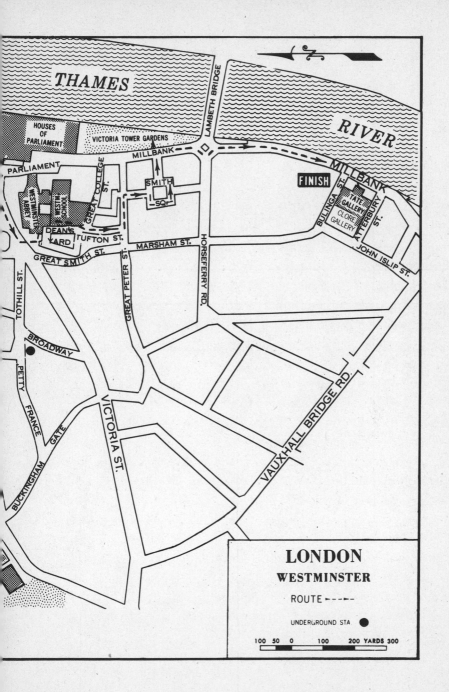

THAMES

RIVER

HOUSES OF PARLIAMENT

VICTORIA TOWER GARDENS

LAMBETH BRIDGE

MILLBANK

PARLIAMENT

GREAT COLLEGE ST.

SMITH SQ.

MILLBANK

FINISH

BULINGA ST.

TATE GALLERY

CLORE GALLERY

ATTERBURY ST.

WESTMINSTER ABBEY

WESTM. SCHOOL

DEAN'S YARD

TUFTON ST.

MARSHAM ST.

HORSEFERRY RD.

JOHN ISLIP ST.

GREAT SMITH ST.

GREAT PETER ST.

TOTHILL ST.

BROADWAY

PETTY FRANCE

BUCKINGHAM GATE

VICTORIA ST.

VAUXHALL BRIDGE RD.

LONDON
WESTMINSTER

ROUTE ----▸-

UNDERGROUND STA ●

100 50 0 100 200 YARDS 300

Walk west along Piccadilly for two blocks to **St. James's Church,** a charming red-brick building designed by Wren. Largely destroyed during the war, the church has been restored. St. James's Church was very stylish in the eighteenth century, and society weddings are sometimes held there still.

From the church turn right into **Jermyn Street,** where you will be lured by the stylish shops. On the left you will find an art-supply store over a hundred years old. A few doors away is a real pharmacy, not a drugstore. A bit farther along, at No. 93, is a marvelous cheese shop, Paxton and Whitfield, boasting probably the most complete selection in London—with almost every variety you have ever heard of. Go inside and look at the huge slabs of English Stilton or Cheddar. Or, stop by Floris, offering a variety of original perfumes. The street is famous for men's fashions (shirts in particular), art galleries, and antique shops.

Return along Jermyn Street and turn right into Duke of York Street to **St. James's Square,** which was laid out by Charles II for fashionable mansions. As you enter the square, the building in the corner to your right is **Chatham House,** formerly the residence of three Prime Ministers, the Earl of Chatham, Lord Derby, and William E. Gladstone, but now the Royal Institute of International Affairs. As you walk around the square, be sure to notice the unusually fine plane trees in the gardens. At No. 14 you will pass the **London Library,** England's most famous subscription library, founded in 1841 and now possessing 600,000 volumes. The British Arts Council, which provides government grants for cultural institutions like the Royal Ballet and various symphony orchestras, is located at No. 4. Continuing around the patrician square, you come to No. 31, a large building at the southwest corner, **Norfolk House,** where General Eisenhower planned the invasions of North Africa and Europe during World War II.

At this end of the square a narrow street a few yards long leads into **Pall Mall,** the center of London's distinguished clubs. Pall Mall received its name from pall-mall, an old French game similar to croquet, played in England at the time of Charles I. Immediately across the street, the large Italian palazzo houses the **Reform Club,** liberal in politics and including a large membership prominent in public affairs, journalism, economics, finance, and the law. For a look at the classic façade of the **Athenaeum,** London's leading literary and intellectual club, walk a few yards to the left beyond the Reform Club to the corner of Waterloo Place.

Returning along Pall Mall you will pass several other clubs on your way to St. James's Street. Turning right into St. James's Street you will notice, in one of the oldest and smallest buildings in the area, the bow windows of Lock's, the well-known hatter, with plumed helmets from the days of the Duke of Wellington on display. A few doors away, at No. 3, there is a very narrow passageway, Pickering Place, cut between two houses and leading a scant hundred feet or so to one of London's charming courts—a secluded corner away from the noise of the city. This was London's last dueling ground, where Georgian gentlemen settled their disputes with rapiers. Turning back from Pickering Place, directly opposite is the massive dark brick Tudor gatehouse of **St. James's Palace,** with its picturesque chimneys dominating the low buildings of the palace behind it. To appreciate fully the dramatic effect of the sixteenth-century clock tower and turrets, look at the palace from a block or so up St. James's Street.

St. James's Palace, built by Henry VIII, was for several centuries the official London residence of the Sovereign, until Queen Victoria moved to Buckingham Palace. Major court functions were held at St. James's Palace; hence the present accreditation of foreign ambassadors "to the Court of St. James's."

When the Queen is not in residence at Buckingham Palace, a changing of the guard takes place at St. James's Palace daily at 11:30 A.M. in Friary Court. At all times a unit of the Brigade of Guards stands sentry duty in front of the palace. Enter **Ambassadors Court** through the passageway west of the gatehouse. Strolling around the quiet courtyard, it is hard to realize you are within a stone's throw of traffic-jammed St. James's Street. **York House,** the residence of the Duke and Duchess of Gloucester, occupies the north side. From the southwest corner of the courtyard you can see silhouetted against the sky the dark-red clock tower and its battlements. On a clear day, this is one of the most romantic scenes in central London. Wander leisurely through Stable Yard and on to **Clarence House,** on the left, the home of the Queen Mother. This imposing mansion, just beyond the palace and off the Mall, was built by the great architect John Nash. **Spencer House,** recently renovated, is now open to the public. There are guided tours, Sunday, 10:45–5:30. Closed January and August.

The Mall, London's majestic boulevard between Buckingham Palace and Admiralty Arch, presents a stately vista. Lined with double rows of plane trees, it has a faded pinkish pavement, whose color comes out sharply in rainy weather. On ceremonial occasions, the flagstaffs along the avenue fly the standards of visiting dignitaries. Behind you and running along most of the Mall, the long classic façade of John Nash's Carlton House Terrace—formerly mansions of the aristocracy—overlooks St. James's Park. You will want to proceed to **Buckingham Palace** to see the changing of the guard at 11:30 A.M., and to visit the **Queen's Gallery** (Tuesday–Saturday, 10:00–5:00; Sunday, 2:00–5:00; closed Monday), showing works of art belonging to the royal family.

Cross over into **St. James's Park,** the most picturesque of London's public recreation areas. Named in the thirteenth century for a female leprosy hospital, the **Sisters of St. James in the Fields,** this oldest of the city's parks was taken over by Henry VIII in 1532 but not opened to the public until the reign of the Stuarts. Patterning his ideas after those of Versailles, the Stuart King Charles II cleaned up the swamps and underbrush and put in trees and new lawns. But as one sees it now, St. James's Park dates from the period of George IV.

Stroll down the walk, which cuts across the broad, well-kept lawns, filled on a fine summer day with Londoners reclining in beach chairs, toward the small suspension bridge. Standing here, with your back to Buckingham Palace, you may see the unusual landscaping of the park, with the somber shades of the Foreign Office well to the right, over the weeping willows. But the most striking view is toward the Horse Guards Parade, with its pearl-gray stone buildings, behind which rise the fantastic Victorian Gothic structures of **Whitehall Court.**

Across the little bridge along the path to the left, is one of London's more fascinating sights—**Duck Island,** a bird and wildlife sanctuary. About 4:00 in the afternoon is probably the best time to see the three species of pelicans (presented by a Russian ambassador years ago) parading near the old Birdkeeper's Lodge on the island, seeking their daily fish ration. Twenty species of colorful wild ducks and geese also inhabit the island and are usually swimming in the lake. Some of the well-dressed men you will notice out for a bit of fresh air may be MPs rehearsing a speech or officials from the Foreign Office.

After this excursion into what might be called a ducal preserve, cross the road by the **Horse Guards Parade.** Here, in the early summer every year, on the Queen's official birthday, the dramatic and stirring ceremony of Trooping the Color takes place. In this magnificent spectacle, the Queen on her charger leads a parade of the horse and foot Guards Brigade, all resplendent in full-dress scarlet-and-blue uniforms, and some, like the mounted band, displaying silver and gold as well.

Climb the few steps into **Downing Street** where, at **No. 10,** the Prime Minister has resided since the days of Sir Robert Walpole. The simple and dignified Georgian brick house was designed by a Harvard graduate, Sir George Downing. A moment later, you are in **Whitehall.** If you happen to be there on a Sunday just before 10:00 A.M., or weekdays at 11:00, hurry along to the left a block or so to the Horse Guards to see the changing of the guard—a colorful ceremony. Opposite Whitehall you'll come to **Banqueting House,** built by Inigo Jones in 1622 for James I, the only part of the palace left untouched by the 1698 fire. Don't miss the splendid Rubens ceiling. (Open Monday–Saturday, 10:00–5:00; closed Sunday.)

From here, walk back along Whitehall past the **Cenotaph,** commemorating the dead in two world wars, to Parliament Square. Before you rises the lofty tower of **Big Ben,** Britain's timekeeper. On the right of the square there is an impressive statue of Abraham Lincoln. Cross the road and enter the courtyard just below Big Ben to visit **Westminster Hall,** the oldest and finest building in the **Houses of Parliament.** When Parliament is in session, you can attend in the **Strangers' Gallery.** Doors open at 2:30.

Westminster Hall, built by William Rufus in the eleventh century, is the only surviving part of the medieval **Palace of Westminster.** Today its noblest architectural feature is its magnificent hammerbeam oak roof dating from 1399. The hall was the site of the Great Council, which preceded Parliament. Later, in the sixteenth century, it was Parliament's meeting place. The chief law courts also sat here from the end of the thirteenth century until 1883. The hall has been the scene of many famous state trials, and a brass marker on the south steps records the spot where Charles I was condemned to death. His successor, Oliver Cromwell, became Protector in Westminster Hall in 1653. His statue stands outside on Parliament Square, and, oddly enough, the statue of Charles I is only a few hundred yards away in Whitehall.

Foreign visitors can get permission to attend sessions of the House of Commons and House of Lords by applying to their embassy or to the Admissions Office in St. Stephen's Hall, opposite Westminster Abbey. The best time to tour the Houses of Parliament with an official guide is on a Saturday or when the house is in recess, between 10:00 and 4:00.

Opposite the House of Parliament is **Westminster Abbey.** Religious worship has been held on this site since A.D. 750, when a Benedictine abbey (the west monastery of the City of London, or Westminster) was built here. In the eleventh century Edward the Confessor rebuilt the abbey, and in the thirteenth century Henry III enlarged it. Its architectural design is early English; its Gothic nave is the loftiest in England. (Open Monday–Friday, 9:20–6:00; Saturday, 9:20–2:00; 3:45–5:00. Closed Sunday.)

Every English sovereign from William the Conqueror to Elizabeth II has been crowned in the abbey. Be sure to see the coronation chair, made by the King's painter for Edward I; it contains the Stone of Scone, used as the coronation seat by kings of Scotland from 850 until Edward I captured it in 1296.

The Henry VII Chapel, a superb example of late Perpendicular Gothic style, with its lovely fan-tracery vaulting, is the abbey's architectural gem. Its nave is embellished by the carved stalls and the colorful overhanging banners of the Knights of Bath.

Westminster Abbey is crowded with countless historic graves and memorials to Britain's great, but Americans should not miss the tablet to President Franklin D. Roosevelt just inside the great West Door near the **Tomb of the Unknown Warrior.** It's a fascinating experience to wander around the abbey discovering the names of sovereigns, statesmen, poets, writers, and actors, on tombs and monuments too numerous to mention. It seems as if every prominent figure in English history is either buried or commemorated by a memorial here.

If you have time, take a turn around the fourteenth-century **Cloisters** and then visit the **Chapter House,** called the "cradle of free Parliaments" because the House of Commons met here from 1352 to 1547. The original thirteenth-century pavement, the best-preserved in England, still retains its brilliant coloring.

Just beyond the Chapter House is one of the most extraordinary museums in London—the **Abbey Museum** in the Norman Under-croft, one of the few surviving parts of Edward the Confessor's church (open mid-March–mid-October, 9:30–6:00; rest of the year, 9:30–4:00). At one time it was customary "at the funerals of Kings or Queens to represent them by a life-sized robed figure, either of wood or of wax, which lay on the coffin as it was borne through the streets." The Abbey Museum contains several remarkable examples of death masks, effigies, and wax figures.

The amazing wooden effigy, a death-mask portrait of Edward III, victor of the battle of Crécy, shows him as he died in 1377, with his mouth and left cheek affected by the muscular contraction that ended his life.

The remarkable death mask of Henry VII is so perfect in detail of bone structure and facial characteristics that it might have been made yesterday. The plaster around the ears has retained small tufts of red and gray hair that may actually have belonged to the dead king.

The full-sized contemporary figure of Charles II dressed in his splendid robes of the Order of the Garter stands in a glass case, resplendent in all details. The effigy of Frances, Duchess of Richmond and Lennox, who died in 1702, represents one beautiful woman who supposedly succeeded in evading his advances. She was the model for the original figure of Britannia on the coinage of Great Britain.

There is also the effigy of Admiral Lord Nelson, commissioned in 1806, a year after his death, which provides the tourist with a supplementary attraction to St. Paul's Cathedral, where he is buried. The figure of Nelson, dressed in his own clothing, was regarded by contemporaries as more lifelike than paintings for which he sat.

Farther along the Cloisters' east walk, an obscure passageway to the left leads to the Little Cloisters. In this secluded garden, where the silence is broken only by the splashing of a fountain, you have a dramatic view of **Victoria Tower** of the Houses of Parliament, which stands higher than Big Ben.

Returning to the main Cloisters, you can stroll through a passageway into **Dean's Yard** and the grounds of **Westminster School,** founded by Queen Elizabeth I and one of the leading public schools in London. In term time, students will be dashing in and out of the fourteenth-century dining hall, where the oak tables are fashioned from timber supposedly obtained from the remnants of the Spanish Armada. From a small garden just off the center quadrangle, there is another striking view of the Victoria Tower rising beyond the garden's old walls.

Making your way from Dean's Yard into Tufton Street, turn left at Great Peter Street, and walk right at Gayfere Street, to **Smith Square.** This is one of those small London squares that add so much character to the city. Here you will find **Transport House,** headquarters of the Labour Party.

Leaving Smith Square by Dean Stanley Street, walk a few yards to Millbank. Across the road is Victoria Tower Gardens, a pleasant park along the river with some good views of the buildings up and down the Thames. A copy of Rodin's *The Burghers of Calais* dominates the gardens.

Follow Millbank for three or four blocks, past one of London's skyscrapers, the Vickers building, to the **Tate Gallery** (open weekdays, 10:00–5:30; Sundays, 2:00–5:30. Closed holidays). Its great collection of paintings and sculpture, second only to that of the **National Gallery** in Trafalgar Square, specializes in the British school since the seventeenth century, French Impressionists and Postimpressionists, as well as distinguished contemporary works. John Singer Sargent and James McNeill Whistler are two outstanding American painters exhibited here; each is represented by a full room. Don't miss the Clare Gallery, housing the splendid Turner collection. These artistic surroundings are a fitting place to end this stroll through the center of London.

Chelsea and Kensington
The King's Road to Hyde Park

As a change from the intensity of sight-seeing in historic and ancient London, you should visit two quite different sections of the **West End** that are residential and off the beaten track. What's more, they are delightful places to walk! Each exudes that peculiar quality of simple dignity and charm in its houses, squares, and quiet, narrow streets that is so characteristic of old London. Each reflects the intimacy of a small community—for London is really a mass of small towns—rather than the hectic air of a bustling world capital.

One is Chelsea, the traditional home of artists and writers, and the other is that part of Belgravia and Kensington just south of

Hyde Park. Neither is usually more than a twenty-minute ride on one of the big red buses from Piccadilly Circus. Yet both are out of the way in the sense that you are not likely to go there in the course of an ordinary visit to London.

A few hours will be ample to wander around both districts, and to absorb the atmosphere of two of the most attractive parts of residential London.

Start at **Sloane Square** to explore the particularly delightful bits of **Chelsea.** (The bus—No. 19 or 22—provides the quickest and most direct transportation to Sloane Square from Piccadilly Circus or Pall Mall.)

Walk down the King's Road past the **Duke of York's Headquarters.** Turn left along Cheltenham Terrace to St. Leonard's Terrace; here you will find some of Chelsea's most distinguished Georgian houses. Across the open playing field of Burton's Court (a game of cricket between units of regiments of guards may be in progress), you will see the tower and cupola of **Chelsea Royal Hospital's** red-brick buildings.

Charles II founded the institution in 1682 for veteran and invalid soldiers and commissioned Sir Christopher Wren to design the buildings. Four-hundred-odd pensioners live here. You should have a chat with these old men wandering around the ground wearing dark blue coats and caps in winter, scarlet in summer. On dress occasions, they are resplendent in their uniforms and black three-cornered hats that date from the days of the Duke of Marlborough. Many proudly display their collections of campaign medals and decorations.

You should visit both **Wren's Chapel,** with its oak carving, and the **Great Hall,** festooned with battle flags and honors from 1698 to the Korean War. The **Governor's House** includes a fine council chamber built by Robert Adam. Pensioners will show you around

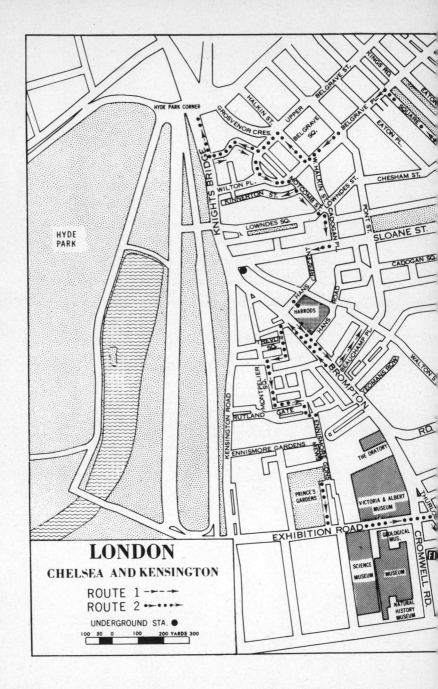

LONDON

CHELSEA AND KENSINGTON

ROUTE 1 ->--->
ROUTE 2 >->-->->->

UNDERGROUND STA. ●

100 50 0   100   200 YARDS 300

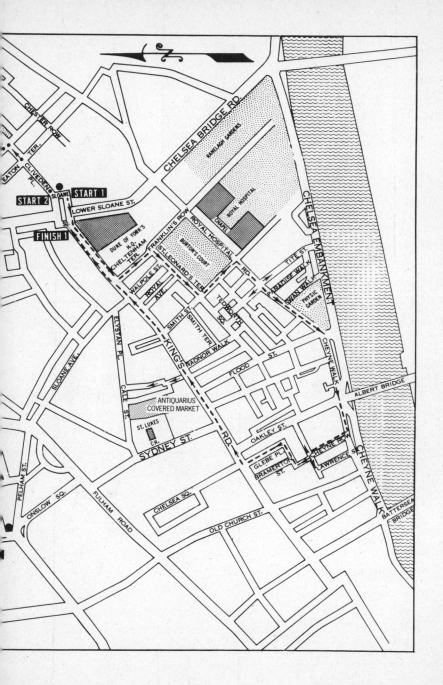

the chapel and Great Hall daily from 10:00 to 12:00 and 2:00 to 4:00; Sundays form 2:00 to 4:00.

After strolling about spacious **Figure Court,** the main quadrangle with its Doric colonnade, you should wander on the south terrace overlooking the gardens where the **Chelsea Flower Show,** Britain's finest collection, is held every spring by the Royal Horticultural Society. The south grounds of the hospital and adjacent **Ranelagh Gardens** are quite extensive and beautifully landscaped with flower beds and shrubbery—a most enjoyable spot for a pleasant promenade under shaded alleys of tall trees.

As you leave the hospital, turn left along Royal Hospital Road and after two blocks you will come to **Tite Street.** You are now entering the Chelsea of literary and artistic tradition. Oscar Wilde lived at No. 34 in magnificent style. James McNeill Whistler built the famous studio, the White House, down on the left. John Singer Sargent resided in No. 31 for twenty-four years and died there. In recent years Augustus John had his studio at No. 33. Just beyond Tite Street, you pass on your left the **Physic Garden,** begun in 1673 by the Society of Apothecaries and still used for botany research. In 1732 the first cotton seed was shipped from here to the southern planters in the American colonies.

Royal Hospital Road runs into the **Embankment** just beyond the Physic Garden. Here you turn slightly to the right by the public gardens into **Cheyne Walk.** You will admire the wrought-iron gates and railings of the distinguished early Georgian houses that face the river. Pause for a moment in front of No. 16, where Dante Gabriel Rossetti and Algernon Charles Swinburne lived, and study these stately mansions, so pleasing architecturally. Several charming balconies overlook the gardens opposite. The popular eighteenth-century coffeehouse, **Don Saltero's,** used to be at No. 18. Now cross Oakley Street and, after passing several eighteenth-century houses, you come to the **King's Head and Eight Bells** on the corner—one of the most delightful pubs in Chelsea. If you are in the mood for lunch, ask for one of the window tables upstairs with a view over the river. Or you can have a snack in the quaint bar downstairs. Artists and writers from the neighborhood frequently gather in the paneled bar and dining rooms, or outside along the street at midday Sunday. It is one of the liveliest "locals" in Chelsea. Leaving the pub, stroll to your left along Cheyne Row, an unusually charming street, shaded by trees, and one of the best-known in Chelsea. You can visit **Thomas Carlyle's house,** No. 24 (open April–October, Wednesday–Saturday, 11:00–5:00; Sundays, 2:00–5:00), and see where the great historian lived for nearly fifty years and wrote his great works. His furniture and books remain as they were nearly a hundred years ago. At the end of Cheyne Row you will come into **Upper Cheyne Row,** a small, secluded street with many gaily painted, low houses. The Chelsea China Works used to be to the left on Lawrence Street, where Henry Fielding and Tobias Smollett lived. In the other direction, toward Oakley Street, there are several attractive modern houses with pleasant gardens.

Cheyne Row, after crossing Upper Cheyne Row, becomes Glebe Place. Continue up Glebe Place to the **King's Road,** so named because it was Charles II's route from Whitehall Palace to Hampton Court. On the right, you will find **Argyll House** at No. 211, regarded as one of the finest examples of eighteenth-century architecture in Chelsea.

The King's Road, Chelsea's main street, is a fascinating place for a promenade. As you wander along, window-shopping for everything from antiques and paintings to odd mementos and old stamps, you are likely to encounter, especially on a Saturday morning, some of Chelsea's colorful characters—actors, writers, or just kids trying to be exotic. The King's Road is by no means merely an antiquarian's delight. Farther along are some of London's most innovative fashion shops. Take your time along the King's Road; it's one of the most interesting of the city's many "high streets."

Just beyond Sydney Street turn into **Burnsall Street,** the second on the left. Down here and in **Godfrey Street,** a continuation on the right, you will see some of the most enchanting little houses in Chelsea. Most of these are former cottages or coach houses that have been rebuilt in the past decades. Now they are painted in pastel shades—blues, pinks, and yellows—and usually belong to well-to-do professionals or business people, since Chelsea has become a highly fashionable residential area. You'll want to visit Antiquarious, a covered market specializing in antique lace and dresses (open Monday–Saturday, 10:00–6:00).

Returning to the King's Road, cross over into Radnor Walk. A few yards farther on the left is the **Chelsea Pottery,** where you can see potters at work producing modern ceramics for sale. Behind the pottery shop you will discover the **Chelsea Forge,** the only one left in the borough. Established in 1780, it makes wrought-iron gates today instead of the carriages it produced years ago.

You now follow the King's Road a short distance to Sloane Square. Before you reach the square, you will pass on the right one of London's largest supermarkets. At Sloane Square you can hop on a bus to **Hyde Park Corner** for the start of the **Kensington** walk. Or if you have the time and inclination (it will take half an hour or so), stroll from Sloane Square through **Belgravia.**

Through Mews and Squares

If you decide to walk, cross Sloan Square to Cliveden Place, then turn left at Eaton Terrace. In a moment you will see **The Antelope,** a delightful pub and intimate restaurant. This is a favorite gathering place for the nearby residents in Eaton Square and the immediate neighborhood. The downstairs bar is very lively, and the small upstairs restaurant has a friendly quality stimulated by its gregarious patrons.

After pausing here for a bit, return to Eaton Gate and walk along the north side of **Eaton Square,** one of London's most elegant residential squares. In recent years these houses have been largely converted into stylish flats. When you reach Belgrave Place, turn left and you will pass Eaton Place, the home of the fictional Bellamy family in "Upstairs, Downstairs." Continue on to **Belgrave Square.** Before the last war the distinguished mansions in this square were among London's finest private dwellings. Now many of them are occupied by foreign embassies.

Continue around the square to the northern corner, where you enter Wilton Crescent, then turn right down Wilton Row. As you saunter along here, you will be entranced by the pastel-colored cottages, formerly stables, that you will discover tucked away in little courtyards. In a moment you will come to **The Grenadier,** a celebrated old pub, once a billet and mess for the Duke of Wellington's First Regiment of Grenadier Guards. Outside the dark brick cottage you will see under a chestnut tree the remaining stone of the duke's mounting block and, in summer, a grapevine that came from Hampton Court. With prints and trophies on its walls, the low-ceilinged interior preserves the atmosphere of the duke's Grenadiers. The duke himself is believed to have often played cards in one of the small dining rooms. His mansion, **Apsley House,** is nearby, by Hyde Park Corner. The ghost of a grenadier officer flogged to death after being caught cheating at cards supposedly haunts the pub during September.

If you wish to visit **Hyde Park Corner,** walk through Old Barrack yard and turn right in Knightsbridge. Otherwise, retrace your steps to Wilton Crescent and on to Motcomb Street.

If you have come by bus to Hyde Park Corner, you begin the walk through Belgravia and Kensington by following **Knightsbridge** for a few hundred yards past the **Lanesborough Hotel,** through an archway on the left, Old Barrack Yard, and on to The Grenadier.

Now make your way around to the right past the stone façades of Wilton Crescent to Motcomb Street. In a moment you will see a narrow entrance to **Kinnerton Street.** There are lots of tiny shops here that are worth exploring, as well as lots of tiny shops here that are worth exploring, as well as little alleyways and courtyards in **Kinnerton Yard** that reveal amusing pieds-à-terre for the country dwellers who keep flats in town.

From **Motcomb Street,** with its art galleries, antique shops, and milliners, follow Cadogan Place one block to **Sloane Street,** the finest shopping street in this part of London. Walk on the other side of Sloane Street toward Knightsbridge to the first turning on the left, Hans Crescent. Then walk for a block or two until you come to **Harrods,** London's leading quality department store. One of Harrods' most exciting departments is the large food shop on the ground floor. Here you can spend lots of time in a serious gourmet-type investigation of all the varied and luxurious foods on sale. The poultry-and-game section offers grouse, venison, English *poussin,* wood pigeon, wild duck, and quail during the summer. The seafood display of kippers and lobsters is arranged most artistically. Even Scottish salmon, as well as Dover sole and other kinds of fish, are laid out on stone slabs.

After you have succeeded in tearing yourself away from these and other enticements, leave Harrods by the **Brompton Road** entrance and stroll along for three blocks to **Beauchamp Place.** This street will captivate you if you like wandering around attractive little shops, for there are all sorts here—shops selling antique silver and brass, shops dealing in old clocks, and china, as well as stores carrying the latest fashions. There is even one called Dog's Baths Requisites, where poodles are shampooed and have their nails clipped.

Now cross Brompton Road and backtrack until you are opposite Harrods. Turn left, walk fifty yards, and you will be in **Trevor Square,** a pleasant rectangle of Georgian houses. From here it is just a step to one of London's smallest, most recherché and picturesque corners—tranquil **Montpelier Square.** The gardens and tastefully planted flower beds beneath large overhanging trees diffuse an air of restfulness that seems almost unbelievable only a few hundred yards from the throbbing noisy traffic of Knightsbridge and Brompton Road. This is one of the delights of residential London that will impress the apartment dweller from New York, who can seldom escape from the din of the metropolis. Nearby you will notice a sign that has been there for years, forbidding street musicians from annoying the residents. Just off the square there is an old Georgian pub where you can have lunch, or simply bread, cheese, and a glass of bitter.

Montpelier Walk, a narrow street at the northwest end of the square, curves around to the left. Almost every house here has a charming front garden full of flowers that the residents have carefully cultivated. Some display equally attractive flower boxes.

You follow Montpelier Walk until you reach a turn to the right where you will spy a passage through a high brick wall, known to the residents as the "hole in the wall." Step through it and keep left a few yards until you came to a mews on the left. Pink, blue, russet, and yellow houses here provide an artistic setting more reminiscent of Provence than of London.

A few yards farther, on Ennismore Street, you approach one of Kensington's classic archways, which leads into **Ennismore Gardens Mews.** The row of pastel-colored cottages, once stables and now small town dwellings, is a picturesque sight facing the back gardens of **Brompton Oratory,** a baroque Roman Catholic Church. This is indeed one of those entrancing out-of-the-way corners of residential London that, when you discover it, grips you with its colorful and artistic atmosphere. Late in the day, the soft rays of the sun through the trees cast a golden glow over the mews. At this hour the high dome of the oratory silhouetted against the sky presents a dramatic sight.

In a moment you will be at **Prince's Gardens,** a well-planted square, from which you exit into Exhibition Road. Walk to the left a few hundred yards to the **Victoria and Albert Museum** (open Monday, 12:00–5:50; Tuesday–Sunday, 10:00–5:50; closed holidays), which contains the nation's great collection of fine and applied art of all countries, styles, and periods. The museum is outstanding in many fields, especially sculpture, ceramics, furniture, costumes, textiles, engravings, and prints. There is a unique collection of Constable's paintings, as well as a fine group of the French Barbizon school. Across the street is the **Science Museum,** illustrating the application of science to the various branches of technology and industry. Next to it stands the **Natural History Museum,** which houses a collection of animals, plants, and minerals (both museums are open daily, 10:00–6:00; Sunday, 11:00–6:00). Either now or on another occasion you should roam through the collections that interest you.

To return to Piccadilly Circus, just walk a block to the left to the South Kensington underground station, or take the No. 9 bus at the top of Exhibition Road by Kensington Gardens.

As you leave these two fascinating districts of residential London, you will feel these walks have only introduced you to charms that you will want to savor more thoroughly at some future time.

Park, Palace, and Promenade

Here is a delightful walk in Kensington, London's fashionable residential section. You will find this route different and unusual. It will offer you lots of interest and variety—**Kensington Gardens** with its colorful herbaceous borders, **Kensington Palace,** the quaint antique shops along Kensington Church Street, and the suburban-type homes off Gloucester Road and on Campden Hill as well as the last town residence of Sir Winston Churchill, and **Holland Park.** This stroll combines historic places, fascinating museums, restful parks, little out-of-the-way shops, and fine homes.

It is a very attractive part of London that many visitors never see because it's somewhat off the beaten track and yet it is very accessible. Not far from Hyde Park by underground or bus, it's the sort of stroll you can easily do if you are in central London and have a couple of hours to spare. Should you have to return for an appointment, you're never far from public transportation or taxi. You can be back in Piccadilly Circus in about twenty minutes at most hours of the day. In short, this is one of the most pleasant walks you can take close to the center of London.

Kensington, through which you will be strolling, derives its name from the Kensings, a Saxon tribe. Queen Victoria was born in Kensington and created it a Royal Borough because of her affection for her birthplace.

If you have been following the suggested walk from Hyde Park Corner to Exhibition Road, you can continue, if you wish, along the route about to be described. Otherwise you should start at Exhibi-

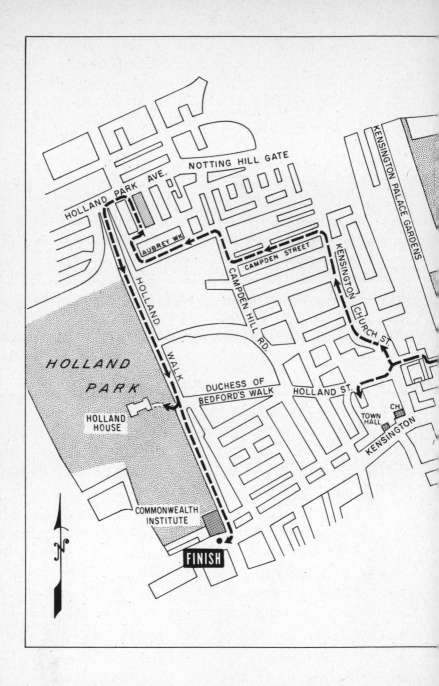

NOTTING HILL GATE

HOLLAND PARK AVE.

AUBREY WK.

CAMPDEN STREET

CAMPDEN HILL RD.

KENSINGTON CHURCH ST.

KENSINGTON PALACE GARDENS

HOLLAND WALK

HOLLAND PARK

HOLLAND HOUSE

DUCHESS OF BEDFORD'S WALK

HOLLAND ST.

TOWN HALL

CH.

KENSINGTON

COMMONWEALTH INSTITUTE

FINISH

N

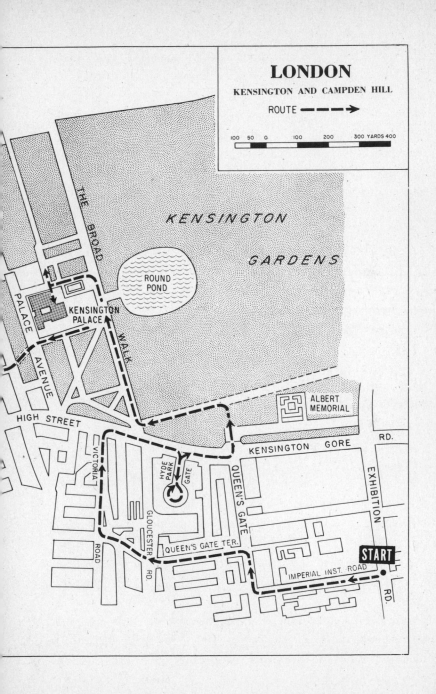

LONDON

KENSINGTON AND CAMPDEN HILL

ROUTE ▪ ▪ ▪ ▪ ➤

100 50 0 100 200 300 YARDS 400

KENSINGTON

GARDENS

ROUND
POND

KENSINGTON
PALACE

THE BROAD WALK

PALACE AVENUE

HIGH STREET

VICTORIA

GLOUCESTER ROAD

ROAD

HYDE PARK GATE

QUEEN'S GATE TER.

QUEEN'S GATE

ALBERT
MEMORIAL

KENSINGTON GORE

RD.

EXHIBITION

START

IMPERIAL INST. ROAD

RD.

tion Road by taking either a tube from Piccadilly Circus to South Kensington Station or a No. 9 bus to the top of Exhibition Road opposite the park.

Begin your stroll from Exhibition Road along **Imperial Institute Road** just opposite the thin golden spire of the modern Mormon Church. On either side of this road you pass the extensive complex of buildings that comprises the **Imperial College of Science and Technology,** one of Britain's leading scientific institutions. The tower on your right was erected in honor of Queen Victoria's golden jubilee.

At the end of the road you will come into broad **Queen's Gate,** a stately avenue lined with tall town houses, mostly built at the end of the last century, that are characteristic of South Kensington. The **Gore Hotel,** famous for its Elizabethan dining room where food of that era is served in an appropriate setting, is at No. 189 Queen's Gate.

Now cross over, and after going along Queen's Gate a block, turn left into Queen's Gate Terrace. In a couple of minutes you will come to **Gloucester Road,** the main shopping street for the neighboring residents.

Just on the other side you enter a corner of Kensington that has a villagelike quality about it. Although one of London's characteristics is the number of small towns that make up this sprawling metropolis, few sections can boast of the charming suburban atmosphere that you encounter when you stroll in the neighborhood of narrow **Victoria Grove.** Take a look down **Launceston Place** at the low two-story cottages. Or just a few yards farther, on the right, turn into **Canning Place** where you'll find delightful houses with big bay windows.

Victoria Road, just ahead, is one of the most pleasant and quiet residential streets in this part of London. Trees shade the walled gardens in front of the three-story family homes. It's hard to realize

ria's dollhouse and toys in the Anteroom. Coronation robes of
King George V and Queen Mary as well as other items of regalia
are on exhibit in the King's Drawing Room. You will also see
Prince Margaret's wedding dress and costumes worn by Queen
Victoria.

Keep to the right past the Sunken Garden, then around the corner of the Palace from the Broad Walk. Go through a gate and turn
right to reach the official entrance of the Palace with its cupola
overhead.

You now cross the wide private road across Kensington Palace
Gardens, known popularly as "Millionaires' Row," which is lined
with many stately mansions with large gardens. A dozen or so of
these houses are now used as embassies. Continue for a couple of
hundred yards along a walk, York House Place, that leads to Kensington Church Street, one of London's ancient thoroughfares, now
lined with antique shops and "in" boutiques. On the other side of
this busy shopping street you will be on Holland Street. The early
Georgian houses and their little front gardens give this street a special character. Holland Street and Gordon Place, just a bit farther
on the left with its charming two-story cottages, are often painted
by artists. The tiny houses on Gordon Place are said to have been
used by ladies-in-waiting to Queen Anne when she resided in Kensington Palace.

Returning to Church Street, there's a pleasant little detour that
takes you into a small garden behind the Church of St. Mary Ab-
bots, whose lofty spire is a Kensington landmark.

Church Street is an excellent place to buy antiques, so walk along
to the left from Holland Street, around the wide bend, and look in
at the different shops. There's a great variety of antiques on sale
here—old silver, china and glass, furniture, objets d'art, old jewelry,
copper and brass, and so forth. You may feel like wandering along

almost to Notting Hill Gate but if not, turn left a few hundred yards farther along at Campden Street.

At the end of this street, which is lined with pleasant two-story houses, you turn right on **Campden Hill Road,** a fashionable residential area since the seventeenth century. Many of the large houses that used to be here have now been replaced by well-designed modern ones, such as those you will pass on **Aubrey Walk,** the first turn to the left. Don't fail to note one of the liveliest pubs in this part of London, the **Windsor Castle,** opposite the reservoir before you turn left on Aubrey Walk.

After a short stroll along this street with its attractive, vine-covered houses, you will come to **Aubrey House,** the site of Kensington Wells, an early eighteenth-century spa. Turn right into Aubrey Road and again right into **Campden Hill Square,** a delightful tree-shaded square. The comfortable homes that surround the square are much sought after.

A few steps down the hill will bring you to **Holland Park Avenue,** a main traffic artery. Turn left and, in a moment or two, sharply left again into Holland Walk, a pedestrian thoroughfare that skirts Holland Park at the top of the rise on your right. A bit farther along the shaded footpath back in the trees you may see the rebuilt **Holland House.** This historic mansion became famous in the eighteenth century as the center of the Whig political and literary circle of which Charles James Fox was a distinguished member. The house was used as Cromwell's headquarters, and William Penn, founder of Pennsylvania, once held the lease. If you stroll into **Holland Park** just past the new Holland Park School on your left, you can enjoy sitting at the outdoor café overlooking the grounds.

Continue along Holland Walk to Kensington High Street. Just to the right you will see a large modern building of original design with a tentlike roof. This is the **Commonwealth Institute.** Its galleries, built around a circular well, display interesting exhibits of the economic and cultural life of the Commonwealth countries. Documentary films are shown in the theater. There is also a library on Commonwealth affairs for students, as well as a restaurant overlooking the lawn. After touring this unusual building, you can catch a bus in Kensington High Street or a tube on Earl's Court Road to take you back to Piccadilly Circus.

2.
Oxford

THE SENIOR UNIVERSITY

North of the High

You should begin your walk through **Oxford** at a particularly scenic spot where you will at once sense the antiquity and beauty of this ancient university. In this way you will get yourself in the right mood to appreciate the history, tradition, and charm of Oxford's towers, cloisters, halls, and gardens.

The ideal place for such a start is **Magdalen Bridge** (pronounced Maudlen), where the London road enters Oxford, for there, before crossing the bridge, you behold that memorable vista—the graceful proportions of the slightly tapering bell tower (believed to be Cardinal Wolsey's design) with its pinnacled turrets soaring above **Magdalen College** and the treelined banks of the Cherwell. To your right, the lovely green meadows below Headington Hill lend a softness to the scene.

After glancing up and down the stream, and seeing student couples renting punts, you pass the late-fifteenth-century tower and enter the grounds of Magdalen College through the main gate from

High Street (known in Oxford as "The High"). The college is open from March–October, daily, 9:00–5:00; November–February, weekdays, 9:00–4:30; Sunday, 10:00–12:00 and 2–4:30.

If you wish to view Oxford from its loftiest perch, ask the college porter at the entrance lodge to obtain permission from a Fellow of the college so you can climb the 144-foot bell tower. From its battlements the panorama of the university can be seen below, and it affords a unique sight of the varying pattern of the colleges and their gardens.

On the left of the gatehouse is the picturesque old seventeenth-century **Grammar Hall** (built considerably later than the founding date of the college, 1458), and on the right the only open-air pulpit surviving in England. After looking around the chapel, a bit farther on the right, you should follow the passageway beneath the **Muniment Tower** to the cloisters. Ascending a flight of steps at the right-hand corner of the cloisters you will reach the distinguished **dining hall,** famed for its lovely linenfold oak paneling, on which hang portraits of famous old members of the college, including a fine painting of Cardinal Wolsey. Note the woodcarving and coat of arms of Henry VIII over the high table.

As you saunter through the cloisters opposite the dining hall, look at the oak beams overhead and the crests of the famous old members of the colleges. Just beyond, to the right, past a fine herbaceous border, you will come to a small stone bridge leading to **Addison's Walk,** named for the great essayist, a former member of the college. Beneath the bridge, perch and pike, safe from the angler, are frequently being fed by visitors.

A stroll around the meadow, only a few hundred yards from the traffic-clogged High, will transport you into a completely rural atmosphere. This walk, under chestnut trees with may and hawthorn blooming pink and white in spring, is perhaps the most charming in

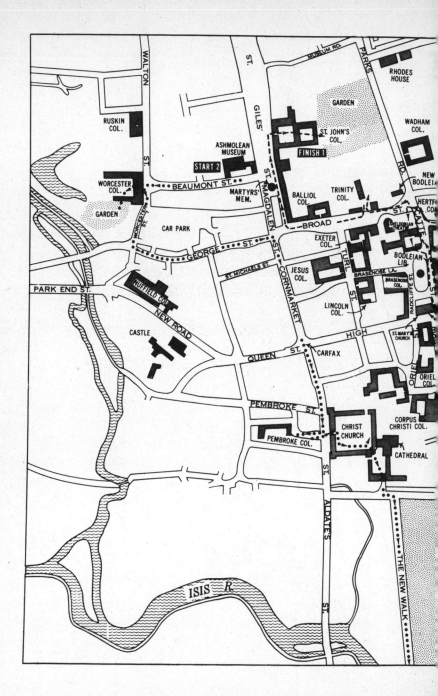

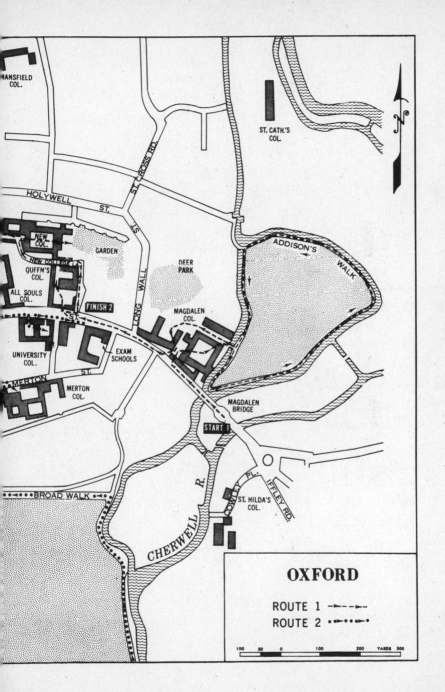

MANSFIELD
COL.

ST. CATH.'S
COL.

N

HOLYWELL ST.

NEW
COL.

GARDEN

DEER
PARK

ADDISON'S WALK

NEW COLLEGE

QUEEN'S
COL.

ALL SOULS
COL.

FINISH 2

MAGDALEN
COL.

UNIVERSITY
COL.

EXAM
SCHOOLS

MERTON ST.

MERTON
COL.

MAGDALEN
BRIDGE

START 1

BROAD WALK

ST. HILDA'S
COL.

IFFLEY RD.

COWLEY PL.

CHERWELL R.

OXFORD

ROUTE 1 ----►
ROUTE 2 •••►••►

100   50   0   100   200   YARDS 300

Oxford. Part of it runs along the meandering **Cherwell,** a stream overhung with willows and only about ten yards wide. At the far end you will find a little footbridge amid luxurious foliage. Pause on the bridge for a few moments and watch the punts go by.

After returning from this twenty-minute excursion, you should visit Magdalen's **Deer Park** just beyond the **New Buildings,** which, despite their name, were constructed in the eighteenth century. There, under a grove of tall and luxuriant oaks, chestnuts, and elms, the sight of the college herd adds a special old-world touch to these academic surroundings. There are about fifty deer, one for each Fellow of the college. Nearby on the left you will spy a lawn on raised ground next to a delightful garden. From this vantage point on the lawn, you have an unusual view of **Magdalen Tower** rising above the college buildings.

You leave Magdalen through the main gate and proceed up The High, universally recognized as one of the finest streets in Europe. In a few moments the famous and graceful sweep of **Queen's** and **All Souls** colleges and the spire of **St. Mary's Church** in the distance come into view. A bit farther on, you should stop at the corner of Queen's Lane and study the college buildings on both sides of the street.

The entrance to **The Queen's College,** founded in 1341, is just ahead on the right. (Open to groups only, by prior arrangement. Write to the College for information.) Pausing under the cupola at the gate, you will be struck by the stately proportions of the eighteenth-century **front quadrangle,** cloistered on three sides. It was designed by Nicholas Hawksmoor, an associate of Wren. Directly ahead, beyond the velvetlike lawn, stands the classic chapel, designed by Wren, and the hall surmounted by a clock tower. The view of this cupola, outlined by the entrance archway, as seen from the outside steps, is particularly effective against the background of open sky.

The finest façade of Queen's—and one of the most magnificent in Oxford—is the west front of the **library,** overlooking the **Fellows' Garden** and surmounted by a stone eagle, the insignia of the founder. But the upper library's interior, with its superb proportions, exquisitely carved dark woodwork, and highly decorated plaster ceiling, has few rivals in England in classic nobility and dignity.

You should now wander along a narrow passageway next to the library in the old **Nuns' Garden,** a restful spot beside **Drawda Hall,** whose gables rise over apple trees and rosebushes. After viewing the college dining hall, ask the porters to let you see the college's collection of silver, including the founder's ancient drinking horn. During term, a trumpet is blown each evening to announce dinner, in accord with the founder's instructions.

Turning left outside Queen's, walk along the winding lane that runs below high stone walls to **New College** on the right. You will notice that the top of the wall is spiked to discourage students from climbing in or out after the college gate is closed.

After passing through the entrance to New College (open during the school year, 2:00–5:00; vacations and weekends, 11:00–5:00), turn sharply to the left to reach what is probably the most peaceful spot in Oxford—the **college cloisters.** Rising above the wood-vaulted cloisters stands the crenelated bell tower, once part of the city wall. While you pause at the far edge of the perfect lawn, dominated only by a venerable ilex tree, you will sense the calm and meditative air of the Middle Ages that has survived the centuries in this place.

New College, founded in 1379 by William of Wykeham, Bishop of Winchester, is the first college whose buildings, most of which still stand, were planned as a college by its founder.

On leaving the cloisters, you should visit the chapel to see the fourteenth-century stained-glass windows, the founder's pastoral staff, and Sir Jacob Epstein's dramatic statue depicting the raising of Lazarus. From the chapel, walk to the left through two quads to a superb wrought-iron gate, the entrance to the college's spacious garden. In the center of the garden is a high mound covered with trees and shrubs, and around the lawn the battlements of the original medieval city wall look down on an exquisitely planned herbaceous border. Here is a perfect spot to sit for a while on a summer day.

Having seen several of the leading colleges, you should now have a look at the finest buildings of the university. Most buildings in academic Oxford belong to the individual colleges, while the university provides the special facilities like the building called **The Examination Schools** and the scientific laboratories used by all the colleges in common.

After leaving New College, you pass under **Hertford College Bridge,** known as the "bridge of sighs." Just ahead you will see the refaced **Sheldonian Theatre,** a smaller copy of the Roman Theatre of Marcellus. It was designed by Sir Christopher Wren, and university ceremonies, such as the granting of degrees, take place in it. The flat, highly decorated ceiling, apparently unsupported, is one of Wren's mathematical achievements. The interior has been repainted as it was in Wren's time. Outside the theater (open 10:00–12:45 and 2:00–4:45; closed Sunday, Christmas, and Easter) the weather-beaten stone heads of classical emperors face "The Broad," Oxford's term for spacious **Broad Street.**

The world-renowned **Bodleian Library** stands next to the Sheldonian. The main gateway, which passes through the **Tower of the Five Orders of Architecture** (Tuscan, Doric, Ionic, Corinthian, and composite) to the Bodleian quadrangle, is opened only on ceremonial occasions. The quadrangle within, dating from the early seventeenth century, was built to house the books Sir Thomas Bodley began to collect in 1602 when he refounded the former university library, which had become dispersed. You should visit the fifteenth-century **Duke Humphrey's Library** and exhibition room. (Guided tours only. Open Monday–Friday, 9:00–5:00 from April–December; Saturday, 9:00–12:30.) Note the painted ceiling and oak beams, and the shelves, which contain old books still arranged in their seventeenth-century classification by size and subject (Theology, Medicine, Law, and Arts). In keeping with Bodley's instructions, a bell is still rung when the library opens and closes. Upstairs are reading rooms with decorative friezes and ceilings. Nearby is the **Divinity School** with its fine stone-vaulted ceilings. The House of Commons met there in 1665 after having been driven from London by the plague. To the south stands the **Radcliffe Camera,** a circular building, mainly a reading room of the Bodleian.

Just a few steps back to The High will bring you to **All Souls College** (open Monday–Friday, 2:00–4:30), the only college without undergraduates, only Fellows. The resident members here are called Research Fellows. Hawksmoor's **twin towers** in the north quadrangle are a familiar feature of the Oxford scene. You should ask the porter at the gate for permission to see the lofty **Codrington Law Library,** an extremely well-designed room where the annual Encaenia luncheon for recipients of honorary degrees takes place in June. Note Wren's great sundial over the library door.

Retrace your steps along **Catte Street;** turn left into The Broad, passing the new Bodleian Library (erected largely through a Rockefeller Foundation grant), and so a few steps beyond **Blackwell's,** Oxford's famous bookstore, to reach the fine entrance gates and extensive grounds of **Trinity College** (open from 2:00–5:00; closed August). Trinity's seventeenth-century ornamental chapel, with its elaborate woodcarving, is well worth seeing.

Continuing along The Broad, you pass **Balliol College,** noted more for its academic excellence than for its monstrous Victorian architecture. After turning right along **St. Giles Street** (known in Oxford as "The Giler"), notice on your left the **Martyrs' Memorial,** commemorating the burning in The Broad of both the Protestant reformers Latimer and Ridley (condemned during the reign of Catholic Queen Mary) and Archbishop Thomas Cranmer in 1556.

St. John's College should not be missed on any tour of Oxford, mainly because of its unusually attractive **garden** (open daily, 1:00–5:00). It is the largest in Oxford and was laid out in 1777–78 in the style of Capability Brown. Its extensive lawn, rockery (one of the oldest in England), and groups of trees, as well as its attractively arranged herbaceous border, make this garden one of Oxford's most delightful havens of repose. **Canterbury Quad,** named after William Laud, Archbishop of Canterbury, who built it, is perhaps the outstanding example of early seventeenth-century architecture in Oxford. Its graceful Italian colonnades are unusually lovely. You should also see the **Hexagon Building,** a modern college dormitory (built in 1960). It has an unusual design in stone and glass and is considered one of the best pieces of contemporary architecture in Oxford.

You will find the gardens of St. John's just the place to end this first stroll through the colleges of Oxford.

Toward the Isis

As a change from touring colleges, you ought to start your second walk in Oxford by spending some time in the oldest museum in the British Isles, the **Ashmolean Museum,** the university's important art and archaeological collection on Beaumont Street, just around the corner from St. Giles (open weekdays except Monday, 10:00–4:00; Sunday and holidays, 2:00–4:00, summer only).

The Ashmolean is particularly distinguished for its rare Egyptian and Cretan treasures, but it also has on exhibition a representative selection of paintings and sculpture ranging from the early Italian masters to contemporary artists.

Straight ahead down Beaumont Street you will see **Worcester College.** Inside the gate on the left is a row of relatively untouched medieval cottages. These were originally separate monastic houses, and the ancient shields over the doorways show the different abbeys with which they were connected. Passing through an archway, you enter a large and delightful garden with noble trees. Its unique feature is Oxford's only lake.

On leaving Worcester, you should turn right into Worcester Street and left into George Street. When you reach the Cornmarket (Oxford's main shopping thoroughfare), you will realize what a busy, industrial city Oxford has become. **Carfax,** the center of the city, is the main crossroad at the end of the Cornmarket. Continuing straight ahead down St. Aldate's, you will see on the left the familiar **Tom Tower** of **Christ Church,** known in Oxford as "The House." (Open weekdays, 9:30–12:00 and 2:00–6:00 [4:30 in winter]; Sundays, 11:30–5:30 [4:30 in winter].)

Before entering the grounds of Christ Church, the most extensive of any in Oxford, you should step back from St. Aldate's a few yards along the lane leading to **Pembroke College** and study the details of imposing Tom Tower. It was completed by Sir Christopher Wren in 1682, after the lower part had been begun by Cardinal Wolsey, Christ Church's founder. Every evening, at five minutes past nine, the great bell tolls 101 times, once for each of the original scholars. After passing through the huge gateway of Christ Church, you will be spellbound by the grandeur and size of **Tom Quad.**

Walking around the stone terrace to the far side, notice the arches built in the walls; these indicate that Wolsey intended to construct a cloister around the quad. In the center of the perfect lawn is a statue of Mercury surrounded by a small pool. Pause for a moment at the archway in the southeast corner of the terrace for an unusual view of Tom Quad, perhaps the most impressive and yet most tranquil quad in Oxford.

Just beyond the archway you should study the magnificent wide stone staircase with its beautiful fan-tracery roof. The **Great Hall** (open Monday–Friday, 9:30–4:30; Saturday, 9:30–12; closed Sunday and holidays) at the top of the stairs, with its elaborately carved oaken roof and superb paneling, is the largest and finest in Oxford. Many interesting portraits adorn the walls, including paintings of Wolsey, who built the hall; Henry VIII, the royal founder; Queen Elizabeth I; Charles Lutwidge Dodgson (Lewis Carroll), a former canon of Christ Church; and William Penn, an old member of the college. In this hall, stage scenery was used for the first time in England, to produce a play for Charles I in 1636.

Outside the hall is **Wolsey's huge kitchen,** the oldest part of the building, still in use and most interesting. The original oak roof is more than fifty feet high. You can see the original spit, which is still operated on special occasions, and a serving table, six to eight inches thick, made in 1734, and used for 210 years. Colorful copper skillets hanging on the walls are used regularly.

Drop by the **picture gallery** (open Monday–Saturday, 10:30–1:00 and 2:00–4:30; Sunday, 2:00–4:30) opened in 1968, it houses a splendid collection of Italian primitives.

Only a few steps away you will find the Norman and early English **cathedral,** which, though small, is the most beautiful in Oxford. Also take a look at the adjoining fifteenth-century **cloisters.**

Before leaving Christ Church, walk along the quad to the

towered gate that leads to **Peckwater Quad** and the **college library.**

Returning through Tom Quad, you should make your way through several passageways of the newer buildings into **Christ Church Meadow.** It is a few minutes' stroll down the New Walk to the river **Isis,** where the gaily colored college barges are tied up. You can make a delightful circular walk along the tree-covered banks of the **Cherwell** (which joins the Isis nearby) back to the **Broad Walk.** As you stroll along this avenue of fine trees, you will see on your right a striking view of the towers of Merton and Magdalen.

Proceeding up the path to Merton Street, past its massive tower, you will reach the entrance to **Merton College** on the right. The College's fourteenth-century **Mob Quad** is the oldest surviving quadrangle in Oxford. The **medieval library** on one side of this simple quad is one of the most fascinating in England (open 2:00–5:00 weekdays [4:00 in winter]; weekends, 10:00–5:00). It has an intimate air, with its old fittings and paneled ceiling. Built in 1371–79, this relic of early Oxford still retains an original bookcase with chained volumes.

On leaving Merton, turn left and saunter along **Magpie Lane** with its odd little houses. Up ahead, the spire of **St. Mary the Virgin Church** looms at the end of the narrow street. If you want a fine view over Oxford, you can climb St. Mary's ninety-five-foot **tower** (open weekdays, 9:00–7:00 in summer; 9:00–5:00 in winter; Sunday, 12:00–5:30). Once again in The High, you turn right to visit **University College,** founded in the thirteenth century. Although Shelley was "sent down" as an undergraduate for publishing a pamphlet on *The Necessity of Atheism* in 1810, the college later repented by erecting a memorial to him. University College was the first Oxford college ever to elect an American as its Master, Professor A. L. Goodhart, who donated the new Goodhart

Quadrangle, one of the best examples of modern architecture in Oxford.

As you approach **Magdalen Tower** and ponder the beauties of the quads, halls, chapels, and gardens, you will realize that such a stroll as this has only served to whet your appetite to spend many more days in the inimitable atmosphere of Oxford.

3.
Cambridge

WHERE THE BACKS ARE FRONTS

From King's to Queens'

"The other place," as Oxonians disparagingly describe **Cambridge,** the junior university, is historically as fascinating as Oxford and in many ways more beautiful. Cambridge's locale in a rural community contrasts with Oxford's in an industrialized area and, with its interesting and lovely surroundings, lends itself to walking, particularly now that many streets in the center have been closed to traffic.

The famous **"Backs"** of the colleges—those sweeping, carpetlike lawns along the languid little river Cam—and the luxuriously colorful college gardens provide a spaciousness unmatched in Oxford. The several colleges along the stream seem to merge into one another; you are not conscious of the walls that separate them. Standing on one of the many picturesque bridges you sense a calm, restful, unhurried air as the branches of the overhanging lime trees sway in the breeze. Altogether, the view of elegant buildings and carefully tended gardens creates the contemplative atmosphere that marks the ideal university community.

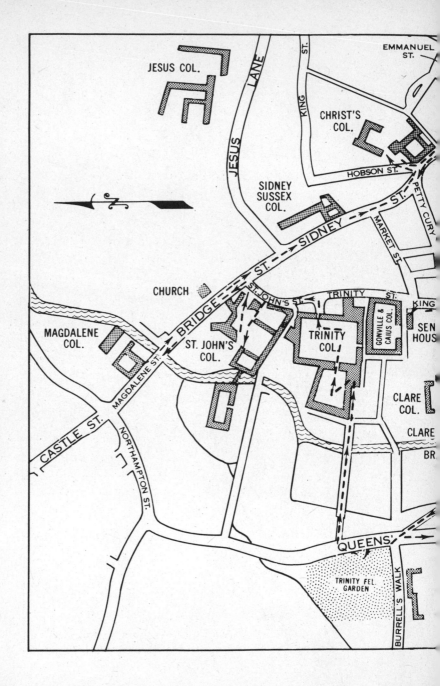

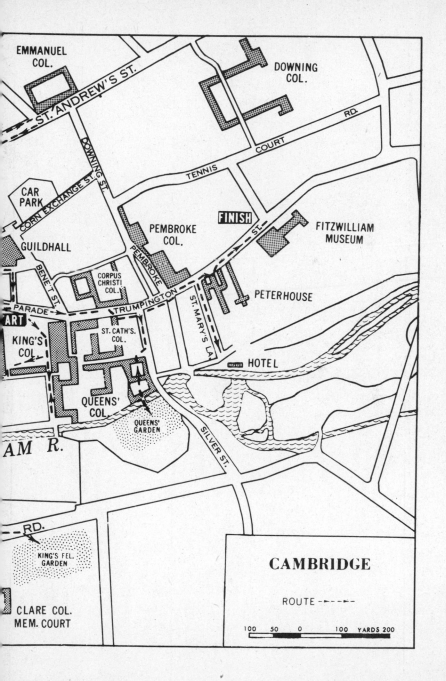

EMMANUEL COL.

DOWNING COL.

ST. ANDREW'S ST.

DOWNING ST.

CORN EXCHANGE ST.

COURT RD.

TENNIS

CAR PARK

FINISH

PEMBROKE COL.

FITZWILLIAM MUSEUM

GUILDHALL

BENE'T ST.

CORPUS CHRISTI COL.

PEMBROKE ST.

PETERHOUSE

PARADE

TRUMPINGTON

ART

ST. MARY'S LA.

KING'S COL.

ST. CATH'S. COL.

HOTEL

QUEENS' COL.

QUEENS' GARDEN

SILVER ST.

AM R.

RD.

KING'S FEL. GARDEN

CLARE COL. MEM. COURT

CAMBRIDGE

ROUTE - - - - -

100 50 0 100 YARDS 200

Upon arrival, as a stroller in Cambridge, you should absorb its unique mood before exploring the byways of the varied college quads. (The colleges are usually open during the daytime, but in term time some may be closed before noon.) To absorb this mood you should get your first impression by entering the main gate of **King's College** and walking to the left down the path that leads to **King's Bridge** over the Cam. Pause on the bridge for a few minutes and face the town. There looms to the left over the close-cropped greensward the pointed Gothic pinnacles of the world-renowned **King's Chapel.** Close at hand are the seventeenth-century stone arches and balustrade of **Clare Bridge,** without doubt one of the most graceful anywhere, which leads to the **Fellows' Gardens.** Behind this bridge, on both banks, rise stately and luxuriant trees with a green richness that only English dampness can create.

In the opposite direction, the half-timbered and deep red brick of **Queens' College** strikes a remarkable contrast in color against the sloping, turfed banks of the river.

On the river below, you will see male and female undergraduates maneuvering their punts by manipulating a huge pole from the rear platform.

After a few minutes spent in absorbing the spirit of Cambridge, you wander back into the main court of King's and approach the glorious **chapel** founded by Henry VI and considered by many the finest example of Perpendicular style in England. Inside the chapel, you will be struck at once by the lofty lacelike fan vaulting in the stone roof of "the loveliest chapel in England," which Henry VIII completed in 1515. The Tudor heraldic carving is highly decorative. The early sixteenth-century stained glass in the great windows was made by both Flemings in England and Englishmen working under Flemish inspiration from Flemish designs. The organ screen, one of Europe's finest pieces of woodwork, carries the arms of

Anne Boleyn. You should inquire when the next service will be held and return, if possible, to hear the celebrated voices of the King's College Choir in this incomparable setting (open weekdays, 9:30–3:45 [5:45 in summer]).

Leaving King's by the gate on the north side of the chapel, you turn left into **Clare College.** Proceed through the old court to **Clare Bridge**—the oldest in Cambridge (1640)—with its famous row of stone balls. Crossing the stream—but stopping for at least a moment to enjoy a still different view of the "Backs"—you pass through handsome eighteenth-century wrought-iron gates. Before leaving the park by the back gate on Queens' Road, you may visit **Clare's Fellows' Garden** (open 2:00–4:00, but not Saturday or Sunday; closed May and June).

A few hundred yards either way on Queens' Road are extensive and delightful gardens—**King's Fellows' Garden** (to the left) and **Trinity Fellows' Garden** (to the right). The variety of the flowers, shrubs, and trees in these well-planned and carefully maintained gardens is quite unusual. The gardens are not open to visitors, but may be admired from Queens' Road.

After passing Trinity Fellows' Garden, cross Queens' Road and take the path leading to **Trinity Bridge,** from which you will get an excellent view of **St. John's College.** Directly ahead, in the grounds of **Trinity College,** is the **Avenue**—one of the finest walks in Cambridge—which leads to New Court. On the left lies the magnificent classic façade of **Sir Christopher Wren's library,** built with cream and pink stone over a covered piazza. Wren's interior design of the beautifully proportioned library "touches the very soul of anyone who first sees it," as Roger North wrote in 1695. The walls and bookcases exhibit the best examples of Grinling Gibbons's wood-carving. The library contains the private book collection of Sir Isaac Newton, one of Trinity's most distinguished sons. You may even find the manuscript of Milton's shorter poems, in his own handwriting, on display among the library's many treasures. (Open weekdays, 12:00–2:00; Saturday, 10:00–12:00.)

The **dining hall** of the college, one of the most magnificent Elizabethan halls in England, with its carved oaken beams, is just off a passage above Nevile's Court and may be open—if the college has someone available—from 2:00 to 4:00. Opposite the entrance to the hall you will notice the colorful portrait of Henry VIII hung on the fine paneling immediately above the high table. Among other interesting pictures is a contemporary portrait of Francis Bacon, painted on wood. Overhead is the Minstrels' Gallery.

On your way out of the hall you should stand for a moment at the top of the stone steps to admire the **Great Court,** the largest of any college in Oxford or Cambridge. All the buildings are in the Tudor-Gothic style except for one section. On the left is Trinity's medieval clock tower, decorated with armorial crests, and in front is Nevile's lovely stone fountain. Near the chapel at the far end are the rooms in which Sir Isaac Newton worked out the proofs of his great scientific discoveries. After wandering around the court, you should stop by the sundial near the fountain and study the noble great tower; then leave the college through the massive Tudor archway.

Just a few yards to the left along Trinity Street stands the imposing stone and brick gateway to **St. John's College,** bearing the elaborately painted and gilded arms of Lady Margaret Beaufort, the founder. In the summer, tourists may seek permission in writing from the Junior Bursar to see the **Combination Room** in the Elizabethan brick second court. This paneled gallery, one of the most stately in England, is nearly a hundred feet long, with a decorated plaster ceiling worked in 1600.

Beyond the third court, the **"Bridge of Sighs"** (somewhat like the one in Venice) over the Cam leads to the delightful cloister in the

New Court. You cannot cross the bridge itself, but you have a fine view of it from the nearby Wren's Bridge. You may walk over Wren's Bridge and wander into the college grounds before returning through the courtyards to the main gate.

A few minutes' walk along Bridge Street will bring you to **Magdalene College** (pronounced Maudlen) to see the fascinating library of Samuel Pepys exhibited in the original bookcases he had made for it. The manuscript volumes of his diary are also in this collection. (The Pepys library is open weekdays, 2:30–3:30 during the first two school trimesters; 11:30–12:30 and 2:30–3:30 during the third trimester and in the summer.)

Returning along Bridge Street, you should look in at the **Round Church.** Built during the twelfth century, it is the oldest of the four round churches in England. A little farther along on the left, across Jesus Lane, Sidney Street brings you to **Sidney Sussex College.** After glancing around its ivy-covered walls, continue to the delightful gardens of **Christ's College** on the left—perhaps the loveliest in Cambridge. (The gardens are open weekdays, 10:00–12:30 and 2:00–4:00.) The mulberry tree on the lawn is supposedly associated with the poet John Milton, Christ's College's most distinguished old member.

If you are interested in the fact that Harvard was founded by an Emmanuel man, walk along St. Andrew's Street a couple of hundred yards to **Emmanuel College.** The college chapel contains a tablet and stained-glass window in memory of John Harvard.

Returning to Sidney Street, you will see opposite you a narrow street called **Petty Cury.** Walk past its old buildings and you will shortly come to **Market Hill,** a shopping center since medieval days. Open stalls display colorful flowers, fruit, and vegetables. A few steps through St. Mary's Street will bring you to **King's Parade.** Across the street stands the classic **Senate House,** where the chief university functions, like the awarding of degrees, take place. Just to the right rises the lovely old **Gate of Honor** of **Gonville and Caius** (pronounced Keys) **College.**

From the Senate House, walk past King's and on the left you will shortly come to **Corpus Christi College,** where you can visit one of Cambridge's treasures—the **old court,** built in 1377 and considered the earliest example of a complete medieval academic quadrangle still standing. Look for the tablet to Christopher Marlowe, who lived in a ground-floor room on the right.

Cross Trumpington Street and turn right into Silver Street to Queen's Lane. Here is the entrance to **Queens' College,** whose fifteenth-century mellow, dark red-brick construction lends a distinct and picturesque quality to its several smaller courtyards. Queens' has the most complete set of medieval college buildings in Cambridge. The embattled turrets of the fifteenth-century gateway are particularly impressive. Wander into the cloister court to look at the old half-timbered **President's Lodging,** with its bay windows supported by wooden columns, surely one of the most charming corners of Cambridge. The large sundial in a nearby court below a sloping red roof adds an attractive touch. Returning through these courts, in one of which lived Erasmus, you cross the famous wooden **"Mathematical Bridge"** (so-called because of the careful calculation of stress that went into its construction) to the college gardens.

Returning to Trumpington Street you should end your tour of Cambridge colleges by visiting the oldest of all, **Peterhouse,** founded by Edward I. Be sure to see the church of **St. Mary the Less** for the tablet to Reverend Godfrey Washington, a Fellow of Peterhouse. The Washington coat of arms displayed here later became the Stars and Stripes. The college **hall** and **buttery** are original late-thirteenth-century buildings.

Just beyond Peterhouse on Trumpington Street you will find the **Fitzwilliam Museum,** containing one of England's most extensive and outstanding collections of all forms of art. The museum is open weekdays from 10:00 to 5:00; Sunday (the Picture Gallery only) from 2:15 to 5:00 (closed Good Friday and the last week in December). The paintings, including excellent examples of English as well as most Continental schools, are well exhibited in light and spacious galleries.

As a suitable end to the day's tour you will enjoy having tea or dinner at the delightful **Garden House** hotel, which you reach by walking down little **St. Mary's Lane,** just north of Peterhouse. The hotel gardens run right along the river. There you might decide, if you can, which spot in Cambridge is the most fascinating of all.

4.
Edinburgh

The Royal Mile

You will find **Edinburgh** a delightful city for walking. It is not only scenically beautiful but full of historical interest. The **old town,** perched on a long, high, rocky ridge, sits in a most dramatic position overlooking the **New Town,** which spreads northward toward the **Firth of Forth.** The old and the new (most of it was built during the late eighteenth and early nineteenth century) are divided by Princes Street. Considered one of the finest avenues in Europe, it owes its reputation largely to the striking view of the old town directly opposite.

Begin this walk in Edinburgh at the west end of spacious **Princes Street,** in full view of the old section, which you should visit first. Rising sharply to the right is **Edinburgh Castle** high on the cliff—in earliest times the stronghold of a Pictish king. Proceeding east, you should enter the beautifully landscaped **Princes Street Gardens** on the right just opposite **Charlotte Street.** As you stroll along, you will enjoy the lawns and flower beds that provide an attractive foreground and brighten the scene of the turreted castle, the stone houses, and the church steeples rising above the rock. At any moment a Scotsman in kilts may saunter by. Take a few minutes to wander through the charming gardens, built on filled ground, the site of a former loch. Midway down the main walk below Princes Street is the impressive **memorial**—a soldier in kilts—erected by Americans of Scottish blood in sympathy to Scotsmen who were killed in World War I. Also note the **Scott Memorial,** a tall, Gothic construction honoring Sir Walter Scott, who resided in Edinburgh for some years. After passing an attractive display of heather— white, purple, and mauve—you will reach the lovely **Floral Clock,** the oldest of its kind in the world. Each quarter hour a cuckoo appears to sound the time. During the festival season (late August to early September) band concerts and displays of Scottish dancing take place in an open amphitheater nearby, and at night the gardens are beautifully floodlit.

At the top of the steps beyond the clock, pause for a moment and look at the skyline silhouette of the houses and churches of the old town. On leaving the gardens, start up **The Mound,** the street that crosses the park into old Edinburgh. On the left are two large buildings designed in the classic style—the **Royal Scottish Academy,** a building of pink stone, and the **National Gallery.** The Academy features contemporary works of art all year round (open Monday–Saturday, 10:00–5:00; Sunday, 2:00–5:00; closed holidays) while the National Gallery houses a fine selection representing most of the major European schools of painting, as well as the most complete collection anywhere of Scottish artists, including Sir Henry Raeburn (open weekdays, 10:00–5:00; Sunday; 2:00–5:00; closed holidays).

Continue to the right up the hill into **The Mound.** As Mound Place turns left into **Ramsay Lane** a bit of the Firth of Forth is visi-

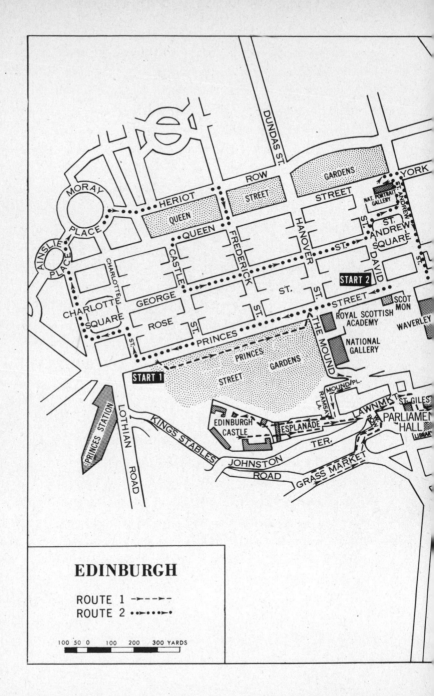

EDINBURGH

ROUTE 1 →--→
ROUTE 2 •--•••→

100 50 0 100 200 300 YARDS

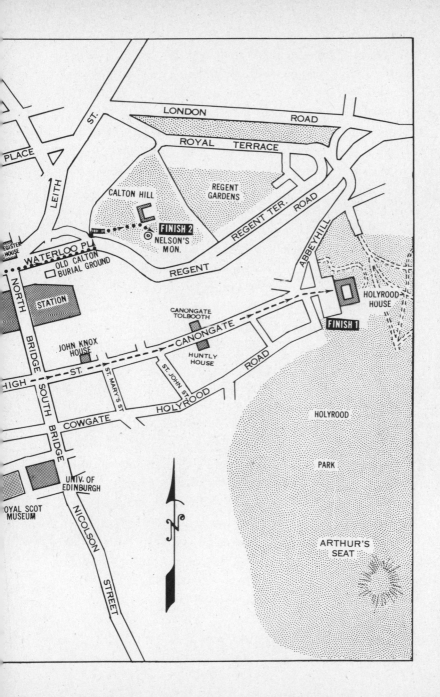

ble in the distance. Keep right past turreted houses to the large **Esplanade,** the castle's parade ground. In former days the burning of supposed witches took place here, but in summer, during the **Edinburgh Festival** season, it is the scene of the stirring military tattoo, a thrilling performance held at night under floodlighting, featuring massed bands. (The castle is open daily, 9:30–6:00 (5:00 in winter; closed weekends in winter.) **Castle Rock** is so steep on three of its sides that it was an almost impregnable fortress.

Statues of the Scottish heroes Robert Bruce and William Wallace on either side of the gateway are reminders that you are on historic ground. Kilted soldiers stand on guard outside the entrance. A steep road winds to the right past the drawbridge and under an ancient prison. In a few moments you will reach a terrace where a battery of old cannon are still in their emplacements. Here you will be rewarded by a magnificent panorama over the city, the wide Firth of Forth, and the hills of **Fife** on the horizon. At the summit, a little farther along, stands the tiny, low stone nonsectarian Norman **Chapel of St. Margaret,** the most ancient building in Edinburgh. It was built in 1073 and restored about a century ago. Some of the original gray stone is still visible in the walls. Fresh flowers in the chapel are changed every week by a group of Edinburgh ladies named Margaret under the patronage of Princess Margaret. In front of the chapel on the ramparts is **Mons Meg,** a huge fifteenth-century cannon. One of Europe's oldest artillery pieces, it fired a stone ball weighing four hundred pounds a mile and a half.

The **Scottish National War Memorial** is located inside **Palace Yard.** In the **Hall of Honor** you will be deeply impressed by the central shrine, consisting of banners, campaign flags, and regimented panels in memory of Scots who fell in two world wars. To see a display of Scottish military uniforms and an exhibit of memorabilia pertaining to the Scottish sailor John Paul Jones, "the Father of the American Navy," you should also stop in at the **United States Museum.** Be sure to see the great **banqueting hall,** decorated with crests of governors of the castle, with its fine hammerbeamed roof on the south side of the quadrangle. It was in the banqueting hall that the early Scottish Parliaments met. Now it houses a collection of armor and ancient weapons. In addition, you should visit the **Royal Apartments,** also in the courtyard, to see the tiny bedroom where Mary, Queen of Scots, gave birth to James VI of Scotland (James I of England). A fascinating display of Scottish regalia— crown, scepter, and sword of state (last carried in state on Queen Elizabeth's coronation visit in 1953)—is on exhibition in the **Crown Chamber.**

After wandering around the castle long enough to absorb its memorable history, return by the **Argyll Tower** with its portcullis leading to the Esplanade. You are now starting on the famous **Royal Mile,** so named because it descends from the Royal Palace in the castle to the Royal Palace of **Holyroodhouse.** It is one of the most renowned walks in Europe, and it promises to become even more so, for an extensive and gradual program of restoring the dilapidated old buildings along the Royal Mile has been in progress for some time.

On leaving the Esplanade you may notice a cannon ball (dating from 1745) embedded in the wall of the first house (1630) on the right just above the central window. A few yards farther along to the left, the **Outlook Tower** is worth visiting and is particularly fascinating for children. In the roof there is a **camera obscura.** The reflection of light through this device enables you to see on a clear day the details of the new town and surrounding country projected on the floor (open daily, 9:30–6:00).

You now enter the wide **Lawnmarket,** so named because the booths of lawn, or cloth, sellers were located here. On either side of the Lawnmarket there are narrow alleyways, or closes, where many distinguished figures lived. In **Milnes Court** on the left you will note a balustrade with curved bars that permitted eighteenth-century ladies in their wide crinoline dresses to pass. The old houses in the closes deteriorated into slums during the nineteenth century, when the new town became fashionable. However, these multistory dwellings are undergoing extensive restoration, so now it is interesting to wander around the closes. Turn right down the steps in front of the church to ancient **West Bow,** a short, steep street lined in canyonlike style with high houses through which royal processions and victims on their way to the execution block passed to and from the castle. At the foot, beyond the old shops, you will come into a large square called the **Grassmarket,** where for several hundred years cattle and grain were sold. Then return by West Bow to the Lawnmarket.

In **James' Court** on the left lived the Scottish philosopher David Hume. Dr. Johnson stayed with his host and biographer James Boswell in the eastern corner. In another close on the left of the Lawnmarket, where the poet Robert Burns lived in 1786, is **Lady Stair's house,** now restored and a museum (open daily, 10:00–5:00; closed Sunday). Under the archway through which you pass from the Lawnmarket, note the tablet, which records that "in a Tavern of 1717 Sir Richard Steele gave supper to a company of eccentric beggars." Opposite is the close where Deacon Brodie lived. He is believed to have been the character whom Robert Louis Stevenson had in mind when writing *The Strange Case of Dr. Jekyll and Mr. Hyde.*

As you wander around the closes or closed courts and down the Royal Mile, try to spot the marriage lintels (stones over the doorways), giving the dates and initials of the original owners.

The Lawnmarket opens into High Street. On the right is **Parlia-**

ment **Square** and the **Cathedral of St. Giles,** whose tower is shaped like the Crown of Scotland. If you look carefully in the square outside the west end of the church, you will see the design of a heart in the cobblestones, which marks the site of the old **Tolbooth,** or prison, popularized in the opening scene of Sir Walter Scott's novel *The Heart of Midlothian.* Although founded in the eleventh century, the cathedral is known primarily as the mother church of Presbyterianism because John Knox, the reformer, was its first minister.

The small **Chapel of the Thistle** (the thistle is the emblem of Scotland's highest order of chivalry), with its exquisitely carved stalls bearing the coats of arms of the knights, is an elegant though recent addition to the church's interior. The fine nave is hung with old battle flags and regimental standards.

At the east end of the square you will see the **Cross of Edinburgh,** which in days gone by marked the center of the city's life as well as the scene of burnings and beheadings and today is used as a forum for official proclamations. On the opposite side of High Street stands the **City Chamber,** or town hall.

The adjoining group of buildings includes **Parliament Hall** (open weekdays, 9:30–4:30; closed weekends) with a lovely hammerbeamed roof, where the Scottish Parliament met from 1639 to 1707. Parliament Hall is now used by lawyers, who pass up and down in their wigs and gowns waiting for their cases to be called in the various courtrooms of the Court of Sessions, the highest Civil Court in Scotland (public admitted). **The Advocates' Library** (open weekdays, 9:30–8:00 P.M.; Saturday, 9:30–1:00; closed Sunday), whose upper room is nobly proportioned, should also be visited. The burial place of John Knox in the courtyard near the cathedral is indicated by a circular spot in the tarmac of the present parking lot.

After passing several closes and crossing the busy junction of

North and **South Bridge** (the **University of Edinburgh** is off to the right), you will come to the picturesque sixteenth-century house on the left where John Knox died in 1572. Inside are many interesting exhibits relating to the "great reformer" (open weekdays, 10:00–4:30; closed Sunday and holidays). Mowbray House next door is considered the oldest private dwelling in the city. An interesting historical collection of toys can be seen in the **Museum of Childhood,** in **Hyndford's Close** (open weekdays, 10:00–6:00; closed Sunday). Look down some of the narrow alleys or closes on the right to get glimpses of industrial Edinburgh, almost obscured in smoky fog. In fact, Edinburgh is called "Auld Reekie" because of the pall of smoke that used to hang over the city in the morning.

After passing what was once **Nether Bow,** the east gate to the old city, you enter **Canongate.** A marriage lintel dated 1677 is over the doorway at No. 185. A few hundred yards farther, on your left, you will see the turrets and projecting clock of **Canongate Tolbooth,** a former courthouse and prison, built in the sixteenth century, that reflects the French influence in Scottish architecture. Today, it is a city museum containing an interesting tartan collection. Adam Smith, the author of *The Wealth of Nations,* which so greatly influenced eighteenth-century economic thinking, is buried in the adjacent churchyard.

On the opposite side of the street is **Moray House,** once used by Oliver Cromwell as a temporary residence. You should visit sixteenth-century **Huntly House** (open weekdays, 10:00–6:00; closed Sunday), a city museum where the local history of Edinburgh is shown in several seventeenth-century oak-paneled rooms. A copy of the National Covenant and John Knox's Psalter are on display. Go through the pleasant tearoom (Scottish scones are served) to a charming courtyard. On one side clay pipes are being made in a small workshop. Also see the typical Scottish kitchen of a hundred years ago. Now turn right just beyond Huntly House and stroll into **Bakehouse Close,** the best-restored of the many closes in the Royal Mile. **Acheson House** (1633), now a craft center, on the east side, is also particularly attractive. **Arthur's Seat,** the rocky mountain that rises above Edinburgh, can be seen in the distance. At the bottom of the hill on the left, the famous **White Horse Inn,** an artistic corner of old Edinburgh, has been restored to its original form.

Just beyond the square is Holyroodhouse, the Queen's official residence, built about 1500 by James IV and for years the Scottish Royal Palace. But before entering its historic grounds, take a turn down Abbeyhill to the left to see **Queen Mary's Bath House,** which dates from the late sixteenth century and was originally a postern gate in the palace's wall.

Holyroodhouse is best known for the period when Mary, Queen of Scots, resided here (1561–67), but the palace as it stands today dates mainly from the reign of Charles II, who rebuilt it in 1671 (open April–October, daily, 9:30–5:15; Sunday, 10:30–4:30; November–March, daily, 9:30–3:45; closed holidays). The long **Picture Gallery** and **State Apartments,** including the **throne** and **dining rooms,** are interesting because of their paneling, ceilings, paintings, and tapestries. The smaller rooms have a lived-in quality, unlike many palaces. Queen Elizabeth II and Prince Philip take up residence in Holyroodhouse every summer. But the most fascinating apartments in the palace are those connected with the tempestuous days of Mary, Queen of Scots. Here, in the main tower—the oldest part of the palace—is located the **secret staircase** and tiny apartment where the bloody murder of the Queen's secretary, David Rizzio, took place before Mary's eyes. In fact, a brass marker in the floor of the audience chamber, outside of the apartment, marks the spot where on March 9, 1566, the corpse lay with its fifty-six dagger wounds.

After touring the palace, you should visit the ruins of the twelfth-century **Abbey Kirk** on the left of the central courtyard. Then stroll around the beautifully landscaped grounds, where each summer the Queen holds a garden party. The artistically planted flower borders, charming rockery, shrubs, carpetlike lawns, and towering trees lend a country atmosphere to the palace park, which seems to nestle so fittingly beneath the high green slopes of Arthur's Seat, Edinburgh's mountainous landmark.

The New Town

Start your stroll through the **New Town** of Edinburgh on Princes Street at the corner of **St. David Street,** opposite the Gothic monument to Sir Walter Scott, Scotland's great historical novelist and poet. As you wander along stately **Princes Street,** you will enjoy indulging in some window-shopping, for Edinburgh's leading stores are located here.

When you reach Charlotte Street, at the west end of Princes Street, turn right and in a minute or two you will be in **Charlotte Square,** one of the most delightful in Edinburgh. The lawns, trees, and gardens of the squares in the new town lighten up the rather forbidding stone of the houses around them. If you walk to the left around the square you will pass the imposing **St. George's Church,** now used for the storing of archives. The delicate detail of the classic façades on the north side is one of the outstanding works of the great eighteenth-century architect Robert Adam.

There is one other spot nearby that is architecturally appealing—the circular **Moray Place,** just two blocks north from the west side of Charlotte Square beyond **Ainslie Place.** At Moray Place turn right on Darnaway Street and walk along **Heriot Row,** with the residents' private gardens on your right and attractive homes on your left, to the next corner. At. **No. 17,** R. L. Stevenson spent his boyhood years. A right turn into Frederick Street and another right at the next corner will bring you into Queen Street. At the next corner take a left turn into **Castle Street,** and in the second block on your left you will come to **No. 39,** an Adam house with a circular window on the ground floor. Sir Walter Scott lived here from 1802 to 1826.

A few yards farther on is **George Street,** which is a half mile long and was originally planned as the main avenue of new Edinburgh. An impressive thoroughfare, wide enough so that parking space is provided in the center, George Street, with its fine buildings and monuments, may strike you as even more distinguished than Princes Street. You can see at the west end of George Street the dome of St. George's Church in Charlotte Square and at the east end the high column in St. Andrew Square.

A few minutes' stroll to the left along George Street will bring you to **St. Andrew Square,** one of Edinburgh's finest. The massive stone buildings around the square—some of them eighteenth-century—house many of Scotland's leading banks and insurance companies. If you look right, toward Princes Street, you will get an unusual view of the **Scott Memorial.** Its tower rises above the crest of **St. David Street,** making it seem as though it were located there instead of on Princes Street, its actual site. At the far end of the square turn left one block down St. Andrew Street to visit the **Scottish Museum of Antiquities** and the **National Portrait Gallery** (open weekdays, 10:00–5:00; Sunday, 2:00–5:00; closed holidays) just around the corner to the left on Queen Street. The Museum of Antiquities contains a varied assortment of Scottish historical objects from the days of the Picts and Romans. John Knox's pulpit from St. Giles' Cathedral and the "creepie," or stool, which Jenny

Geddes is believed to have thrown at the Dean's head when he was reading Archbishop Laud's liturgy in 1637, are also on exhibition. In the National Portrait Gallery you will find paintings by Sir Joshua Reynolds and bronzes by Sir Jacob Epstein.

Return along St. Andrew Street to Princes Street and then turn left to **Register House,** the repository of Scottish national and historical records. This building is regarded as an excellent example of Robert Adam's design (open weekdays, 9:00–4:45).

Just a few yards ahead, along **Waterloo Place,** you can locate on the right the **Old Calton Burial Ground,** where you will be interested in a monument to the memory of Abraham Lincoln and the Scottish-American soldiers killed during the American Civil War.

Continuing along Waterloo Place, take a turn to the left and climb a flight of steps to the top of **Calton Hill.** From here you can see a magnificent panorama spread below—the new town at the foot; to the right, the **Firth of Forth,** the port of **Leith,** and the **North Sea;** and in the other direction the ridge of the **Royal Mile** and **Arthur's Seat.** The **two monuments** on the crest of Calton Hill are quite unusual: one a row of classic pillars, intended as a memorial of the Napoleonic Wars, which, if completed, would have been a reproduction of the Parthenon; and the other a telescope-shaped tower, in memory of Lord Nelson.

As you walk around the Observatory on the top of Calton Hill looking out over Edinburgh, with its striking contrast of ancient and modern, you are at the right spot to end your walk in this picturesque and lovely capital of Scotland.

PART TWO

The Continent

5.
Copenhagen

THE CITY OF COPPER ROOFS

Skirting the Canals

Copenhagen's lively, intimate atmosphere, the charm of its delightful old houses and squares, and its stately palaces with their copper roofs and beautiful parks has made this Scandinavian capital increasingly popular, particularly with Americans. Also, you will discover, like most visitors, that the Danes are a friendly, hospitable people with whom you will feel at home. Incidentally, English is really a second language in Copenhagen, which makes it easier for many tourists to find their way.

The center of the **old city** through which you will walk has not only considerable historical interest but also the seafaring spirit of a throbbing harbor and free port. One of the attractions in walking around Copenhagen is the considerable variety that you encounter—medieval streets, fascinating palaces and churches, canals and quays, and the fashionable shops, all comparatively close together and in one general area.

As a convenience to the stroller, this walk through Copenhagen

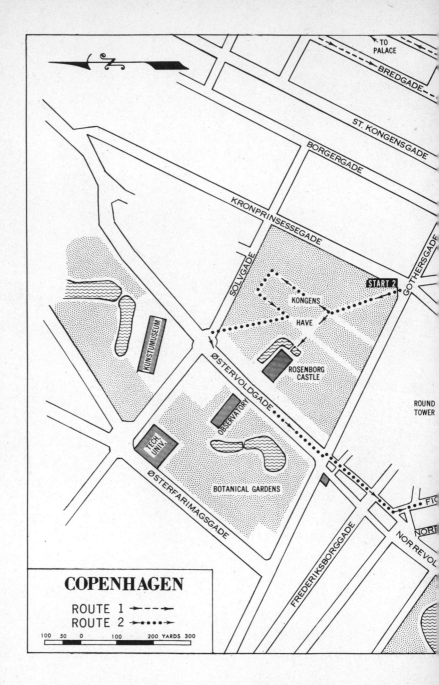

TO PALACE

BREDGADE

ST. KONGENSGADE

BORGERGADE

KRONPRINSESSEGADE

GOTHERSGADE

SOLVGADE

START 2

KONGENS

HAVE

KUNSTMUSEUM

ØSTERVOLDGADE

ROSENBORG CASTLE

ROUND TOWER

OBSERVATORY

TECH UNIV.

ØSTERFARIMAGSGADE

BOTANICAL GARDENS

FI

NOR

FREDERIKSBORGGADE

NØRREVOL

NOR REVOL

COPENHAGEN

ROUTE 1 ➤---➤
ROUTE 2 ➤•••➤

100 50 0   100   200 YARDS 300

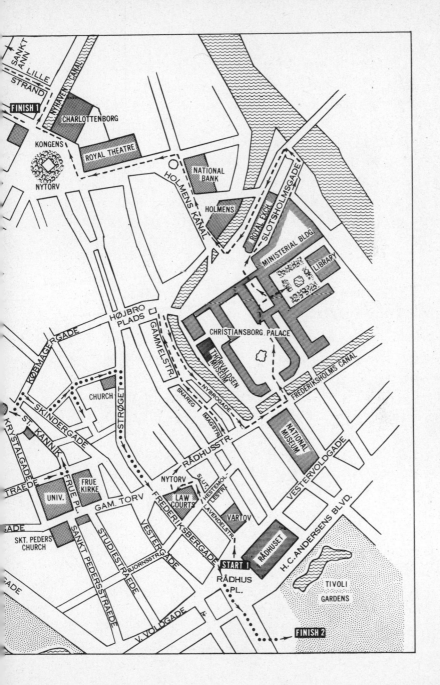

FINISH 1

SANKT ANN LILLE
STRAND
NYHAVEN CANAL
CHARLOTTENBORG
KONGENS
NYTORV
ROYAL THEATRE
NATIONAL BANK
HOLMENS KANAL
HOLMENS
ROYAL EXCH.
SLOTSHOLMSGADE
MINISTERIAL BLDG.
LIBRARY
HØJBRO PLADS
GAMMELSTR.
CHRISTIANSBORG PALACE
THORVALDSEN MUSEUM
FREDERIKSHOLMS CANAL
KØFMAGERGADE
CHURCH
STRØGE
SKINDERGADE
SNAREG
NYBROGADE
MAGSTR.
ST. KANNIK
KRYSTALGADE
RÅDHUSSTR.
NATIONAL MUSEUM
VESTERVOLDGADE
TRAEDE
FRUE KIRKE
FRUE PL.
UNIV.
GAM. TORV
NYTORV
S.LUT
HESTEMOL-
LESTR.
LAW COURTS
FREDERIKSBERGADE
LAVENDELSTR.
VARTOV
SKT. PEDERS CHURCH
STUDIESTRAEDE
SANKT PEDERSSTRAEDE
VESTERGADE
BJORNSSTRAEDE
START 1
RÅDHUSET
RÅDHUS PL.
H.C. ANDERSENS BLVD.
TIVOLI GARDENS
GADE
V. VOLDGADE
FINISH 2

has been divided into two parts, each of which should require about half a day. The first part includes the oldest section as well as the palaces of Christiansborg and Amalienborg. The second stroll covers the park, Rosenborg Palace, and the university and shopping sections.

You should begin your walk (in the morning, if possible) in the center of Copenhagen at the **City Hall Square,** or **Rådhuspladsen.** When you stand in front of the Palace Hotel, by the column depicting two Vikings blowing their horns, you are at the spot where some of the oldest habitations were located in earliest times, for Copenhagen's history goes back to the Stone Age.

If you have the stamina to climb the 300 steps to the top of the tower, you will be rewarded by a panoramic view of the old town, Rosenborg Castle, and the port (tours in English, Monday–Friday at 10:00, 12:00, and 2:00; Saturday at 12:00). Opposite the City Hall tower, you enter the old part of town by turning left into **Lavendelstraede.** Mozart's widow, who later married a Danish diplomat, lived at **No. 1** from 1813 to 1819. Now cross Hestemøllestraede, named for a mill that was driven by horsepower, and wander under the arch along a little winding street, Slutterigade. After passing through another arch you will be in **Nytorv,** the new marketplace. The classic building on the left with the large Ionic columns is the **City Courthouse;** formerly, it was the Town Hall until the new one was erected in 1906. Søren Kierkegaard, the famous Danish philosopher, was born next door in 1813.

From Nytorv turn right into **Radhusstraede,** where you will find some quaint old brass and copper shops. You may be attracted by the ground-level display windows and wish to browse around them for a bit. These houses were built in 1795, after the second great fire.

At the second corner turn left into the narrow street **Magstraede,** once the shoreline of the old town. It still preserves the atmosphere of early days. The two red-brick gabled houses on the right are about the only bourgeois homes dating from 1650 that survived the first conflagration, which devastated Copenhagen in 1728. Several of the Dutch-style houses on this curving street have antique shops in the basement. On the other side of Knabrostraede, Magstraede changes its name to Snaregade, although it continues to be just as narrow. The ancient house at **No. 5** is unusual for its fine timber beams and original early eighteenth-century, hand-fashioned blown glass windowpanes. Cross over to the opposite side to **No. 10** and look at a semicircular courtyard below ocher-colored buildings (1792). For a bit of variety, stop in at **No. 4** to see the series of amusing modern frescoes depicting the different owners who have lived there since 1397.

Straight ahead is **Gammel Strand,** which faces the **Frederiksholms Canal.** At the far end of the street you will come to one of Copenhagen's most picturesque scenes, the old red-faced women cleaning and selling fish. In the midst of the stalls, there stands a granite monument of a typical fishwife to personify the spirit of this colorful market.

Bishop Absalon's statue is in the square in front of you, **Hojbro Plads.** This medieval warrior founded the town where Christiansborg Palace stands. You can see the foundations of this and later castles when you visit Christiansborg. Beyond the statue, the corner house with pilasters was the home of the Melchior family; in the second-floor drawing room Hans Christian Andersen used to read aloud his popular fairy tales.

Return now along Gammel Strand, where there is a very good fish restaurant, **Fiskehusets.** Across the canal you will notice two buildings; the one with a green cupola is **Slotskirchen,** the castle chapel. (Excellent free concerts by the **Copenhagen Boys' Choir** are held in the chapel during the winter.) Next to it on the right is the important **Thorvaldsen Museum** (open daily, 10:00–5:00, except Monday,) featuring the famed Danish sculptor's neoclassical works as well as his collection of Danish painting. You should pay particular attention to the very fine old houses on your right.

Continuing along the canal, you follow **Nybrogade** to the end. Looking back along the canal, there is a superb view from here of the copper steeple of the **Nikolaj Church** reflected in the water. Now turn left on the Fredericksholms Canal, and you come to the **National Museum.** This museum contains, among other things, important and interesting ethnographic and prehistoric collections related to Danish culture. The museum has been rebuilt to make room for new collections and was totally refurbished in 1992. The main entrance is on Ny Vestergad. (Open June–September, Tuesday–Sunday, 10:00–4:00; October–May, Tuesday–Friday, 11:00–3:00; Saturday, Sunday, and holidays, 12:00–4:00.)

Cross the bridge opposite, at the corner of Ny Vestergade, with its exquisite rococo pavilions on either side. To the left is another view of the row of attractive houses, which have survived the centuries. Also, you will see the high sloping roof of **King Christian IV's huge brewery.** The canal itself is full of interest and activity, because in summer big wooden-hulled sailing ships and small steamers tie up at the wharf.

You now enter **Christiansborg Palace** and make your way over the cobblestones to the royal riding ring straight ahead, attractively landscaped with rows of pollarded trees. The curved archways and the symmetrical buildings on either side are the only remains of the original eighteenth-century palace. You can visit the state departments and the Danish parliament. (Guided tours in English, May–September, Tuesday–Sunday, 11:00, 1:00, and 3:00; October–April, Tuesday, Thursday, and Sunday, 11:00 and 1:00.) The building on the left is the indoor **riding hall,** and on the right are the **King's stables,** which you may be able to enter for a peep at its beautiful interior. If you happen to be here on Wednesday or Sunday between 2:00 and 4:00, stop in to see the old **court theater** also on the right, which now houses a **museum of Danish dramatic art.**

At the end of the open space, you walk under a colonnade to the right of the large palace and go into the courtyard of the **Folketing,** the Danish Parliament. In the building on the right you will see five low arches. Through the arches and down a couple of steps you will come to the most delightful part of Christiansborg, the marvelously landscaped gardens of the red-brick **Royal Library** directly facing you. The statue on your right depicts Søren Kierkegaard. Here is a most inviting and quiet place to sit for a while, under the birch trees, near the lovely large rose garden around the square pond. This enclosure used to be a naval harbor long ago.

With the library behind you, turn right and go through a low passageway into a large square in front of the palace. To the right along the canal is the old corn exchange, built in 1624, one of the most interesting and unusual Dutch Renaissance buildings in Copenhagen. It now houses the stock exchange. (Closed to visitors.) Saunter along **Slotsholmsgade** on your right to get a better view of the exchange and, especially, its corkscrew spire of four entwined dragon tails rising above its green copper roof. From the end of Slotsholmsgade you can see another twisted spire. This one has an external staircase and is across the busy harbor in the old part of **Christianshaven.**

Now go left around the **Royal Exchange,** or **Borsen,** to the canal on the far side. Here you will sense the busy life of the port. Ships for other parts of Denmark and for Sweden dock along the wharves to your right. As you stroll along the quay you will pass barges from the Danish islands, selling fruit, flowers, and vegetables—a gay and colorful sight. Every twenty minutes after 10:00, boats leave from here for **Langelinie,** a favorite promenade for Copenhageners, which runs along the harbor. From Langelinie the famous **bronze statue** of **The Little Mermaid** looks out to sea. In the early 1970s, radical students cut off the Little Mermaid's head. The city of Copenhagen was in an uproar until its mascot was made whole again. If you have an hour or more to spare, this trip will give you a good idea of the nautical side of Copenhagen.

Cross the bridge where you see the sign reading "Ring II" on the Havnegade to reach the **Holmenskirke** on your left, the site of a sixteenth-century anchor foundry for the Danish Fleet. You follow the broad avenue, **Holmens Kanal,** to the large square, **Kongens Nytorv,** which is pleasantly landscaped with attractive flower beds inside a ring of pollarded trees. **The Royal Theatre** for opera, drama, and ballet is on the right. **Grumstrup,** a leading antique dealer, is a little farther, located behind the theater (F. Holmens Kanal). Just beyond you will notice a beautifully proportioned building of dull red brick, built in the late seventeenth century. This is **Charlottenborg,** now the home of the **Royal Academy of Art.**

If you keep to the right around the square, you will reach **Nyhaven,** where sailing ships often are tied to the pier. This street along the canal, a popular hang-out for sailors, is filled with picturesque old houses, now cheap restaurants and seamen's dives. A short distance along Nyhaven will bring you to Lille Strandstraede, an interesting street, where you turn left. When you reach **Sankt Annae Plads** just a little farther along, turn right a few yards for the memorial bust of President Franklin D. Roosevelt, which the Danes erected after World War II.

You now walk along **Amaliegade** to the left for a few minutes to visit the **Amalienborg Palace,** the residence of the Danish Queen.

Enter the royal square through a colonnaded arch. The spacious courtyard with a fine equestrian statue in the center is most impressive. Four distinguished rococo mansions of lovely proportions occupy the four corners. The residence of the Queen is at the far right; other members of the royal family occupy the other buildings. At noon, when the Queen is in residence, the ceremony of changing the guard takes place. You leave the square on the left until you come to **Frederick's Church,** and then return to Kongens Nytorv by **Bredgade.**

If you started this stroll in the morning, you probably are ready for a good lunch. Around the square are several attractive restaurants—one is **Stephan A' Porta**—where you can relax and enjoy the tasty open sandwiches that the Danes prepare so well.

Rosenborg to Tivoli

If you take your second stroll through Copenhagen in the afternoon, start before 2:00. You should begin at the entrance to **King's Garden (Kongens Have).** To reach it from Kongens Nytorv, you walk a few blocks along Gothersgade through a dull business section to the corner of Kronprinsessegade.

The King's Garden, Copenhagen's first public park, was originally planted in the French style. Its extensive lawns (as green as those in England) and luxurious trees and shrubbery make this park exceptionally charming. A few steps inside the entrance you will reach an avenue of trees, then straight ahead you will see **Rosenborg Palace,** which used to be the King's summer home. To the left, beyond a narrow avenue of lime trees, you will have a glimpse of the Round Tower and **Our Lady's Church (Vor Frue Kirke).**

Take the path branching to the right and at the end you will come to a good statue of Hans Christian Andersen, surrounded by a bed of flowers. From here keep to the left past the herbaceous border to the parterre rose garden by the moat that flows around the palace. This is a delightful spot to pause for a moment while you study Rosenborg's rather fancy seventeenth-century exterior.

You leave the park by the **Queen's Gate** in the far corner and then turn left down Øster Voldgade and go a few hundred yards to the entrance of **Rosenborg Palace** (open June–August, daily, 10:00–4:00; May, daily, 11:00–3:00; November–April, Tuesday, Friday, and Sunday, 11:00–2:00). Inside there is a museum with exhibits pertaining to the Danish royal family, including the Crown regalia and an unusual collection of china, glass, and paintings.

On leaving the palace, continue along Øster Voldgade a few blocks into Nørre Voldgade. At the Nørreport underground station, turn left into Fiolstraede, the beginning of Copenhagen's **Latin Quarter.** You are now approaching the university section. As you wander along **Fiolstraede,** you will be enticed by the mass of old copper and brass bowls, plates, and so forth, hanging outside the many antique shops. Several secondhand bookshops display their wares on outside racks. At the corner of **Krystalgade** you will find a lovely ocher half-timbered house that dates from 1734.

A block farther along you will reach Frue Plads, the square dominated by **Our Lady's Cathedral** (open weekdays, 9:00–5:00; Sunday, 12:00–4:30) and the old buildings of the **University of Copenhagen,** founded in 1479. Across the courtyard, beyond a large tree, you will see the **Konsistorium,** a building of red brick and the oldest in the city. Opposite the front of the cathedral you should walk through an archway opposite the church (Nørregade II) into the delightful courtyard of the **Bishop's Palace,** shaded by trees and vines. Practically next door is **St. Peders Church** with a beautiful herb garden. The quarter is noted for its avant-garde boutiques and bookshops.

Return to the cathedral square and beyond the university on the far side saunter along Store Kannikestraede to **No. 10** where, in a quiet courtyard, you will discover a charming old house. This timbered building of varied height has a warm ocher coloring. The vine-covered walls and small fountain lend great charm to this out-of-the-way corner of Copenhagen. Just a little farther along the street you will come to the seventeenth-century **Regensen,** the university's oldest dormitory. Here you will see another charming courtyard, ivy-covered buildings with tile roofs, a clock tower and belfry, and, just above, the upper part of the **Round Tower.** (Open June–August, weekdays, 10:00–8:00; Sunday, 12:00–8:00; in winter, weekdays, 10:00–4:00; Sunday, 12:00–4:00.)

You should climb the wide spiral ramp of the tower—Czar Peter the Great once did it on horseback. The tower, built in 1637, was an observatory until a century ago. From the top you get an excellent and close impression of Copenhagen's old houses, with their gabled, sloping roofs and tree-shaded courts.

After climbing the Round Tower, you should wander around the nearby streets and visit two attractive squares. From the Round Tower go left a few yards on Købmagergade, then right on Skindergade, and in a moment left on Niels Hemmingsgade to Gråbrødretory, a square of great charm and quaintness. The eighteenth-century gabled houses are painted in pastel colors. There are several elegant antique shops on the square.

Return to Niels Hemmingsgade and on the other side of Valkendorfsgade you will come to **Helligandskirken** (Church of the Holy Ghost). You are now on **Strøget,** Copenhagen's famous and crowded main shopping street, which is really five streets continuing one another. Just across Strøget is a pleasant square with a flower market, from which you get a good view of Christiansborg Palace. **Illums Bolighus,** perhaps the city's leading department store and a center of modern design, is nearby (Østergade 52) and well worth looking around.

Now walk to the right past the many shops along Strøget toward Gammel Torv, and then on Frederiksbergade back to City Hall Square. Cross the busy square and shortly, on the left side of wide **Vesterbrogade,** you will reach the entrance to **Tivoli,** the world-famous amusement park. Even though you will want to return one evening for dinner (try the **Balkonen** for fine cuisine, and a taste of the great variety of entertainment—concerts, outdoor vaudeville, and pantomime shows, as well as the traditional "Fun Fair") it's pleasant to sit, perhaps by the lake, in these beautifully landscaped gardens—a fitting finish to these strolls through attractive Copenhagen.

6.
Amsterdam

HOLLAND'S CITY OF CANALS

The Old Town

Amsterdam combines business with art—the modern with the old—an active commercial port with the charm of the days of Rembrandt. It's a colorful city, with flower markets along the quays and music in the streets. It's a city of some fifty canals. But unlike Venice, most of Amsterdam's waterways are lined with cobblestoned streets.

In fact, there are two Amsterdams: the old town dating from the thirteenth century and the new, which developed some three hundred years later. Both are intensely interesting, quite different from other important European cities, and steeped in the history of the seventeenth century, when Holland with her Hanseatic merchants was a world power.

The art lover will be attracted to Amsterdam because it was the home of Rembrandt and because its world-famous Rijksmuseum houses probably the greatest collection of Dutch art to be seen anywhere. Those who admire fine old houses will derive much pleasure

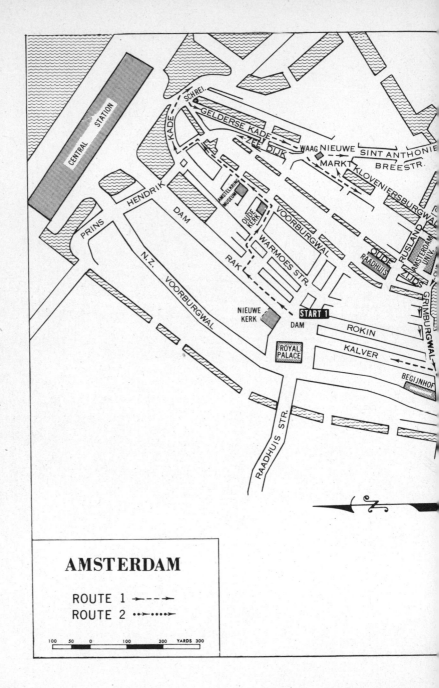

AMSTERDAM

ROUTE 1 —--→
ROUTE 2 ••••••••→

100   50   0   100   200   YARDS 300

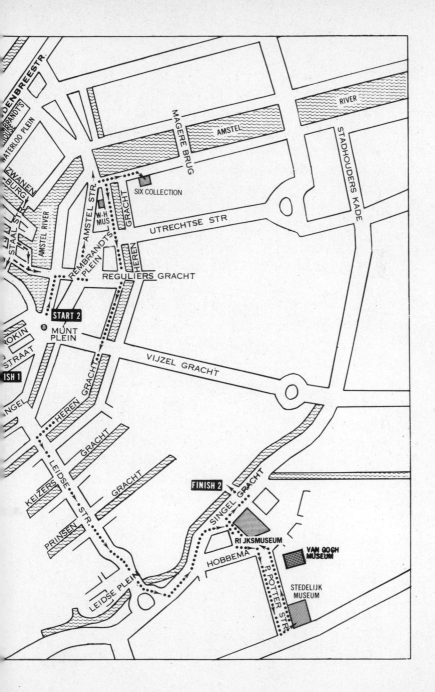

from the fascinating gabled residences of the great Dutch merchants that line the broad canals in the newer section. And if you like to stroll about a city where you continually encounter enchanting views, Amsterdam will delight you with its long vistas of tree-lined canals spanned by graceful bridges. Combine all this with the throb of a vigorous commercial community, its busy harbor teeming with activity, and you have an unusually attractive tourist center.

Here is a modern metropolis—one of the greatest ports in Western Europe—built on piles driven into the sand and composed of seventy islands. Although you will always sense the bustle and activity in Holland's financial and trading capital, you will find that the quiet and picturesque canals best express the spirit of this ancient city.

As you walk around Amsterdam, you will understand that its charm does not depend on the artistic views from its bridges or the stillness of its broad canals. It springs from a combination of sights and sounds and from the vivacity of the residents, reflected in its street life. Thousands of cyclists seem to overwhelm motor traffic. Concertina players can be heard, helping to satisfy the city's centuries-old craving for music, although carillons every quarter hours from church towers in the old section of the city are a more traditional feature of the city's musical life. Not only do the people of Amsterdam love music, but they adore flowers, which, during the growing season, seem to be everywhere—in markets, window boxes, barges, gardens, and parks.

Amsterdam, now a city of close to one million people, looks back on the sixteenth and seventeenth centuries as the period when it became a great commercial and cultural center. It won its freedom in 1578 during the Netherlands War of Independence. Shortly afterward, merchants and artists began to move to Amsterdam from Antwerp and Ghent; the size of the city doubled in the closing years of the sixteenth century. A few years later Amsterdam became the foremost trading port of Europe, and not long thereafter, Rembrandt, Bol, Van Ruysdael, and others established its artistic reputation.

For your convenience, two walking routes are recommended, the first concentrating on the **old town** and the second mainly centering on the **newer city** (built up during the seventeenth and eighteenth centuries) with its stately homes, its broad, peaceful canals, and its great museums.

Begin your first walk (women should wear flat shoes because of the brick sidewalks) at the **Dam**—the center of Amsterdam life—the huge open square in front of the Royal Palace (open June–August, daily, 12:30–5:00; September–May, Tuesday and Thursday, 2:00–4:00). The Dam is the central point around which the **five canals** that mark off the old section of the city fan out in concentric semicircles.

The Royal Palace, an imposing brick building that was originally the **Town Hall,** is a remarkable structure because its foundations rest on thousands of piles driven into the ground. The palace has recently been modernized to receive heads of state; the Queen resides here for only one symbolic week per year. The palace's **Great Hall** has an impressive air, particularly on state occasions, when thousands of candles sparkle from the large glass chandeliers.

The **Nieuwe Kerk,** Holland's coronation church and one of Amsterdam's oldest, stands opposite the palace at one end of the square. If you go inside to visit the burial place of Dutch heroes, you will notice the church's unusually fine vaulted wooden ceiling.

In Amsterdam there are many narrow streets down which cars tear at a terrific pace—so watch your step.

Stroll along the wide Dam a couple of blocks to a small square, **Beurs Plein.** At the far right-hand corner, go left in front of a red-brick building, then right down an alley, Paternoster Steeg, and across busy Warmoes Straat, the oldest street in the city. Straight ahead you will see the **Oude Kerk,** founded in 1309. This typical Dutch town church is worth examining for its spacious interior, stained-glass windows, and 223-foot sixteenth-century spire. Note the tiny houses built into the church tower on either side of its base. These were formerly stables for the horses of rich worshipers.

Now stroll along the right side of the church and walk to the left along the picturesque **Voorburgwal.** Looking across the canal, you will be enchanted by the ancient houses that actually lean forward. Look up and you will see the hoisting beam, a particular Amsterdam phenomenon, that has been used for hundreds of years to raise furniture and merchandise from barges to the upper floors.

Turn left and proceed along the canal a few yards, and shortly you will come to the **Amstelkring Museum** (open weekdays, 10:00–5:00; Sunday and holidays, 1:00–5:00), which contains a collection of Roman Catholic objects. Opposite, there are some fine rococo houses with stone pediments.

Before turning to the left on Zee Dijk to **Prins Hendrik Kade** in the inner harbor, turn around and look back along the colorful canal. Near the wide bridge you will find the wharves, where glass-covered excursion boats leave frequently, both during the day and in the evening, for an hour's delightful cruise through the network of canals—a trip you will enjoy even more after touring the city on foot, for then you will recognize many of the interesting places you have already visited.

Just to the right along the waterfront, past the bridge that leads to the railroad station, you will find around the corner an ancient stone tower, the **Schreierstoren,** which now houses the Master of the Port of Amsterdam. A tablet on the tower commemorates Henry Hudson, the discoverer of the Hudson River in New York, who sailed past here in the *Half Moon* in 1609. Another and more sentimental stone plaque on the opposite side shows a woman weeping as the ships sail away. As you stand facing the **Gelderse Kade**—the wide canal that runs into the harbor—you will be interested in the varied ornamentation of the houses, especially that of the shipchandler's warehouse on the right.

If you want to stroll along what was one of Amsterdam's famous old dikes and is now a street, turn right for a moment on Stormsteeg to **Zee Dijk.** But if you do, be prepared to confront a rather disreputable section of Amsterdam, for this is the sailor's **red-light district.**

Turn back, and at the end of the Gelderse Kade you will find yourself in the **Nieuwe Markt**—still an active street market—where the seventeenth-century gatehouse, called the **Waag,** houses the **Amsterdam Historical Museum** (open weekdays, 10:00–5:00; Saturday and Sunday, 11:00–5:00; closed January 1). Rembrandt painted his famous *Anatomy Lesson* in one of the upper rooms that formerly were guild chambers. The museum's **Jewish collection** is a most interesting chronicle of Amsterdam's Jewish community, which for several hundred years played such a vital role in the growth of the city and whose destruction by the Nazis is also recorded in a special exhibition.

A few minutes' detour from Nieuwe Markt along **Kloveniersburgwal** to **No. 12** will bring you to a two-hundred-year-old herb shop. You might like to putter about here and watch the shopkeeper weigh the herbs in his brass scale.

At the far corner of the Nieuwe Markt you will find **Sint Anthoniebreestraat,** leading to the Jodenbreestraat and **Rembrandt's house,** with its red wooden shutters (open weekdays, 10:00–5:00; Sunday and holidays, 1:00–5:00; closed January 1). This is just beyond the bridge, from which you have a good view along the canal to the left. The house is now one of the most interesting museums in Amsterdam. The interior has been restored and is very much as it was when Rembrandt lived here from 1639 to 1658. The art collection contains a fine group of his etchings, watercolors, and drawings.

From Rembrandt's house, turn left along Zwanenburgwal beside the canal and continue over the bridge. On the right, the spire of the **Zuider Kerk** rises in the distance. Just beyond the bridge, you will come to the juncture of the canal and the **Amstel River.** Here is a good spot to rest for a bit on a bench and look out over Amsterdam's network of waterways.

On the other side of the bridge you will be in Staal Straat; in a moment you will come to an old wooden drawbridge. To your right, the tree-lined **Groenburgwal** with the towering steeple of the Zuider Kerk at its end makes a picturesque scene. Now turn left and walk around the quay by the Amstel. Turn right to the 's-Gravelande Veer, then left; at the center of the bridge, look across the river and you will have a good view of the **Mint Tower.**

Turn around and then go straight along the canal Kloveniers Burgwal, which flows into the Amstel, then across the steel drawbridge on the left and turn right for perhaps a hundred yards along the canal to an archway. Colorful barges will very likely be moored to the quays.

You make your way down the dark, narrow, cloistered passageway lined with secondhand bookstalls and called Oudemanhuispoort. On your right the delightful courtyard shaded by a majestic copper beech is enclosed by the ivy-covered buildings of **Amsterdam University,** a seventeenth-century municipal institution with 30,000 students of 140 different nationalities. After wandering about the courtyard and browsing among the prints and maps farther along the passageway, you come out and cross a little bridge to your left. The scene you will see along the tree-lined **Oude Zijds Canal** is one of the most paintable in old Amsterdam. At the next corner to your right you will discover a tablet on an old brick house identifying it as the **Fluwelenburgwal** or Velvet Town Wall, a residence of the wealthy or velvet-clothed citizens.

Stroll across the bridge into Grimburgwal, and on to the wide Rokin. Just ahead you will be in the **Spui.** Cross Kalver Straat, one of the city's most crowded shopping streets, usually jammed with pedestrians. Take the Gedample Begijnen Sloot on your right. Then turn left through a little gateway, and you will discover a charming and quiet oasis, the **Begijnhof.** This is a somewhat circular group of old, narrow brick houses where, following a characteristic Flemish custom, widows and elderly women live. Each gabled house with its white window frames has a little garden in front facing the common lawn and overhanging trees. Notice the leaning tower of the brick church in the courtyard. The whole effect of the houses with sloping tile roofs, the old church, and the brick walk around the central lawn will captivate you. It's as if an old Dutch painting had come to life.

After this delightful interlude, continue along the Spui to the **Singel,** then turn left and you will be fascinated by a **floating flower market.** If you don't find what you want on the street, you can climb aboard the barges moored to the cobbled quay and join Dutch housewives as they shop for flowers and shrubs. It's one of the most unusual and attractive flower markets you will encounter in Europe. As an extra touch, you can hear the bells of the Mint Tower chime the hour. Enthusiasts for flower decorations should be sure to visit the shop on the other side of the canal, where flowers and plants are artistically arranged in special containers. It is called the **Aziatische Bloemsierkunst,** No. 506 Singel.

Now that you have started your shopping, return to the Spui and turn either left or right on **Kalver Straat,** where many of Amsterdam's most popular stores are located. This is just the place to interrupt your walk through old Amsterdam, either for shopping or for luncheon. There are several good restaurants nearby, including the 't **Binnenhofje** in the Singel or **Five Flies** at 294 Spuistraat. Both have an old-world atmosphere but are fairly expensive.

By the Canals to the Rijksmuseum

The Mint Tower, on Munt Plein, an Amsterdam landmark and favorite meeting place, is the best starting point for your second walk, through the **newer section** of the city. Years ago the city's coinage was minted in this old rounded brick tower surmounted by a belfry.

Walk along the **Amstel River** straight ahead and turn right at the bridge along Halvemaansteeg. After a short block you will be in the **Rembrandts Plein,** a small green square bordered with flowers and enlivened by sidewalk cafés and places of entertainment. Continue along Amstel Straat to the bridge over the river. From here you will see, on your right, one of Amsterdam's most famous and most picturesque bridges, the **Magere Brug.** Its characteristically Dutch balance levers are well known to devotees of Van Gogh and other Dutch painters.

Now you are about to walk along the first of the three wide parallel canals that give such a feeling of nobility to the newer part of the city. (You should also walk through this section at night when the houses are floodlit.) The most beautiful and distinguished of these tree-lined promenades is the **Heren Gracht.**

After returning to the Amstel Straat approach to the bridge, you will find the Heren Gracht, the first turn to your right. Stand for a moment on the bridge and look down this lovely canal. The house on the far corner has particularly beautiful brickwork.

To visit the **Six Collection** at 218 Amstel, just across the Heren Gracht, you must obtain a card of introduction by applying to the director of the Rijksmuseum. One of the finest private art galleries in Holland, its collection was started by Rembrandt's patron Jan Six. Its masterpiece is Rembrandt's painting of his friend Six, certainly one of the artist's greatest portraits.

Now return to Heren Gracht and saunter along the tree-covered quay. As you wander past the four- and five-story narrow brick mansions with their decorative stone garlands, you will get an idea of the kind of life Dutch aristocrats lived in the seventeenth and eighteenth centuries. Now many of the houses are occupied by banks, law offices, and business firms. It's also a fashionable neighborhood for wealthy young married couples. If by chance you should notice a door that is open, perhaps a discreet inquiry will result in an invitation to see the rich ornamentation of the interior decoration done in the French style of that period. You might stop in at the **Willet-Holthuijsen Museum,** the building with fine metal and stone works at No. 605, where furniture, glass, porcelain, and objets d'art from the sixteenth to the nineteenth centuries are on exhibit (open weekdays, 10:00–5:00; Saturday and Sunday 11:00–5:00; closed January 1).

No. 284, once the Van Brienenhuis, an early eighteenth-century mansion, is now occupied by the **Hendrick de Keyser Society.** It is no longer open to visitors; however, you may obtain special permission by writing the society well in advance of your visit.

At the second bridge, **Reguliers Gracht,** you have a fine view of the canal in each direction. Often private sailboats are moored along the quay.

Continue your stroll along the curving canal until you reach Koningsplein; turn left, cross the bridge, and you enter the Leidse Straat. Most of Amsterdam's quality stores, as well as the city's finest restaurant, **Dikker and Thijs,** are located here. As you walk along, you will cross two other broad canals, the **Keizers Gracht** and the **Prinsen Gracht.** At No. 672 Keizers Gracht, drop by the **Van Loon Museum,** a seventeenth-century town house recently opened to the public (open Monday, 10:00–5:00; Sunday, 1:00–5:00). Continue to No. 263 Prinsen Gracht to **Anne Frank's house,** a memorial to the young Jewish girl who recorded the Nazi occupation in her shattering diary and who perished in a concentration camp (open June 1–September 1, 9:00–7:00; Sunday and holidays, 10:00–7:00; September 1–May 30, 9:00–5:00; Sunday and holidays, 10:00–5:00). Notice that the trams make their stops on the bridges. Return to Leidse Straat and continue to the **Leidse Plein,** where the **Municipal Theatre** is located. Just beyond the square you cross **Singel Gracht,** a wide and curving canal.

Turn to the left through the beautifully landscaped little park. Across the canal, rose gardens decorate the banks. In a couple of blocks you will come to the world-renowned **Rijksmuseum** on your right (open weekdays, 10:00–5:00; Sunday and holidays, 1:00–5:00). Its collection of Dutch paintings is unrivaled; Flemish and Italian artists are also well represented. In addition, the gallery has fine exhibits of Dutch arts, crafts, and sculpture. But if you have only a limited amount of time, you will want to concentrate on Rembrandt's *The Night Watch, The Jewish Bride, The Staalmeesters,* and the other fine examples of his work. Also, you will be thrilled by the superb, though few, Vermeers on exhibit.

If you prefer modern art, you may wish to limit your time in the Rijksmuseum and save yourself for the **Stedelijk Museum,** just two blocks behind it, which contains works by twentieth-century Dutch painters and many French Impressionists (open daily, 11:00–5:00; closed January 1).

Next to the Stedelijk, at Paulus Potterstraat 7, is the renowned **Van Gogh Museum,** opened in 1973. Its resolutely modern architecture and vast, sunlit interior is a perfect setting for the master's works, which deserve an extended visit (open daily, 10:00–5:00; Sunday and holidays, 1:00–5:00; closed January 1).

After reveling in this artistic feast you will feel like sitting quietly and enjoying tea or a drink, so cross the Singel Gracht and find a table on the attractive outdoor terrace of the **Lido** overlooking the canal. This is just the spot to contemplate the fascinating places you have visited while strolling through Amsterdam.

7.
Bruges

THE WORLD OF THE MIDDLE AGES

To the Lake of Love

Bruges is unique. The medieval and Renaissance worlds have miraculously survived in this Flemish city. Here, encircled and intersected by quiet waterways, the past has been preserved for the enjoyment of the present. Though there are a few other relatively untouched medieval towns in Europe, none is quite so accessible to the mainstream of tourist travel, for Bruges is only fifteen miles from **Ostend,** on the English Channel, and sixty from **Brussels.**

When you cross the outer ring of canals and enter the **old city,** you feel at once transported into the days of Bruges' greatest glory, the fourteenth century. Then, through its trade both in wool and cloth with England, its status as a Hanseatic town, and its commercial ties with Italy, Bruges was one of the great trading and artistic centers of northern Europe. In those days the medieval guilds flourished, and the wealthy Flemish merchants made possible the northern Renaissance.

Today as you wander down the narrow streets past the ancient houses and along the tree-lined quays, the spirit of old Bruges lingers on. The reflections of the ivy-covered buildings and tall Gothic towers in the waters of the canals remind you of the time when Bruges, at the junction of the trade routes between the Baltic and the Mediterranean, was the home of humanism, when Italian bankers sat for Van Eyck, and Memling painted his marvelous triptychs.

Being so concentrated—it's hardly a half mile from one side to the other—and packed with such fascinating detail, Bruges is perfect for the tourist who wants to do his sight-seeing on foot. In fact, you couldn't properly see the city any other way. By walking, you have time to stop and admire the picturesque corners, medieval towers, and lovely façades with which Bruges abounds.

Before starting on your walk, you should buy a museum card, which entitles you to a reduced rate, is transferable, and can be purchased at any museum or at the **Bruges tourist office** located in the **Government Palace** at No. 7 in the **Markt,** or Market Place.

Let us start our walk here in the **Market Place**—the main square of Bruges. There before you rises the impressive, lofty **tower**—one of the most significant Gothic structures anywhere—soaring above the fourteenth-century market house. (Open April–September, 10:00–5:15; October–March, 10:00–11:45 and 1:30–4:15.) Stand well back in the square so you can see the graceful turrets of the 280-foot belfry. The world-renowned **carillon,** which is composed of forty-seven bells, is played every quarter of an hour. Come back for a carillon concert some evening. (Open June–September, Monday, Wednesday, and Saturday, 9:00–10:00 P.M.) Listening to its majestic tones is a thrilling experience.

As you start toward the tower, you may be surprised to note that it leans slightly to the southeast. If it is a clear day and you want to

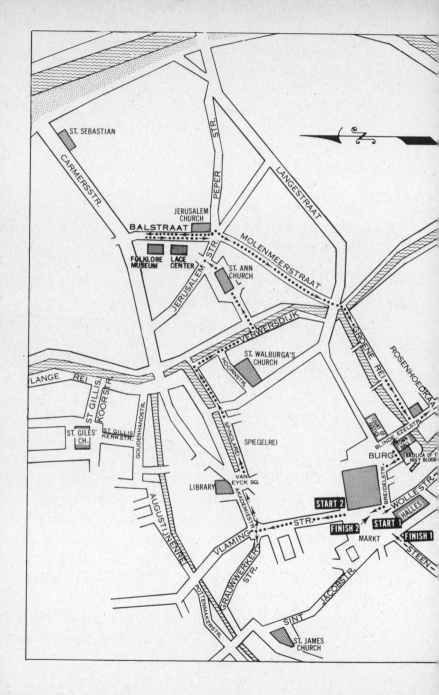

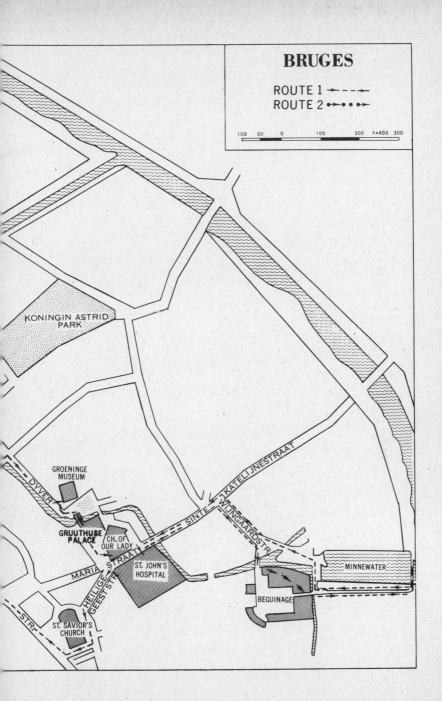

BRUGES

ROUTE 1 — — —
ROUTE 2 •—• • •—•

100 50 0 100 200 YARDS 300

KONINGIN ASTRID
PARK

KATELIJNESTRAAT

GROENINGE
MUSEUM

DYVER

SINTE

WIJNGAARDSTR.

GRUUTHUSE
PALACE

CH. OF
OUR LADY

MARIA STRAAT

HEILIGE GEEST STR.

ST. JOHN'S
HOSPITAL

MINNEWATER

BEGUINAGE

STR.

ST. SAVIOR'S
CHURCH

enjoy a wonderful view of the city and the sea, you may climb some 360 steps to the top.

Wander around the square to look at the old **guild houses** opposite the bell tower. The **Fishmongers' Guild** can be easily spotted by the fish-shaped sign on its building.

Now follow Wollestraat along the side of the bell tower to the bridge over the canal. Then turn right along the **Dyver,** an embankment shaded by chestnut, linden, and weeping beech trees, and lined with cream- and gray-colored houses. From March to late October, pick up a souvenir at the **Flea Market** on Saturday and Sunday afternoons. Just to the left, enter a gateway to a rose garden. This will bring you to the **Groeninge Museum,** the city art gallery (open daily, 9:30–5:00, April–September; daily except Tuesday, 9:30–12:00 and 2:00–5:00, October–March; closed holidays). You should go in to see the important paintings by such great Flemish artists as Rogier van der Weyden, Jan van Eyck, Hans Memling, and Gheerardt David, as well as Belgian contemporary art. A fifteenth-century Van Eyck, painted on wood, is remarkable for the extraordinary quality of its blues and reds.

At the end of the quay, the **Gruuthuse Palace** (open daily, 10:00–11:30 and 2:00–4:30, April–September; daily except Tuesday, 10:00–12:00 and 2:00–4:00, October–March; closed holidays) is well worth a visit for its fine collection of objets d'art, silver, china, and musical instruments, as well as lace and pottery, for which Bruges is still famous. The building itself is a splendid medieval mansion decorated with great fireplaces, beautifully tiled floors, and rich wood carving. The exhibits and furniture are arranged to show how people lived during the fifteenth and sixteenth centuries. You will find the kitchen fascinating, with its huge brick fireplace. Giant hooks hold kettles and pots. There is a huge iron caldron that was used for washing utensils. The motto above the fireplace, *Plus est en vous* ("You can always do better"), will amuse you. A less attractive relic is an eighteenth-century guillotine, formerly used in Bruges.

A little farther along is the **Church of our Lady** (open daily, Monday–Saturday, 9:00–11:30 and 2:30–5:00; Sunday and holidays, 2:30–5:00). Its tower is 375 feet high. Inside, you will be excited by Michelangelo's exquisite marble statue of the Virgin and Child in the south transept. The great sixteenth-century artist Albrecht Dürer expressed his admiration of the statue on a visit to Bruges.

Although these two museums are interesting, you should save your most intensive sight-seeing for what is probably the finest art collection in Bruges, the **Hans Memling Museum** in what was formerly **St. John's Hospital** just across the street through an archway from the Church of Our Lady. The Memling masterpieces are hung in a corner of the fifteenth-century early Gothic hall. Its high roof, original oak beams, and huge windows give it an atmosphere of great spaciousness. The six outstanding works in the former **Chapter Room** include *The Shrine of St. Ursula* (perhaps the most notable), *The Mystic Marriage of St. Catherine,* and *The Adoration of the Magi.* (April–September, open daily, 9:30–5:00; mid-January–March, 9:30–12:30 and 2:00–5:00; closed holidays.) In addition to the Memling Museum, you should visit the cloisters, the seventeenth-century pharmacy, and the portrait gallery. (Since 1977, the hospital services have been located in Ruddershove, a suburb of Bruges.)

As you leave, glance up at the sloping tile roofs against the background of the lofty church tower. This is one of Bruges' many picturesque touches.

Turn right along **Maria Straat** to the nearby bridge. Pause for a moment and study the odd angles of the old houses on either side. Now continue on Sinte Katelijnestraat to the third turning on the right, Wijngaardstraat, which you follow to the canal.

As you cross the bridge to enter the beautiful grounds of the thirteenth-century **Beguinage** (a modified nunnery founded by the Beguines, a charitable community of lay women), stop for a moment and look at the delightful vista in both directions. Below you there will probably be many swans adding a decorative note to the placid canal waters. In Bruges, they say the swans are kept in the canals because of an ancient legend. While you are enjoying this peaceful scene, black-frocked Benedictine nuns may pass to and from the Beguinage (open April–September, Monday–Saturday, 9:30–12:00 and 1:45–5:30; Sunday and holidays, 10:45–12:00 and 1:45–6:00; October, November, and March, Monday–Saturday, 10:30–12:00 and 1:45–5:00; Sunday and holidays, 10:45–12:00 and 1:45–6:00; December and February, Wednesday, Thursday, Saturday and Sunday, 2:45–4:15).

Walk into the quiet courtyard enclosed by trim whitewashed houses and shaded by lime trees. You will find the Beguines' house most charming and it will give you an idea of the meditative life led by the Benedictine Sisters who live there now. You leave the delightful grounds on the far side through the south gate, cross a bridge, and, after passing through a brick gate, you face the **Minnewater,** or the **Lake of Love**—a harbor during the Middle Ages. From the stone bridge at the far end, near the fourteenth-century tower, you have a fine perspective of the diverse foliage, reflected in the water in the foreground, and the spire of Our Lady's Church in the distance.

There is a small turreted brick castle on your right, partly hidden by copper beeches. Return along the tree-sheltered path to the old lockhouse. From here turn slightly right, past the little green where the swans are preening themselves, into Wijngaardstraat. To the left on **Walplaats** you will probably see elderly women making lace in the doorways of their homes. Just to the right you will once again be in Sinte Katelijnstraat. After you pass Our Lady's Church, take the left fork, Heilige Geeststraat, to the **cathedral, St. Savior's Church,** the oldest in Bruges. Its interior is well proportioned and includes a **museum** with several fine Flemish paintings. (The church is open all year, Monday–Saturday, 8:00–11:30 and 2:00–6:30; Sunday and holidays, 8:00–11:30 and 3:00–6:45. The museum is open in July and August, Monday–Saturday, 10:00–12:00 and 2:00–5:00; Sunday and holidays, 3:00–5:00; the rest of the year daily, 2:00–5:00; Sunday and holidays, 3:00–5:00; closed Wednesday and January 1.) But if you feel you have done enough sight-seeing, just walk around the cathedral and follow Steenstraat for about three hundred yards back to the Market Place.

If you started the first walk in the morning, you may have returned to the Market Place in time to lunch at one of the two good restaurants in the square, the **Huyze Die Maene** or the **Civière d'Or,** decorated with original paintings by Toulouse-Lautrec and Renoir. Bruges also has several excellent pastry shops, so keep that in mind for now or later.

Reis and Waterways

Begin the second stroll by following Vlamingstraat for two blocks to **Theater Plaats,** where you will find a fourteenth-century residence at **No. 33,** occupied centuries ago by merchants from Genoa. Turn left down Grauwwerkersstraat to No. 35. On this site was a building, which belonged to the Van der Beurze family, where merchants gathered in the fifteenth and sixteenth centuries to transact business. Hence the word "bourse" or "beurze" came into use for commercial centers all over the world. Now return to Vlamingstraat and cross into Akademiestraat; a few yards farther on, you come to **Jan van Eyck Square,** one of Bruges' most historic sections. There are several interesting narrow streets here where you can wander. On one side of the square stands the fifteenth-century **Customs House,** which contains the **Public Library.** Inside you may see the exhibit of paintings by William Caxton, who printed the first book in English and who lived in Bruges during the fifteenth century.

The square overlooks a **wide canal**—one of the loveliest scenes in Bruges. Gray and white brick and stucco houses with tiled roofs face one another across the canal. At the far end you will see a fine white house that looks like a French hunting lodge. It was once the Spanish Embassy. Walk along the quay on the right, **Spiegelrei,** to the first bridge. Look back at the Van Eyck statue and the Gothic tower above. Continue along the quay to the end, study the lovely houses, and turn right on Verwersdijk. Pause on the first bridge for the fine vistas on both sides. Just ahead is the mellowed brick **Church of St. Ann.** Its simple exterior contrasts with its impressive Renaissance interior, which has the carved woodwork and brass candelabra so often seen in Flemish paintings. Just behind the church, by taking a right turn, you will come to the **Jerusalem Church,** noted for its stone altarpiece and stained-glass windows, the oldest in Bruges (1483). For admission, you must ring the bell at the gate on the right. (Open Monday–Friday, 10:00–12:00 and 2:00–6:00; Saturday, 10:00–12:00 and 2:00–5:00; closed Sunday and holidays.)

Follow Belstraat to No. 14, and drop by to visit the **Lace Center,** where people of all ages learn the traditional craft of lace-making. (Open daily except Sunday and holidays, 10:00–12:00 and 2:00–6:00.) Then proceed to admire the **Folklore Museum** at Nos. 27–41. This group of ten seventeenth-century houses has been restored; it's like stepping back in time. (Open daily, April–September, 10:00–12:00 and 2:00–5:30; October–March, 10:00–12:00 and 2:00–4:30; closed Tuesday and holidays.)

Now take Molenmeerstraat opposite the Jerusalem Church, make a left turn at the end, and in a few yards cross the bridge. Then turn right along the **Groene Rei,** one of the most delightful canals in Bruges. The **first bridge** you come to dates from the late fourteenth century and is the oldest of all.

As you saunter along here, you will be entranced by the effect of the ivy-covered buildings on the opposite side, the huge overhanging trees, and the greenish water of the canal.

In a few moments you will reach the **fish market,** which is located under a colonnade. Turn left and in a few yards you will be on the Rosenhoedkaai. Here, by the **Brick Tanners' Guild building,** is one of the most romantic and beautiful sights in Bruges—the old brick houses on the other side of the canal and, soaring above them, the magnificent belfry tower and spire of Our Lady's Church. Many artists, including Sir Winston Churchill, have found this an irresistible setting, beautifully modulated by the reflections in the water at different hours of the day.

When you can drag yourself away from this incomparable scene, walk back toward the Fish Market past the Tanner's Guild (now an exhibit of modern handicrafts) and the ancient Duke of Burgundy hotel (its dining room, hung with an unusual collection of modern paintings, has a wonderful location overlooking the canal).

Linger for a few minutes on the bridge by the Fish Market. You will be fascinated by this charming corner of Bruges—with the old buildings along the quay, the hanging gardens and luxuriant trees shading the water, the donkeyback bridges, and the Gothic towers and spires. Motor launches leave from the dock just below the bridge for a tour of the canals—a delightful half-hour trip which you might make as a finale to your visit. It's particularly attractive after dark, when many of the buildings and towers are floodlit.

From the bridge walk along the Blinde Ezelstraat to the **Burg,** or **Castle, Square,** named after the fortress formerly located here that belonged to the Dukes of Burgundy and which was then protected by moats. Here you can hire a horse and carriage for a romantic ride (daily from 10:00–6:00).

Several interesting ancient buildings of varied architectural styles surround this small square. The first one you should visit is in the left-hand corner, the **Basilica of the Holy Blood** (open in summer, 9:30–12:00 and 2:00–6:00; in winter, 10:00–12:00 and 2:00–4:00; closed Wednesday afternoons). This Romanesque chapel is really divided into two chapels, an upper one and a lower one. The **upper chapel,** Gothic in design and ornate in decoration, contains the relic in which, it is said, there are drops of Holy Blood brought from Palestine in 1150. Every year in early May the relic is carried in the colorful religious **Procession of the Holy Blood.** The **lower chapel** is a magnificent example of Romanesque architecture and a striking contrast to the upper chapel. Next to the chapel is one of the oldest and finest Gothic town halls in northern Europe. (For admission, ask the caretaker.) Its exterior turrets are quite striking, and, on the inside, the **Great Hall** has a magnificent vaulted fourteenth-century roof and nineteenth-century murals depicting the history of Bruges. The gold boss in the ceiling is original. If you have time, you might look through the adjacent eighteenth-century **Court of Justice,** particularly to see the unusual black marble chimneypiece in the Court Room, which was made in 1526.

After visiting these interesting buildings, stroll a few yards along the narrow Breidelstraat back to the Market Place. When you have completed these two strolls, you will agree that Bruges is incomparable—a precious, enchanting, and beautiful heritage of Western culture.

8.
Brussels

MODERN CAPITAL
WITH AN OLD-WORLD AIR

The Upper Town

Brussels, Belgium's cosmopolitan capital, has a genuine appeal for the tourist as well as the business executive or government official visiting this headquarters of the European Community and NATO. Though it is an old city—more than a thousand years older than the country it governs—you will be struck by its modern, up-to-date air. Yet this twentieth-century vitality you sense as you stroll about Brussels hasn't spoiled those sections that are reminiscent of the late Middle Ages and the days of the Hapsburgs when the trade corporations were the center of the city's life. Many buildings are in the process of being renovated.

In recent years this city of just under a million people has been divided into an upper or newer, and a lower or older, section.

You should start your walking tour of Brussels at the **Palais de Justice** in the upper town. Stroll over to the terrace from the square in front of this huge building. Here you have a good view over the lower town. You can use the automatic guide that presents a brief

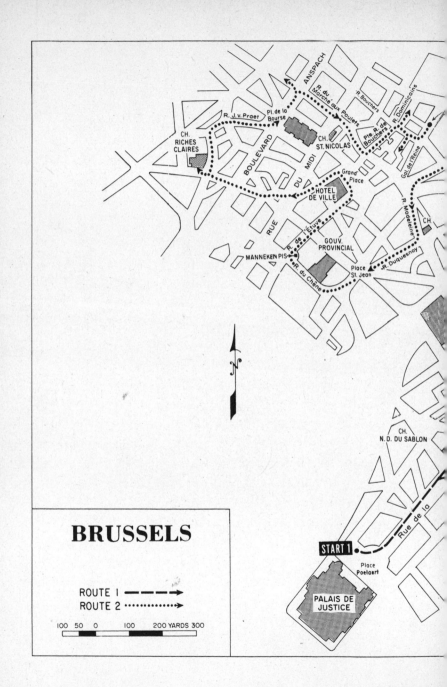

ANSPACH

R. du
Marché aux Poulets

R. Bouchers

R. Dominicains

R. J. v. Proet

Pl. de la
Bourse

Phe R de
Bouchers

R. Pte de l'Reine

CH.
RICHES
CLAIRES

BOULEVARD

CH.
ST. NICOLAS

DU MIDI

Grand'
Place

Gal. de l'Reine

HOTEL
DE VILLE

R. Madeleine

CH

RUE

R. de l'Étuve

GOUV.
PROVINCIAL

MANNEKEN PIS

R. du Chêne

Place
St. Jean

R. Duquesnoy

N

CH.
N. D. DU SABLON

Rue de la

START 1

Place
Poelaert

PALAIS DE
JUSTICE

BRUSSELS

ROUTE 1 ————▶
ROUTE 2 ●●●●●●●▶

100 50 0   100   200 YARDS 300

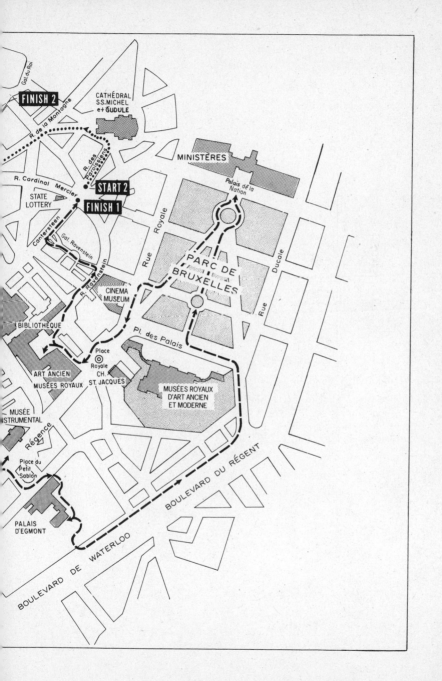

recorded talk in English on the city and its main buildings, such as the ancient **Town Hall,** that you see before you.

The **Palais de Justice,** called the Mammoth by local residents, is the largest building erected during the nineteenth century and covers a much greater area (five acres) than St. Peter's in Rome.

From the **Place Poelaert,** named for the Palais' architect, you follow the left side of the Rue de la Régence for about five minutes until you come to the **Rue des Sablons.** On the left is the elegant **Place du Grand Sablon,** the center of the antiquarians' district. You may feel like looking around some of the antique shops that face the square. A flea market in antiques and rare books takes place here in the open square on Saturdays and Sundays from 9:00 to 2:00.

The pure Gothic Church of **Notre Dame du Sablon** on the **Rue de la Régence** was founded during the fourteenth century by the guild of crossbowmen.

On the corner just across the avenue from the church is the **Musée Instrumental,** a fine museum of musical instruments (open Tuesday–Saturday, 2:30–4:30; Sunday, 10:30–12:30; closed holidays).

The little park opposite the **Place du Petit Sablon** is one of the most charming in Brussels and one of the most unusual in Europe. Forty-eight bronze statuettes, representing the various trading corporations of Brussels, rest on columns that circle a delightful garden with flower beds and a fountain at the end. You will be fascinated to inspect in detail the different figures of the ancient guilds—the fisherman, cobbler, saddle maker, archer, and so forth.

When you leave the park just above the fountain, have a look at the interesting old house on the right-hand corner of the square. Built in 1610, it is now a restaurant, **Au Duc d'Arenberg.**

Cross the street and enter the courtyard of the **Palais d'Egmont,** a classic eighteenth-century mansion, where international receptions are held. You pass under an archway and by keeping to the right come into the attractive, wooded park which the palace faces. This is a pleasant place to wander for a bit. The tower of the Palais de Justice looms in the distance. You will notice **Beethoven's statue** and recall his Egmont overture. Count Egmont was a hero of the Low Countries' resistance to Spain.

Continue along the cobblestoned alley by which you entered the palace grounds and pass beside the ivy-covered building in which there are artists' studios, then go under an archway and through a large entrance doorway into the wide **Boulevard de Waterloo.**

Turn left along this fine avenue with its attractive luxury shops and in a few minutes you will come to a small square, the **Place du Trône.** The large classic building on your left is the Royal Palace. It stands in extensive grounds well back from the impressive entrance gates.

A left turn along the **Rue Ducale** will bring you to the front of the nineteenth-century palace, with its eighteenth-century wings, which is landscaped with beautifully planted sunken gardens.

Now you should cross over to the **Parc de Bruxelles.** Belgium won its independence here in 1830. Earlier it was a hunting preserve of the Dukes of Brabant. Stroll down its broad tree-lined promenade, past the pond, toward the eighteenth-century **Palais de la Nation,** which you can see facing you. It now houses the **Belgian Parliament** (guided tours for groups only).

From the large pond in the park you follow the walk that will bring you out at the corner of the **Rue Royale** and the **Place des Palais.** Just across from the Rue Royale is the **Palais des Beaux Arts,** Brussels' cultural center, which is used for concerts and exhibitions, and houses the **Cinema Museum.**

A minute or two from this corner of the park is the **Place Royale.** This classic square, with the **statue of Godefroy de Bouillon,** leader of the First Crusade, in the center, is in eighteenth-century French style. The royal church of **St. Jacques sur Coudenberg** stands at the far end.

The **Royal Museums of Fine Arts** combine the Musée d'Art Ancien and the adjoining Musée d'Art Moderne. The latter opened in 1984. The building on the Place Royale houses temporary exhibits, while the permanent collections are below street level, with twentieth-century Belgian sculpture, painting, and drawing. (Open daily, except Monday, 10:00–1:00 and 2:00–5:00; closed holidays.)

The **Musée d'Art Ancien** (open daily except Monday, 10:00–12:00 and 1:00–5:00) is on the corner of the square, its entrance facing Rue de la Régence. You should devote some time to visiting this outstanding art gallery, notable especially for its collection of Flemish and Dutch paintings.

When you come out of this museum, turn left along the **Rue du Musée** to see the charming **Place du Musée** on the left. The stately **Bibliothèque,** or **Royal Library**, with its fine collection of engravings, medals, and coins, faces the square. Its illuminated manuscript collection is well worth visiting (open to groups only, upon request). While here, be sure to visit the sixteenth-century Gothic-style **Nassau Chapel,** where temporary art exhibits are held; the **Book Museum,** devoted to Belgian writers such as Ghelderode and Verhaeren (open Monday–Saturday, 2:00–4:45; closed Sunday and holidays); and the **Printing Museum,** where you can admire printing presses from the eighteenth to twentieth centuries (open Monday–Saturday, 9:00–5:00).

From the Place du Musée it's only a moment or two before you enter the curving **Rue Ravenstein.** Art galleries and antique shops line this street, but the most interesting building is just opposite, when you stand at the point where the street curves into the Rue Montagne de la Cour. This red-brick turreted building is the late fifteenth-century **Hotel Ravenstein.** It is the only remaining patrician house of this period and has an attractive inner courtyard.

A few steps farther will lead you to the **Albertina,** a complex of buildings and exhibition halls that are built around a landscaped garden. Standing above the garden, you can see the spire of Brussels' **Town Hall.**

Continue on the Rue Ravenstein to the entrance on the left of the large **Galerie Ravenstein.** This is a huge modern office building with a circular glass dome in the central hall. You will pass various shops selling paintings and antiques, as well as a cafeteria, before you emerge on the far side of the building on Rue Cantersteen. A few steps to the right will bring you opposite one of Brussels' glass skyscrapers, formerly a luxury hotel and now housing the State Lottery.

The Lower Town

You should commence your walk through the **lower town** and the older section of Brussels at the large **Saint Michel Cathedral,** only a few minutes along the **Rue des Paroissiens** and on the slope of the upper town. This Gothic church, built from the thirteenth to the fifteenth centuries, possesses sixteenth-century stained-glass windows and a fine carved wooden pulpit.

Walk down the **Rue Ste. Gudule,** in front of the church, and then bear left on the Rue de la Montagne past the gabled houses with their ancient façades. Keep to the left after crossing the junction of several streets and continue along the **Rue de la Madeleine.** The houses on this street, one of the oldest in Brussels, are particularly attractive with their baroque façades, gables, and balconies. Don't miss the delightful little **Church of the Madeleine,** nor its eighteenth-century bell tower.

At this point turn right into the Rue Duquesnoy and at the Place St. Jean cross over into the **Place de la Vieille-Halle-aux-Blés,** which is lined with old houses. You now bear right into the **Rue du Chêne.** A brick house on the left dates from 1697 and others are from the eighteenth century. If you look along the **Rue de Villers,** on the left you will see part of the old city wall with a battlemented tower.

The **Manneken Pis,** Brussels' famous bronze statue of a small boy creating a fountain, is just ahead on the corner of the **Rue du Chêne** and the **Rue de l'Étuve.** More than three hundred years old, this mascot of Brussels is regarded as its "oldest citizen." It has been stolen several times and was even broken up during the War of the Austrian Succession. But it has always been restored and put back in its place. The manikin has an entire collection of costumes with which he is dressed on special occasions. Nearby shops sell photographs of him wearing the various uniforms and suits of clothes.

Turn right on the Rue de l'Étuve and in a few yards you will come to an arch. The recumbent statue is of **Evrard 't Serclaes,** a fourteenth-century Brussels liberator. There is a story that if you touch the figure's arm or his dog's nose you will have good luck for a year—and then you have to return to Brussels for it to continue.

You now enter the heart of Brussels, the **Grand' Place,** one of the finest squares in Europe. Dominated by the tapering spire of the **Hotel de Ville,** or **Town Hall,** the square preserves the spirit of the ancient trade guilds. Although the original buildings had to be restored after the bombardment of 1695, the Gothic and baroque character of the guild houses, with their picturesque gables, balustrades, statues, and gilded decoration, has remained as a re-minder of the trade corporations' central role in the history of Brussels. Be sure to return at night to see these dramatic buildings under floodlighting.

First look around the square to get an overall impression of the different buildings. Opposite the Town Hall is the large Gothic-style **Maison du Roi,** formerly called the House of the Bakers. This is of quite recent construction—the latter part of the last century. Inside the Maison du Roi is a museum retracing the history of Brussels; on the third floor you can see the collections of costumes for the Mannekin Pis. (Open daily, 10:00–12:30 and 1:30–5:00 [4:00 in winter]; Sunday, 10:00–1:00; closed holidays.) One of the finest corporation houses is the **House of the Archers,** which dates from 1691. You can identify it by the portraits of Roman emperors that decorate its façade. Notice No. 6—**House of the Boatmen.** Its gable is in the form of the stern of a ship. Six houses on the southeast side of the square make up the **House of the Dukes of Brabant,** the home of various guilds. You will have a fascinating time just strolling around the square looking at the unusual details of these houses and browsing in the antique and lace shops. No. 10 is the **House of the Brewers.** Here you can visit a brewery museum and a reproduction of an old brewery (open 10:00–12:00 and 2:00–5:00; closed Saturday afternoon, Sunday, and holidays; closed Saturday 10:00–12:00 from November to March).

One of the finest restaurants in Brussels, **La Maison du Cygne,** is at No. 2 Rue Charles Buls in the **House of the Butchers,** just where you entered the Grand' Place.

Before you visit the **Town Hall,** you will observe that the left side of the building, which was built first (1402), is wider than the right side, which was added in 1444. The tower was added later. The statue of Brussels' patron saint, the **Archangel Michael,** surmounts the spire. In the courtyard you will see Brussels' official distance marker. It is interesting to tour the Town Hall (open Tuesday–Friday, 9:30–12:15 and 1:45–5:00 [4:00 in winter]; Sunday, 10:00–12:00 and 2:00–4:00; closed Saturday and holidays) to see the baroque **Great Council Chamber** and the **Salle des Mariages** where Brussels couples have their civil wedding ceremony performed.

Leave the Grand' Place by the side of the Town Hall on the Rue de la Tête d'Or. In a moment you will pass another of Brussels' odd fountains at the corner of the Rue du Marché au Charbon and the Rue des Pierres, **le Cracheur** (the Spitter). Water pours from the man's mouth as though he were spitting. Now turn left on the Rue du Midi from the Rue du Marché au Charbon—an old street—then right on the Rue du Lombard. Cross **Boulevard Anspach,** Brussels' main shopping street, then continue for about one hundred yards on the Rue des Riches Claires to the **Church of Notre Dame aux Riches Claires,** built of Spanish brick. You are now in the oldest part of the city.

From the rear of the church stroll left along the Rue de la Grande-Île. In a few yards you will come to the **Place St. Géry,** named for the river island that was once on this site. Brussels was born on this spot in A.D. 580 when St. Géry built a little chapel here.

Now turn into Rue Jules van Praet and you will see Brussels' **Bourse** in front of you. Stroll to the left along the busy Boulevard Anspach. If you would like to visit the city's great fruit, vegetable, and fish markets, take a short detour by turning left for one block at the **Rue du Marché aux Poulets.** You will note that many of the streets in this area are named for markets of one kind or another.

Cross the Boulevard Anspach and walk along the other side of the Rue du Marché aux Poulets and continue into the **Rue du Marché aux Herbes,** which, as its name suggests, used to be a vegetable market in the Middle Ages. Along here you will discover little passageways off the street that are called "impasses." Down one of them is an excellent restaurant, **Bon Vieux Temps,** which has lots of atmosphere of days gone by.

About one hundred yards farther along the Rue du Marché aux Herbes turn left into a narrow street, the **Petit Rue des Bouchers.** This section of the old city is full of intriguing little streets and restaurants. **Chez Vincent** is a colorful seafood restaurant on the Rue des Dominicains. Stroll along the Rue des Dominicains or turn from the Rue des Bouchers into a tiny passageway, the **Rue d'une Personne** (just wide enough for one person).

After exploring these byways, a few yards farther along the Rue des Bouchers will lead you to the center of Brussels' popular shopping arcades—the **Galerie du Roi** and the **Galerie de la Reine.** Here you will want to wander up and down these glass-covered arcades, lined with smart shops—a pleasant place to finish these walks through this modern capital with an old-world air.

9.
Paris

The Right Bank
Place de la Concorde to Place des Vosges

Paris's unique beauty and elegant charm take time to absorb. Walking is the ideal way to sense the mystique of this captivating city—a mystique that has exerted a magnetic attraction on visitors throughout the ages.

The river **Seine** flows through the center of Paris, dividing the city into the Right and Left Bank. A walk on the **Right Bank** will introduce you to various phases of Paris—modern and ancient, fashionable and simple. You will enjoy vistas that reveal the magnificence and splendor of the city. Also, you will discover out-of-the-way places where fascinating events in French history have occurred.

You will appreciate this walk more if you take it slowly and easily, with an occasional rest, perhaps at some pleasant café along the way or in one of several parks you will visit.

If you wish, divide this walk into several separate ones. Actually, the walk divides itself, since the route covers various aspects of Paris, some comparatively modern, some ancient, some elegant, some bourgeois or working-class.

Start in the morning at one of Paris's most magnificent squares, the **Place de la Concorde.** The Seine flows alongside. Cross the vast Place de la Concorde, one of the largest in the world (the traffic makes it an adventure for nimble pedestrians, but perhaps you'll want to play it safe, hugging the river and going around the Place). Enter the Tuileries gardens by the steps near the **Orangerie,** the small building overlooking the river, where Claude Monet's famous murals *Les Nymphéas* are on view (open weekdays except Tuesday and holidays, 9:45–5:15). Stop for a few seconds on the terrace's balustrade facing the Place, and linger over the majestic scene: the 75-foot granite **obelisk from Luxor** in the center (its companion may be seen in New York City's Central Park), flanked by spectacular fountains and, beyond it, Jacques-Ange Gabriel's colonnaded twin mansions in the style of Louis XV. The recent cleaning of these buildings has made the Place lovelier than ever.

Before the Place was enlarged in 1854 by Jacques-Ignace Hittorff, the site had already become famous. For here, between 1793 and 1795, during the French Revolution, the dreaded guillotine had ended the lives of Louis XVI, Marie Antoinette, Danton, Robespierre, and nearly three thousand others.

As you look down on this splendid square and along the expansive **Champs-Élysées,** note the five **Marly horses,** sculptured in marble. (They have been replaced with copies; the originals are on view in the new Richelieu wing of the Louvre.) They command the entrance to this avenue, which, broad and beautiful, climbs ever so slightly to the **Arc de Triomphe** at the **Étoile** more than two miles away.

You are now only a couple of hundred yards from the **Jeu de**

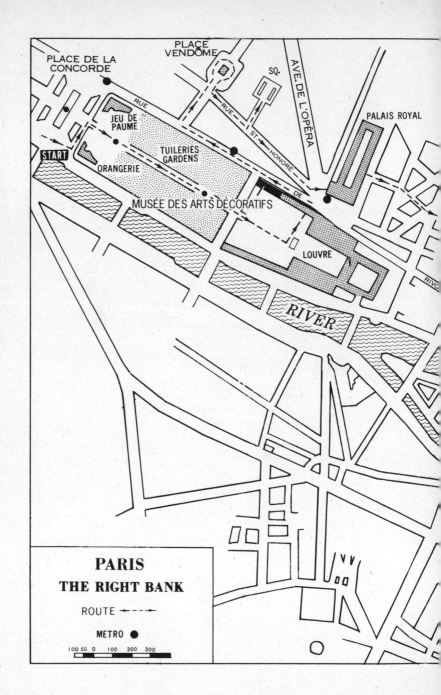

PARIS

THE RIGHT BANK

ROUTE - - - →

METRO ●

100 50 0   100   200   300

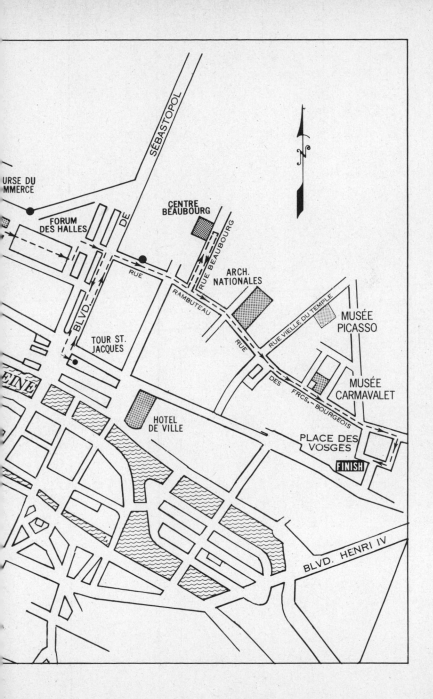

Paume, the building along the terrace at the corner of the Place de la Concorde and the Rue de Rivoli, which used to house one of the world's greatest collections of Impressionist paintings, which are now in the Orsay Museum. The **Jeu de Paume,** so named because it was originally built as a royal tennis court in 1851, was a gallery of Impressionist paintings until 1986, when the Impressionists were moved to the d'Orsay Museum, to be replaced by exhibitions of contemporary art. Now restored, the Jeu de Paume has had major successes with their Dubuffet and Elsworth Kelly shows. (Open Tuesday, 12:00–9:30; Wednesday–Friday, 12:00–7:00; Sunday, 10:00–7:00; closed Monday.)

Below the terrace, midway between the Jeu de Paume and the Orangerie, are a spacious octagonal fountain, and nearby, attractive rose-bordered gardens. From here you can gaze along the tree-lined **Grande Allée** to the great **Arc du Carrousel,** and beyond it to the **Louvre,** originally a royal palace and now one of the world's greatest museums. The Louvre is an absolute must for anyone visiting Paris. It is being totally renovated and this entails the temporary closing of some sections. The "Grand Louvre" project created by former President François Mitterand includes the restitution of the Richelieu wing to the Louvre. (It formerly housed the Ministry of Finance.) The internationally known architect, I. M. Pei, revamped the exterior, and the Cour Napoleon, formerly marred by cars and buses, is now a vast space for visitors. It includes a bookstore, restaurant, and an auditorium. The courtyard is illuminated by a modern glass pyramid, which is the main entrance to the museum. The pyramid caused some controversy when it was first unveiled, but now Parisians and tourists alike have become rather fond of it. Sixty-nine feet high and 108 feet at its base, the pyramid is surrounded by fountains, water basins, and three miniature pyramids. (Open daily, except Tuesday and holidays, 9:00–6:00; Monday and

Wednesday, 9:00–9:45 P.M.) A few yards from the fountain, on the side toward the Orangerie, you will find Aristide Maillol's statue of the *Femme Couchée,* erected in honor of Paul Cézanne.

Although formal in layout, the **Tuileries gardens** have a distinct charm because young children are usually to be seen playing along the graveled alleys, sailing boats among the carp in the round pond, riding on the merry-go-round, or sampling an ice cream at one of the stands under the trees.

When Jean-Baptiste Colbert, Minister of Finance under Louis XIV, undertook the beautification of Paris in 1664, he commissioned André Le Nôtre, designer of the great gardens of Versailles, as landscape-gardener of the Tuileries. The result of his efforts was so successful that Colbert favored reserving the gardens for royal use, but eventually he yielded and opened them to the public. Today, their sixty acres are much the same as they were in Le Nôtre's time.

Rambling along the gravel walk, past many statues of classical design, you will shortly find yourself in Le Nôtre's formal gardens, whose borders of seasonal flowers contrast effectively with the green lawns. Off to your left are the rounded leaden roofs of the six-story buildings along the Rue de Rivoli. When you stand in front of the Arc du Carrousel—a Napoleonic reproduction of the Arch of Severus in Rome—you may be surprised to notice that, although the vista before you appears to follow the laws of French architectural symmetry, in reality the central wing of the Louvre is not in a straight line with the Arc De Triomphe at the Étoile, the Place de la Concorde, and the central walk in the Tuileries gardens.

Napoleon I reviewed his battle-scarred regiments near the arch. The nearby gardens and those between the two facing wings of the Louvre are on the site of the old **Tuileries Palace,** to which Louis XVI was taken by the mob in 1789, when he was brought from Versailles, and from which he left for the guillotine in 1793. Later, both Napoleon I and Napoleon III lived in the palace, which was finally burned by the Communards in the Revolution of 1871.

After turning left at the Place des Pyramides for a look at the gilded statue of Joan of Arc, you turn left again at the **Rue de Rivoli** and wander along of one of Paris's most fascinating shopping streets. Note the uniform façades of the buildings facing the Tuileries. You will be lured by the many little stores under the arcades that run almost to the Place de la Concorde, with their infinite variety of wares: handbags, handkerchiefs, jewelry, hats, perfumes, china, and so forth. **Angelina,** an elegant tea shop with irresistible pastries, is at No. 226. Thus fortified, take a look at the **Musée des Arts Décoratifs** at 107, Rue de Rivoli (open weekdays, 12:30–6:00; Sunday, 11:00–6:00; closed Monday, Tuesday, and holidays), which contains decorative art in daily life from the Middle Ages to today—furniture, wallpaper, porcelain, glass, and toys. The boutique on the ground floor sells beautiful replicas of jewelry, scarves, pottery, and glass, but be prepared to spend a pretty penny here.

When you reach the corner of the Rue de Castiglione, turn right for a stroll around the splendid **Place Vendôme,** which you can see ahead of you beyond the Rue St. Honoré.

Much of Paris's charm is found in her many squares, some of which are huge, some tiny. They are representative of different periods in her long history. Most of them reflect the esthetic talent of the French, but none is more harmonious than the one you have now reached.

The Place Vendôme, named for the Duc de Vendôme, illegitimate son of Henry IV, whose mansion was located here, was planned by the great architect Jules Hardouin-Mansart at the beginning of the eighteenth century. He laid out the square and designed the harmonious limestone houses with their sloping roofs. These buildings are so treasured that they have now been declared historical monuments and no alterations are permitted to be made to the façades or roofs. The old-fashioned lampposts on the sidewalk lend an enchanting atmosphere, especially at night.

The **imposing column** in the center of the Place, modeled on Trajan's Column in Rome, although considerably higher, was erected by Napoleon I to commemorate his victories in Germany and Austria. The covering bronze bas-relief plaques, now weathered by time, came from captured cannon that were melted down after the Battle of Austerlitz. A **statue of Napoleon** as a Roman emperor surmounts the monument.

As you wander leisurely around the Place, on your left is the **Ritz Hotel** of worldwide reputation. You might stroll through its lobby and long shopping gallery, noting the small but charming garden and looking in at its famous "Hemingway" bar.

Return to the Rue St. Honoré and try a diverting brief detour by taking the first left, the Rue du Marché St. Honoré, to browse among the many little shops—fascinating *épiceries, pâtisseries,* and *boulangeries* that make Parisian marketing such a colorful and delightful experience. The **Place du Marché St. Honoré** at the end of the street, now undergoing reconstruction for some as yet unrevealed destiny, was formerly the **Place des Jacobins,** a center of the French Revolution.

Back in the Rue St. Honoré you are following the route down which the tumbrels of the French Revolution rolled, carrying aristocrats on their way to execution. Today the street is characterized by many antique and leather-good stores.

In a few minutes you reach the junction of the Rue St. Honoré and the Avenue de l'Opéra, where the **Place André Malraux** is located. Joan of Arc was wounded in 1429 at this spot, then a gateway to Paris.

Cross the square and enter the Palais Royal at the far end of the Square on the left, next to the **Comédie Française**. But first, perhaps you'd like to stop on the right and have an *apéritif* or *café au lait* at the **Café de la Régence,** where Napoleon once played chess, before browsing in the Comédie Française gift shop. Here you'll find books and videotapes on French theater, as well as delightful small presents (plates with quotes from Molière, matchbooks, agendas) all beautifully wrapped in the traditional red and gold Comédie Française colors.

The **Palais Royal,** built by Cardinal Richelieu in the seventeenth century, was later inhabited by Louis XIII and, for a short period, by Louis XIV. During the eighteenth century the gardens and the quadrangle's galleries were the favorite promenade of Parisians; after the Revolution gambling houses were established there. Today, however, the Palais Royal has an air of silence. The long symmetrical arcades on either side of the gardens, planted with elms and lime trees, extend from the **Galerie des Proues,** so named because it is decorated with prows of ships, to the **Théâtre du Palais Royal.** Note the double colonnade between the **Cour d'Honneur** and the **rose gardens.** In the small shops along the arcade you can purchase old stamps or coins and other antiques.

At the far end near the Théâtre du Palais Royal, beyond the fountain in the center, is one of Paris's finest and most expensive restaurants, the **Grand Véfour.** It is among those exclusive Parisian restaurants where wealthy gourmets gather in historic surroundings for a quiet evening of serious eating and the finest of chateau-bottled wines.

A glass door midway along the colonnade on the right just opposite the fountain will lead into the Rue de Valois. Turn right and walk a few yards beyond the immense Banque de France until you reach Rue du Colonel Driant.

A couple of blocks east, just beyond the domed **Bourse du Commerce,** you come to what was formerly the famed **Les Halles.** What used to be the central market in Paris was moved in 1969 to Rungis, near Orly Airport—a terrible blow to the native Parisian and the tourist alike. The "belly of Paris" has become a vast underground shopping center, the **Forum des Halles,** officially opened in the fall of 1979. Fashionable luxury boutiques abound. A large garden pleases the neighborhood's ecologists, who would like to preserve at least some semblance of beauty in an otherwise bustling commercial enterprise. Old-time visitors to Paris will share the native's nostalgia for the magnificent iron pavilions of the old Les Halles— which the French government, incomprehensibly, saw fit to demolish. Take a moment to visit the **Espace Grévin** (open weekdays, 10:30–6:45; Sunday and holidays, 1:00–7:00), a lively reconstruction of Parisian life from 1885 to 1900, and the **Cousteau Oceanic Park.** Modern audiovisual technology allows the visitor to explore the ocean floor or crawl inside a blue whale. This homage to Cousteau's explorations and discoveries is not to be missed (open Monday, Tuesday, and Thursday, 12:00–7:00; Wednesday, Saturday, Sunday, and holidays, 10:00–7:30; closed Friday).

Before leaving the area of Les Halles, stop in to see the high Gothic vaulting at the **Church of St. Eustache,** which is opposite the former markets on the left. It is considered by many to be second only to Notre Dame in beauty among the churches in Paris.

Two short blocks to the east you reach the long Boulevard de Sébastopol. At this point you should turn right for five minutes or less along the boulevard to the Place du Châtelet to see the lovely Late Gothic **Tour St. Jacques,** an elegant Paris landmark built in the early sixteenth century and originally part of the **Church of St. Jacques-la-Boucherie.**

Retracing your steps along the boulevard to **Rue Rambuteau,** continue along this street crowded with stalls, food shops, and throngs of people from the neighborhood until you reach the corner of Rue Beaubourg. Here you can visit the huge, ultramodern Georges Pompidou National Center of Art and Culture, better known as the **Centre Beaubourg.** Opened in 1977, its controversial exterior, which resembles an intricate network of brilliantly colored pipes, could be compared to a surrealistic ship that has sailed into the wrong port. Some consider the Centre Beaubourg an eyesore in an otherwise charming traditional quarter. On the other hand, stout defenders claim the museum succeeds in demonstrating that art cannot be cut off from daily life. It encompasses a National Museum of Modern Art, a Center of Industrial Creation, a Public Information Library, an Institute of Music Research, a *cinémathèque,* and a children's workshop, where four- to twelve-year-olds become familiar with creativity. (Open daily except Tuesday, 12:00–10:00; Saturday and Sunday, 10:00–10:00.) **The National Museum of Modern Art** is among the best of its kind in the world. You can discover Fauvists, Cubism, and high-quality contemporary art. Particularly interesting is the reconstruction of Brancusi's sculpture *atelier.* Go up to the fifth floor and enjoy the unique panoramic view of Paris rooftops.

Return to the Rue Rambuteau until you reach the old turreted buildings of the **Archives Nationales.** This museum contains magnificent mural paintings as well as France's great historical documents. It is worth stopping at the entrance from the Rue Rambuteau on the left to see the elegant court of honor of the **Hôtel de Soubise,** one of the finest architectural structures within the Archives group of buildings. **The Museum of French History,** on the first floor, contains famous original historical documents: a letter written by Joan of Arc, the Edict of Nantes, Napoleon's testament.

From here you enter **Rue des Francs-Bourgeois,** with its many old mansions, in the **Marais** district. This quarter, now the center of hundreds of workshops producing millinery, costume jewelry, and piecework for the stylish fashion houses, still maintains its traditionally cosmopolitan atmosphere. Its great period was during the seventeenth and eighteenth centuries, when its graceful mansions and palaces belonged to fashionable noblemen. In those days this was the center of Parisian artistic and cultural life. Now you can still search out many architectural gems of that day alongside the more recent tenements.

Look up and down the narrow **Rue Vieille du Temple** as you cross it, and stop on the left at **No. 87** to see the little courtyard of the **Hôtel de Rohan,** also part of the Archives Nationales.

Take the Rue de Thorigny to the Hôtel Salé, which houses the magnificent Picasso collection. This seventeenth-century palace was completely restored to become the Musée Picasso. Picasso's heirs donated more than 200 paintings, 3,000 drawings, sculptures, ceramic pieces, and books, as well as Picasso's personal art collection to the French state, which exempted them from paying inheritance taxes. All the major periods in the artist's creative development are represented. Notice the superb wrought-iron staircase and the sculpted ceiling.

In a few minutes you will be at the **Musée Carnavalet,** a Renaissance mansion and, since 1880, the Museum of the City of Paris. Its entrance is in the Rue de Sévigné around the corner to the left from the Rue des Francs-Bourgeois (open daily except Monday and holidays, 10:00–5:40). Mme de Sévigné lived here from 1677 to 1696, during which time she wrote her well-known letters. Among its many other exhibits, the museum contains prints and models of old Paris (including some which show the evolution of the streets you have just traversed), a wrought-iron shop and tavern signs from the fourteenth to the eighteenth centuries, and a collection of seventeenth-, eighteenth-, and nineteenth-century costumes.

A couple of hundred yards farther on, across the Rue de Turenne, you reach the oldest large square in Paris, the **Place des Vosges.** Henry IV ordered that this first of the *Places Royales,* laid out in the early seventeenth century, be constucted so that the uniformity of the façades and the roofs of the four-story houses would create an architectural effect of geometric unity, a sight rare in Paris. Today in the restored Place des Vosges the rose-colored brick and white-stone classical buildings, with their arcades and dormer windows jutting out of slate roofs, are practically unchanged from the days when Cardinal Richelieu lived at **No. 21.** About two hundred years later Victor Hugo lived at **No. 6,** now a museum containing his drawings, as well as furniture he designed. (Open daily except Monday, 10:00–5:40.)

After the Revolution the square received its present name for a reason rather remarkable in France. New taxes had been imposed, and since the Department of the Vosges was the first to pay them, its citizens were honored in this unusual way.

As you stroll around this gem of the seventeenth century it is easy to imagine the festive life led by the nobility in these stately mansions.

This is the moment to drop in at a little café called **Ma Bourgogne,** frequented by working people of the quarter, at the corner of the Place and Rue des Francs-Bourgeois. Here you can get snacks, sandwiches, and *pâté de campagne.* If you feel like lunching at an exellent, though expensive, restaurant on the square, try the **Coconnas** in the opposite corner. While enjoying this respite after strolling through the historic and fascinating Marais, you may find yourself contemplating the present calm of the Place des Vosges, haunted with memories of the days when Louis XIII, more than three hundred and fifty years ago, reviewed splendid parades on horseback in this same square.

The Left Bank
The Sacred Mount

This walk through the **islands in the Seine** and on the **Left Bank** will take you to some of the most fascinating parts of old Paris. As you will not want to be rushed while wandering around these out-of-the-way corners, it is advisable to divide this walk into two sections, perhaps one in the morning and the other in the afternoon.

In any case you should start at the east end of the Île St. Louis by the **Pont de Sully**—preferably in the morning. If, however, you are continuing the walk that finished at the Place des Vosges, you follow the Boulevard Henry IV from the **Place de la Bastille,** the site of the hated Royalist prison that was destroyed during the French Revolution. Incidentally, the key to the Bastille is now in the United States, at Mount Vernon, having been presented by the Marquis de Lafayette. The square is dominated by the **Opera-Bastille,** Paris's new—and controversial—opera house, which opened in 1990. The architect Carlos Ott designed a hypermodern, functional building, allowing for instant changes in scenery. Esthetically, Opera-Bastille is not to everyone's taste. Its sober gray exterior is not unlike a prison's (a reminder of the original Bastille prison?) and the pristine marble foyer is somewhat cold. The neighborhood, which used to be working-class, has become *très chic,* where artists' lofts and yuppies abound.

The **Île St. Louis** resembles a small provincial seventeenth-century French town set down in the midst of Paris. It is a backwater of the busy city, with the sleepy air of an earlier age. After all, it is named after Louix IX or Saint Louis, often called the Father of Paris, who was born in 1215, the year the Magna Carta was signed.

Many artists and writers, as well as wealthy residents seeking

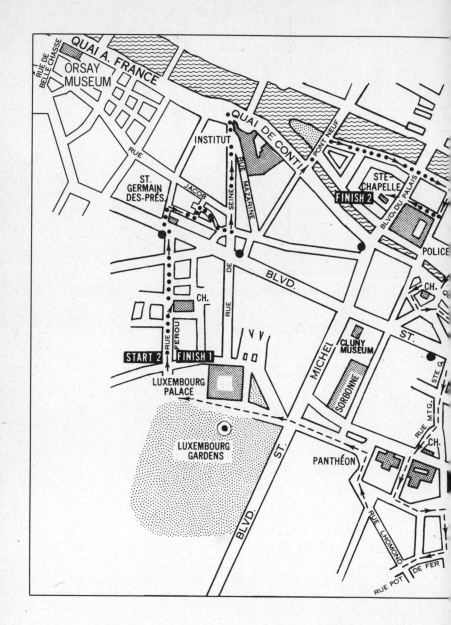

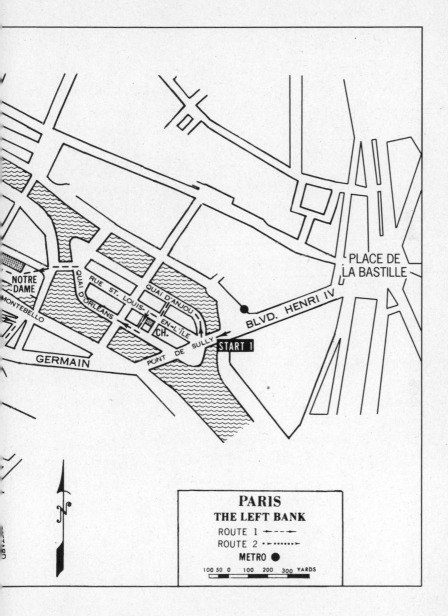

NOTRE DAME

MONTEBELLO

QUAI D'ORLEANS

RUE ST. LOUIS-

QUAI D'ANJOU

EN-L'ÎLE

CH.

GERMAIN

PONT DE SULLY

START 1

BLVD. HENRI IV

PLACE DE
LA BASTILLE

PARIS
THE LEFT BANK
ROUTE 1 ←---→
ROUTE 2 ·····→
METRO ●

100 50 0   100   200   300 YARDS

quiet, have established themselves here in apartments, or some-times even penthouses, in converted three-hundred-year-old man-sions.

On setting foot on the island from the bridge, glance down the narrow Rue St. Louis-en-l'Île in front of you. Now turn right along the **Quai d'Anjou,** which, shaded by tall elm trees, runs along the embankment above the Seine. The nineteenth-century artist and caricaturist Honoré Daumier lived at **No. 9.**

The first distinguished mansion you reach is the noted **Hôtel de Lauzun,** at **No. 17,** a typical nobleman's private residence, built in the middle of the seventeenth century and named after a fabulous Don Juan of the time who lived there. Two hundred years later the writers Théophile Gautier and Charles Baudelaire both resided in this exquisite town house. Today it belongs to the municipality of Paris and is used to entertain distinguished guests of the city. (Visits organized by the Caisse Nationale de Monuments; tel. 44-61-20-00.)

A few yards farther on, turn left along the Rue Poulletier and then right along the main thoroughfare, the **Rue St. Louis-en-l'Île,** which bisects the narrow island lengthwise. Overhead on your left an old clock in the tower of the **Church of St. Louis-en-l'Île** juts out above the street.

As you stroll past little shops and cafés you will be relieved to note the relative absence of motor traffic. Turn left at the next cor-ner on Rue des Deux-Ponts and shortly you will find yourself on the opposite side of the island, at the **Quai d'Orléans,** which is lined with gray and cream-colored houses.

The view of **Notre Dame** from the Pont de la Tournelle on your left is an artist's favorite. It is well worth stopping for a few minutes to absorb the dramatic and memorable sight of the cathedral's famed medieval flying buttresses and towers.

As you saunter along the Quai d'Orléans you see Notre Dame rising above the ivy-covered quay from a slightly different angle. You may want to stop for lunch at No. 42, **Au Gourmet de l'Île,** a friendly, inexpensive, crowded bistro with vaulted ceilings and simple wooden tables.

From the Quai d'Orléans you cross the iron footbridge over an arm of the Seine to the park behind Notre Dame. To your right the lovely Late Gothic **Tour St. Jacques** rises above the stream. While you are walking through the little **cathedral park,** a group of black-frocked priests may pass on their way to Notre Dame, giving the scene an appropriate touch. Why not follow them under the trees and through the beautifully kept gardens along the side of this great cathedral of Paris, which was in the process of construction for nearly two hundred years, from 1163 to 1345. Its location has been a religious site since the time when a Roman-Gallic temple stood here. Pause in the gardens along the quay to look up at the glorious **towers,** the **rose window,** the **spires** above, and the characteristic **gargoyles.**

When you reach the front of the cathedral, continue to the **statue of Charlemagne** on the far side of the square, the **Place du Parvis Notre Dame,** to get a proper perspective of Notre Dame's magnificent façade and towers. The cathedral as we see it today owes much to Viollet-le-Duc, who restored it in the 1840s following the damage and deterioration it suffered during the Revolution and thereafter.

After examining the famous figures around the three **portals** decorated in wrought iron, you will want to spend some time (either now or later) studying the interior, especially the glorious seven-hundred-year-old stained-glass rose window over the main entrance, as well as those on either side of the nave. You may even wish to climb one of the bell towers to view old Paris and the Seine with its many bridges.

For another and perhaps lovelier view of Notre Dame, cross the **Pont au Double,** to the left from the cathedral's front, to the **Place René Viviani.** Walk across this tiny square, which boasts a locust tree well over 250 years old, to the twelfth-century **Church of St. Julien le Pauvre.** This is a delightful bit of the most ancient section of Paris. To your right you will notice the quaint old houses with their uneven roofs. Turn left into the picturesque **Rue Galande,** possibly the oldest street in Paris. You are now in the **Latin Quarter.**

Although you will be tempted to follow these narrow old streets indefinitely, continue on the Rue Galande (look to your right at the **St. Severin** church, which is worth a visit) to the junction with Rue Lagrange. Cross this street and follow the Rue de l'Hôtel Colbert. In about fifty yards turn right into the Rue de la Bûcherie, then in a few yards go left on Rue du Haut Pavé into the **Quai de Montebello,** where there are several good and moderately priced restaurants.

You leave the quay by turning right into the Rue de Bièvre, a narrow street almost opposite the Pont de l'Archevêche. Don't be surprised if you see policemen and guards protecting this unassuming street. Former President Mitterand's private residence is located here. After crossing the Boulevard St. Germain at the Place Maubert, turn slightly left into the **Rue de la Montagne Ste. Geneviève,** named for the earliest of Paris's patron saints. As you walk up the hill, known for ages as "The Sacred Mount," you are on the road originally built by the Romans that led from Paris to Lyons and Italy. Here, in the heart of old Paris, you may be entertained by a singer leaning over a decorative window box above a wrought-iron balcony. A golden horse head over an old house signifies a "Boucherie Chevaline" (shop for horse meat).

After crossing the Rue des Écoles, you bear right at a little square where several streets meet. Ahead of you, past charming old houses on either side of the street, is the **Church of St. Étienne du Mont,** a most attractive combination of Late Gothic and Renaissance architecture. Go in to see the beautifully carved sixteenth-century stone rood loft, the last one in Paris. It was used before the adoption of the pulpit.

In front of the church rises the dome of the **Panthéon,** the secular Temple of Fame where the "ashes of great men" have been enshrined since the French Revolution.

Hereabouts, practically every street (as you will note from the names) and many buildings and monuments are sacred to the memory of early Paris—including the **Paris of the Romans,** still preserved in the Roman baths in the grounds of the **Musée de Cluny** at the corner of Boulevard St. Michel and Boulevard St. Germain, (open daily, except Tuesday, 9:45–12:30 and 2:00–5:15)—and to the **Paris of scholarship** since the thirteenth century, when Louis IX's confessor, Robert de Sorbon, set up a theological college there, which was the origin of the Sorbonne. The Musée de Cluny is dedicated to the Middle Ages and is best known for its magnificent tapestries, in particular *The Lady and the Unicorn.* Stop by some afternoon to attend a concert of medieval music given in the museum.

A few hundred yards down the Rue Clotilde, flanked by the rear of the Panthéon and the **Lycée Henry IV,** you will come into the Rue de l'Estrapade, which you follow to the left for a few yards; then take a slight bend to the left on the Rue Blainville to reach a charming little square, the **Place de la Contrescarpe.** From this little square, surrounded by attractively weather-worn houses, five narrow streets stem in various directions. The most fascinating is the lively **Rue Mouffetard,** dating from the thirteenth century, which twists down a steep slope to the right and is usually jammed with yuppie residents of the quarter darting in and out of the many shops—the greengrocer's with heaps of vegetables, a tiny bistro, and the bakery with long crusty *baguettes* and other inviting shapes of delicious bread and *pâtisseries*. Nearby a bearded student strums a guitar in a wine shop and bar. The Rue Mouffetard is rich in local color and activity, with its market stalls and shops that give it the character of an Eastern bazaar. (The shops usually close from 12:30–3:30.) Formerly working-class, this street has become both fashionable and expensive.

Turn right in Rue Pot de Fer into the rather dull Rue Lhomond, then, after going through the little square, take a sharp right on Rue Clotaire to the **Panthéon.** Designed by Jacques-Germain Soufflot in the style of Agrippa's Pantheon in Rome, the church was partially financed by the proceeds of three state lotteries. Inside are the tombs of Jean-Jacques Rousseau, Voltaire, Honoré-Gabriel Mirabeau, Victor Hugo, Émile Zola, Anatole France, and many other distinguished political and literary figures.

As you leave the Panthéon and stand on its front steps you can see, directly before you, down the Rue Soufflot to the Luxembourg Gardens with the Eiffel Tower in the distance. This is the quarter of the **Sorbonne.** The university buildings of the many graduate schools can be seen from the Rue Soufflot down the Rue St. Jacques to the right. These streets are usually crowded with students.

Entering the **Luxembourg Gardens** at the Place Edmond Rostand, turn right under the lime and chestnut trees to the lovely Médicis fountain, designed as an Italian grotto. The Italian influence pervades the **Luxembourg Palace** and gardens, named, however, for a French nobleman who sold the **Petit Luxembourg** (beyond the main building) to Marie de Médicis, the Florentine wife of Henry IV. The large palace, which she had constructed between 1615 and 1620 in the style of the Pitti Palace in Florence, is now the home of the French Senate.

The Luxembourg's ornamental gardens, with their informal meandering walks, are located on the site of an ancient Roman camp. In front of the palace is a small artificial pond, surrounded by colorful flower beds. Spend a delightful half hour wandering around the gardens and end up by the **Orangerie** beyond the palace. You will be surprised to see palm trees growing outdoors in front of the Orangerie. This park, the largest on the Left Bank, is still a great favorite among the quarter's students and bohemians, as it has been since the seventeenth century. It is an animated and charming spot, with many children at play and many elders at ease.

If you have taken this stroll from the Île St. Louis during the morning, by now you will probably be looking for a good place to lunch. There are many inexpensive restaurants around the Place Edmond Rostand where you entered the gardens. Or you can walk along the Rue de Médicis to one of several better restaurants in and around the **Place de l'Odéon.**

The Luxembourg to Sainte-Chapelle

Begin your second walk through the literary and artistic Left Bank in front of the **Luxembourg Palace** on the **Rue de Vaugirard,** the longest street in Paris. Turn right after a couple of blocks down the Rue Férou to the **Place St. Sulpice** and the church of the same name, the second largest in Paris. Its organ is world-famous.

From here it is only a few hundred yards to the **Boulevard St. Germain.** You go along the narrow Rue des Canettes ("the Street of the Ducklings") to the right as you emerge from the church. Then walk past the old houses on the Rue des Ciseaux just to the right and across the Rue du Four, with its many chic boutiques.

The Romanesque **Church of St. Germain des Prés,** the oldest in

Paris, stands across the boulevard on the site of an eighth-century Benedictine abbey. Immediately behind the church and its graceful eleventh-century stone tower, on the Rue de l'Abbaye, you will notice remnants of the original abbey.

The two cafés on the opposite side of the square, **Les Deux Magots** and the **Café de Flore,** separated by a narrow street, are famous as centers of the existentialist movement and the meeting places of writers. Plan an entire morning for the **Musée d'Orsay,** where you can walk from St. Germain des Prés by following the boulevard and taking a right on the Rue de Bellechasse. Formerly a railroad station built by the architect Victor Laloux in 1900, its façade was inspired by the Louvre. Technological progress turned it into a ghost station, where prisoners of war arrived in 1945; Orson Welles used the décor in his film *The Trial;* and it housed several theatrical companies. Under Presidents Giscard d'Estaing and Mitterand, the station was converted into a museum of nineteenth-century art from the Impressionists to Art Nouveau and opened in 1986. Particularly striking is the ground floor with its high, arched ceiling. You should return one evening for a concert of chamber music. (Open from 9:00–5:30; Thursday until 9:15; closed Monday and holidays.)

Return to the church of St. Germain des Prés (if your feet hurt after the Musée d'Orsay, cross Boulevard St. Germain and hop on the 63 bus) and walk right, along the Rue de l'Abbaye, then take the first street to the left, the short Rue de Furstenberg, which leads to one of the most enchanting miniature squares in Paris, the **Place Furstenberg.** Here in the shade of four magnolia trees and the square's antiquated, ornate lamppost there is a strange and quiet air. The nineteeth-century painter Ferdinand Delacroix had his studio at **No. 6.** You will be delightfully surprised to come upon several antique shops, among the most tasteful in Paris.

Leaving this lovely oasis, so near the bustling traffic along the Boulevard St. Germain, turn right into the twisting, narrow **Rue Cardinale.** Above you rise picturesque houses in varying shades of gray and ocher, with window boxes beneath slanting roofs and crooked chimneys. Now turn left and cross the fourteenth-century Rue de l'Échaudé, and then left to the junction of the Rue de Seine and Rue de Buci. Here you are in the midst of the neighborhood **marketplace.** *Pâtisseries,* grocery stores, vegetable stalls, and fish and meat markets cater to the many customers who crowd the street and sidewalks. Have a drink at the corner bistro while you watch the shoppers fight their way through the hawkers, and listen to the housewives, jamming the little streets, shout to the truck drivers who are trying to get through with their loads of perishable foods. This is usually one of the liveliest scenes in Paris.

Now stroll down the **Rue de Seine** toward the river. This street is a great center of **art galleries, bookstores,** and **print shops.** The art galleries feature not only the traditional artists, but especially the work of the younger generation who may well be the famous of tomorrow. Wander in and out, even if you are only browsing.

The end of the Rue de Seine turns into the Quai Malaquais. On your right is the imposing **Institut de France,** home of the renowned **Académie Française,** established by Cardinal Richelieu. Among other things, its forty scholars are charged with the responsibility for a dictionary of the French language, the first edition of which appeared in 1694. Four other academies—literary, scientific, political, and artistic—whose members are outstanding scholars, comprise the distinguished Institut. You should look around the inner courtyard of the seventeenth-century building.

Now cross the quay to the **Pont des Arts,** the picturesque footbridge that crosses the Seine. From the center of the bridge there is an admirable view. To your right is the triangle-shaped Vert Galant at the tip of the **Île de la Cité.** Above this little park rises the tapering spire of Sainte-Chapelle. To the left you'll see the figures and gargoyles of the **Tour St. Jacques.** In the opposite direction is the sweep of the **Louvre** and the graceful **Pont du Carrousel.** You will want to linger on this bridge for a while.

Returning to the quay, you'll be intrigued by the continuous rows of bookstalls with their books, prints, maps, and memorabilia of Paris. A few hundred yards left along the **Quai de Conti,** across the stream of traffic, is the **Hôtel des Monnaies**—the mint that houses a collection of French money since Merovingian days and is open to the public (Monday–Saturday, 10:00–6:00; the workshops where modern coins are minted can be seen Tuesday and Thursday, 2:15–3:00; Wednesday until 9:00; closed Monday and holidays).

Ahead of you is the **Pont Neuf** which, despite its name, is Paris's oldest bridge (dating from 1578), as well as its most popular. The Pont Neuf marked the beginning of bridges without houses. Cross it as far as the Île de la Cité. There, under the statue of **Henry IV,** the famous seventeenth-century entertainer Tabarin, along with jugglers, songsters, and clowns, attracted crowds of Parisians to the teeming fairgrounds of the day. Their main locale was just to the right, the **Place Dauphine.** One of the first of the royal squares (built in 1607), it was one of the busiest marketplaces in Paris until about a hundred years ago.

Before leaving the little **Place du Pont Neuf,** descend the steps behind Henry IV's statue to the **Vert Galant** park, a popular playground for little children. Stand for a few minutes alongside the hopeful fishermen at the point of the island under the shade of the overhanging trees. As you look downstream, from one bridge to the next, you will agree that this is one of Paris's most enchanting and peaceful spots.

Returning to the rose-colored brick and stone houses of the

Place du Pont Neuf, follow the **Quai de l'Horloge** to the **Conciergerie,** the noted prison of the Revolution, which is still in use. During the Revolution its inmates included Louis XVI, Marie Antoinette, Danton, Robespierre, and hundreds of others before they were sent to the guillotine. Many of its medieval halls and cells are now open to the public (9:30–6:30 daily, except holidays). At the corner is the **Tour de l'Horloge,** where the first clock tower in Paris was built in 1370. From here there is an incomparable view of the Tour St. Jacques against the sky.

After crossing the Boulevard du Palais, walk past the **Tribunal de Commerce** to the colorful central **Flower Market,** crammed with stalls and shops displaying cut flowers and plants of many varieties.

Return to the Boulevard du Palais by taking a right turn into the Rue de Lutèce, beyond the flower mart. This street runs along the building occupied by the **Prefect of Police.**

Now cross the boulevard and enter the **Cour du Mai** in the **Palais de Justice** to visit one of the truly glorious sights of Paris— **The Sainte-Chapelle** (open daily except holidays, 9:30–6:30).

This masterpiece of Gothic architecture was built by Louis IX (Saint Louis) between 1246 and 1248 to house holy relics he received from Baudoin, Emperor of Constantinople. They were later removed to Notre Dame. You enter the **Lower Chapel,** originally reserved for pilgrims. Its rather drab appearance only heightens the suspense until you climb the winding stone staircase to become dazzled by the brilliance of color and graceful lines of the **Upper Chapel.** This chapel, designed for the royal family, is world-famous for its magnificent **stained-glass windows** illustrating some fifteen hundred Biblical scenes. These windows are rivaled only by those in Chartres Cathedral for their radiant splendor and remarkable workmanship. The rich color of the dark reds and blues is extraordinary. To stand in the nave and see the sun streaming through the hundreds of glass panels (60 percent of the originals remain) is one of the great artistic experiences, not only in Paris but in all Europe. Here is the perfect spot to end this walk through old Paris.

Quartier Invalides
To the Eiffel Tower

This is an afternoon walk that includes some of Paris's most interesting and scenic places. Its starting point is very accessible, and the entire walk is located in the same general area of the city. You won't have any great distances to cover, so you can spend some time visiting the Musée Rodin and the Invalides. You will finish at the Eiffel Tower late in the day, in time to enjoy the wonderful panorama of Paris in the soft afternoon sunlight.

Start on the terrace of the **Palais de Chaillot** at the **Place du Trocadéro.** From this vantage point a magnificent scene opens up before you. The view of the Eiffel Tower soaring to the sky is extraordinarily dramatic and beautiful. The **École Militaire** at the end of the green lawn seems framed underneath the Eiffel Tower. To your left you see the dome of the Invalides with the Panthéon in the distance. In a city where you are repeatedly carried away by so many superb vistas, this is surely one of the most impressive.

Turn right along the Avenue du Président Wilson to the Place d'Iéna, and in a moment you will reach, on your right, the **Musée d'Art Moderne de la Ville de Paris** (open 10:00–5:30, 8:30 Wednesday; closed Monday and holidays) with a fine selection of twentieth-century art, including works by Matisse, Derain, Braque, Soutine, and Chagall.

Continue on the Avenue du Président Wilson to the Place de l'Alma and wander along the **embankment of the Seine** in the direction of the Place de la Concorde. If it is springtime as you walk down the alley of carefully pruned chestnut trees on the Cours Albert I, the cone-shaped blossoms will be flowering through the green leaves. If it is midsummer, the trees will already be turning a slightly rust color. But in any season, the long vista of triple rows of chestnuts between the riverbank and the musty gray buildings will put you in the proper mood to savor the allure of Paris.

You will notice the **Bateaux-Mouches** moored to their wharves. They are glass-enclosed river steamers, on which you will probably want to cruise, preferably at night, between the **Île St. Louis** and the **Bois** to see the many artistically illuminated monuments along both shores of the Seine.

As you cross the Place du Canada the golden horses of the Pont Alexandre III loom up on the right through the trees. The **Cours la Reine** that extends to the Place de la Concorde is also an avenue shaded by chestnuts. It was laid out by Marie de Médicis in 1616 in order to display her Florentine import, the revolutionary sprung carriage that drastically altered seventeenth-century transporation.

On the far side of the Place du Canada return to the embankment so that as you walk you can study the elaborate décor of the Pont Alexandre III (built in 1900), which expresses so well in its fancy statuary and lamps the ostentatious style of the turn of the century.

Pause for a moment at the **Pont Alexandre III,** the only single-span bridge over the Seine. Then, as you turn right to face the bridge's gilded statues gleaming in the sunlight on top of the four stone pylons, there lies before you across the river the broad sweep of the esplanade in front of the domed Hôtel des Invalides.

In a few minutes you will come to the **Place de la Concorde.** Here you turn right at the fountain that splashes in front of the obelisk. Cross the **Pont de la Concorde,** which leads to the Palais

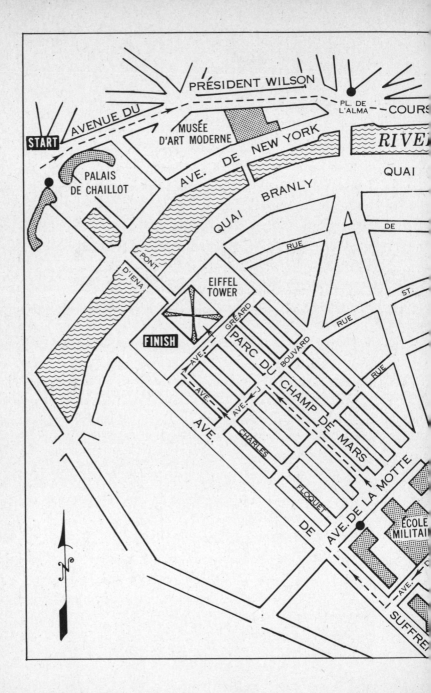

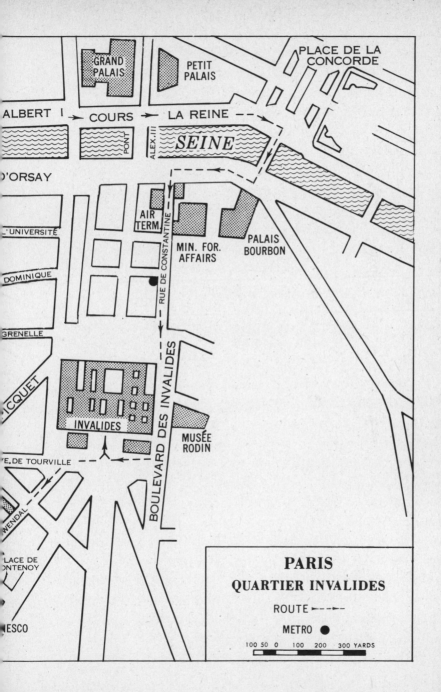

GRAND PALAIS

PETIT PALAIS

PLACE DE LA CONCORDE

ALBERT I → COURS → LA REINE – – –

PONT ALEX. III

SEINE

D'ORSAY

L'UNIVERSITÉ

DOMINIQUE

GRENELLE

AIR TERM.

RUE DE CONSTANTINE

MIN. FOR. AFFAIRS

PALAIS BOURBON

ICQUET

INVALIDES

BOULEVARD DES INVALIDES

MUSÉE RODIN

E. DE TOURVILLE

WENDAL

LACE DE ONTENOY

ESCO

PARIS

QUARTIER INVALIDES

ROUTE ► - - ►

METRO ●

100 50 0   100   200   300 YARDS

Bourbon. There's a remarkable view from the bridge—**Notre Dame** on your left and the highly decorative and resplendent Pont Alexandre III on your right. Looking back toward the Place de la Concorde and its classic buildings, you see **the Madeleine** at the end of the Rue Royale. Note how architecturally harmonious with the buildings in the square the Madeleine is.

You turn right past the **Palais Bourbon,** where the Assemblée Nationale—the lower house of the French Parliament—meets. Its façade was designed during the Napoleonic period to balance the Grecian front of the Madeleine. Continue beyond the **Foreign Office** on the **Quai d'Orsay** and turn left on Rue de Constantine. Across the street is Paris's air terminal and, as you walk along, you'll see on the right the large Esplanade and the golden dome of the Church of the Invalides.

There is one of Paris's many pleasant little parks at the corner. Why not stroll by the flower beds and watch the children playing in the sand?

The **Musée Rodin** (open daily, except Monday, 10:00–6:00, April–September; 10:00–5:00, October–March) is a bit farther up, on the wide **Boulevard des Invalides,** just across the intersection of the Rue de Varenne. Formerly the eighteenth-century **Hôtel de Biron,** this sumptuous mansion with its extensive garden was Rodin's studio during the last ten years of his life. Some years before his death he agreed to leave his sculptures to the nation if the government would exhibit them in this building. You will want to spend a while studying the expressive marbles of this great master, especially such famous pieces as *The Thinker* and *The Kiss.*

On leaving the Musée Rodin, cross the Boulevard and take the first right from the Avenue de Tourville and walk to the front of the **Church of the Invalides,** where Napoleon's remains are enshrined in an open crypt under a sarcophagus of red porphyry, a stone used for burials in Imperial Rome. This is also the resting place of many of Napoleon's greatest generals, as well as the heart of Marshal Sébastien de Vauban, the fortress builder. Marshal Ferdinand Foch, Supreme Commander of the Allied Armies in World War I, is the only recent French hero to be buried in the Napoleonic crypt. The splendid interior of the church is elaborately decorated. To see several interesting personal **relics of Napoleon,** such as his sword and hat, go down into the crypt, where the emperor's death mask is also exhibited. You may want to visit the **Musée de l'Armée,** devoted to military history and art (open daily, 10:00–6:00; closed holidays).

Not very far from the Invalides is UNESCO's unusual modern building, which has a particular appeal to those interested in contemporary architecture. To reach it you cross the Avenue de Tourville on leaving Napoleon's tomb and take the second left into the Avenue de Lowendal. You will see the **UNESCO Building** on the left at the Place de Fontenoy. It's worth taking a guided tour so you don't miss such unique features as the interior columns, which are circular at the base and square at the top, as well as the various conference halls designed and decorated by artists of each donor country. Also, see **Picasso's mural,** which has been quite controversial. Outside, there are such **contemporary works of art** as a mural by Joan Miró, a huge mobile by Alexander Calder, and a statue by Henry Moore. Be sure to look around Isamu Noguchi's delightful Japanese garden, which is not far from an extraordinary spiral cantilevered staircase.

Now cross the street from UNESCO to the **École Militaire,** France's military staff college, founded by Louis XV, and turn left. Skirt this large building by taking the Avenue de Suffren to the right until you reach the Avenue de la Motte-Picquet. Here you again take a right and you will be in the Place Joffre.

You are now facing the stately park of the **Champ de Mars** with the base of the gigantic Eiffel Tower spanning the width of its promenade at the far end. The Champ de Mars, originally an eighteenth-century parade ground, was the scene of popular demonstrations during the French Revolution. You will enjoy exploring the informal **gardens** on your right, for they are full of luxurious shrubbery and trees, as well as attractive flower beds. A small lake, cascades, and grottoes add to the charm. As in other Parisian parks you will see little toy horse carts provided for children at a modest fee.

When you reach the Avenue Joseph Bouvard, turn left across the main promenade lined with carefully pruned trees. On the far side, turn right into the second street, the **Avenue Charles Floquet,** to get an idea of the mansions, now mostly apartments, that were residences of stylish Parisians early in the century.

After a couple of blocks, turn right on the Avenue Octave Gréard, which will bring you to the base of the **Eiffel Tower.** You can take the elevator to one of the **three stages** (the top platform is 898 feet above ground). It's an exciting experience to watch Paris open up below you as the elevator ascends inside the framework of steel girders. If you don't want to go all the way up to see the tremendous panorama of Paris and its suburbs, the second platform commands an extensive view over those areas you are likely to visit and has the advantage of being close enough to the ground so that you don't have that remote feeling of being in an airplane. Then, too, you can pick out prominent landmarks more readily. A restaurant is on the first platform—a scenic spot to enjoy afternoon tea with Paris spread out at your feet.

Montmartre
La Butte by Day

Almost every visitor to Paris goes up to **Montmartre,** and usually at night. You will probably dine in or near the Place du Tertre, wander about the many art galleries, and stop by at a cabaret or café. But you will find it more interesting, though perhaps not as exciting, to walk around Montmartre by daylight, preferably early in the morning, before busloads of tourists crowd the narrow streets. It is a delightful and very different little section of Paris—just a few blocks on the top of La Butte (or hill). Even though it may be "touristy," the winding little streets and byways off the Place du Tertre are fascinating, and many are unspoiled. There's quite a bit to see and do in this picturesque village or commune of Montmartre.

The historical origin of the word Montmartre seems uncertain. Some stories ascribe the name to Mont des Martyrs where, according to tradition, three saints, including St. Denis, were beheaded. However, in its catalogue the Musée du Vieux Montmartre states that the word Montmartre comes from Mons Martis, because on this hill the Romans had built a temple consecrated to the god Mars.

A rural community until the last century, Montmartre was known for its plaster quarries, from which the term plaster of paris is derived. Artists and writers have been drawn to Montmartre for many years, but around the turn of the century it became particularly famous as the haunt of the Impressionist painters. Montmartre is still full of artists, as you will see when you wander about its nooks and corners. The old picturesque atmosphere abounds, and even one of the famous Montmartre windmills has survived.

Start your walk through Montmartre at the **Place Clichy,** the famous locale of cabarets, cafés, and the Moulin Rouge. Stroll along the Boulevard de Clichy into the Boulevard de Rochechouart, to the Rue Dancourt. Turn left along this street and at the **Place Dancourt,** one of Paris's attractive small squares, go around the **Théâtre de l'Atelier,** which as the Théâtre de Montmartre was one of the

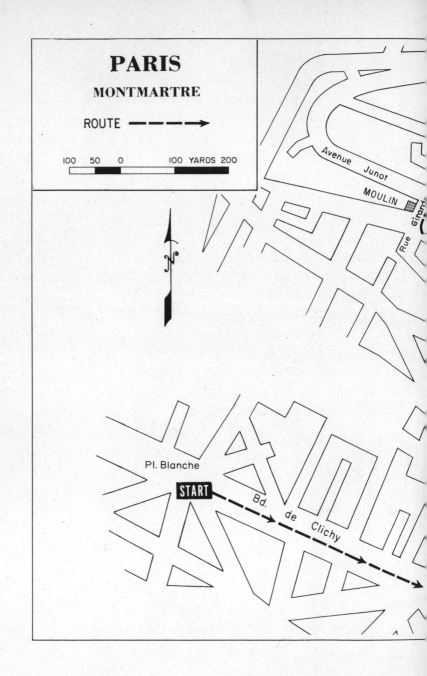

PARIS

MONTMARTRE

ROUTE ---->

100 50 0 100 YARDS 200

N

Avenue Junot

MOULIN

Rue Girard

Pl. Blanche

START

Bd. de Clichy

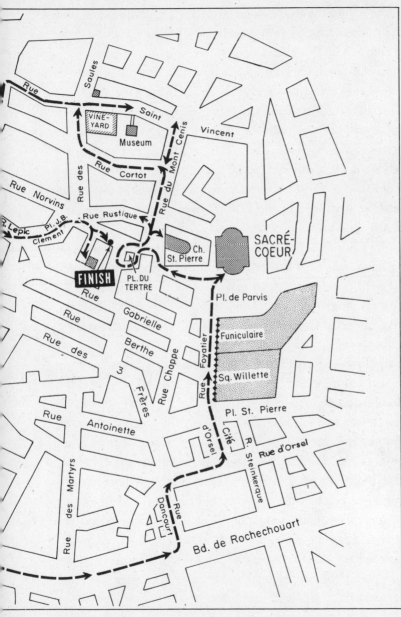

oldest in Paris, into the **Rue D'Orsel.** At the **Rue Steinkerque,** turn left, and in a moment you will come to the old-fashioned funicular that will take you up the steep slope.

This in itself is an amusing experience. You are quite likely to find the car crowded with women and children from the neighborhood, all chattering at a great rate. As the car ascends, you will notice a small park on your right. In a few minutes you will be at the top, 328 feet above the Seine. Climb the steps to the terrace in front of **Sacré-Coeur.** A wonderful panorama of Paris unfolds below. Straight ahead you can see **Notre Dame** and the **Panthéon** just behind it, while to your right the **Eiffel Tower** pierces the horizon. (You are about on a level with its second landing.)

The white Church of Sacré-Coeur, one of the most familiar landmarks in Paris, was built in Romanesque-Byzantine style between 1876 and 1914. You may wish to wander around its vast, dark interior and look at the modern stained-glass windows. One of the world's largest bells, **La Savoyarde,** weighing nearly nineteen tons, hangs in the tower.

From the basilica, turn right on **Rue Azaïs,** then right again on the **Rue St. Eleuthère** and left into the center of Montmartre, the **Place du Tertre.** This small square, similar to those in French provincial towns, is enclosed by old-fashioned, gray, weather-beaten houses and restaurants. It is a great popular gathering place at all hours of the day and night. In warm weather the center of the square, under the trees, will be filled with tables where patrons of the adjacent restaurants are served. The narrow cobblestone street around the square is usually crowded with visitors, either watching the different artists at work or inspecting their paintings displayed on easels. A typical Montmartre painter may be dressed in beret, colorful blue jeans, and a gray sweater, applying his or her paint with a palette knife. Just on the left you might see a bearded artist cutting out silhouettes with scissors. At the corner of the square you will notice this somewhat faint red lettering on a gray building, "Commune Libre du Vieux Montmartre Mairie," an association founded by the artists in the *quartier,* which has a mayor and corporation but no legal significance. No. 3 was the first legal **town hall** of Montmartre (1790) and here Georges Clemenceau, France's premier in World War I, was mayor in 1871. In front of **Chez La Mère Catherine,** the square's best-known restaurant, you have a characteristic view of the domes of Sacré-Coeur.

Turn left from the square past the **Café La Bohême** into the Rue du Mont Cenis, and on your right you will see the old parish **Church of St. Pierre.** Originally a Benedictine abbey, it is the third oldest church in Paris and an example of early Gothic architecture. The four Roman columns inside are ruins of the temple that was erected here. The choir's rib vaulting is the oldest in Paris. Step out into the garden for a moment. When you are standing in the center look up at the church's Gothic tower contrasted against the Byzantine-style dome of Sacré-Coeur.

Returning to the **Rue du Mont Cenis,** in about fifty yards you will come on your left to a tiny street or passageway, the Rue Rustique. Wander down here for a minute or two—it's a Utrillo scene come to life, so typical of Montmartre with its old-fashioned lampposts and window boxes overhanging the alley. Everywhere you turn there is a charming sight on this unspoiled street.

As you stroll along the Rue du Mont Cenis and the streets that run off it, you are bound to be attracted by the various art galleries. Some, of course, deal in rather inferior paintings, but others are quite reputable, though the prices are not as low as in certain parts of the Left Bank.

Walk to the end of the Rue du Mont Cenis and look down over

the terraces below that lead to one of the main industrial quarters of the city.

Now turn back a few yards and right on the **Rue Cortot** (Renoir lived at **No. 12**) and right again on the **Rue des Saules.** As you go down the hill, you will pass on your right an amazing sight, a vineyard in the heart of Paris. The last of many that produced the wine of Montmartre, the terraces of **Clos Montmartre** are well tended. The picking of the grapes is an occasion for much festivity every year.

Turn right along the **Rue St. Vincent** past the vineyard and go into a garden on the right to visit the **Musée du Vieux Montmartre** (open 2:30–6:00, except Monday and holidays). This collection of memorabilia about Montmartre, in a house surrounded by trees and shrubs above the street, is well worth visiting. In addition to prints and posters, there are fascinating models of Montmartre and the section just below the hill. You will get a better idea of the distinctive character of Montmartre's history by spending a little time in this museum than in any other way.

Return to the corner of the Rue St. Vincent and the Rue des Saules, where you will see a little two-story brick cottage beneath a tree with a gnarled stump. This is the **Lapin Agile,** Montmartre's most famous cabaret (open after 11:00 at night except Monday). The sign above the door with the phrase "Poèmes et Chansons" depicts a rabbit balancing a bottle of wine on his arm and was painted by A. Gill, from which the cabaret took its name. At one time such noted artists as Picasso and Utrillo used to meet here. Come back in the evening to hear the entertainers sing songs of old Montmartre.

Continuing along the Rue St. Vincent you will pass, on the left, dilapidated cottages with old chimney pots. At the end of the street you will come to a little park on the right.

Now go left up the hill and climb the steps on the **Rue Girardon.**

After you pass a playground on the right, you will see a windmill above the building on the corner of the Rue Lepic. This is the **Moulin de la Galette,** a celebrated dance hall, the scene of Renoir's great painting. This windmill is the last of several that used to stand on La Butte a hundred years ago.

After you turn left along the **Rue Lepic** (Van Gogh lived at **No. 54**), you will notice weathered houses with red and gray shutters standing above little gardens. There's a little triangle of green on the right, the **Place J.B. Clément,** and to your left trees and a vine-covered wall rise above the street. Now you will pass more art galleries in the popular **Rue Norvins.**

Take a right turn into the narrow Passage Trainée for a couple of minutes until you come to the **Musée de Cire** (open daily, 10:00–12:00 and 2:00–6:00). This is a wax museum where fourteen tableaux depict different periods in the history of Montmartre. Some scenes show Montmartre artists like Toulouse-Lautrec, others the period of the French Revolution with Danton and Lafayette, still others present the days of Clemenceau. Tours through this interesting museum are conducted in English.

Just opposite the museum you can enjoy a wonderful view of Paris over the typical slanted rooftops and chimney pots of the nearby houses.

Now return to the Rue Norvins and continue just a few yards to the **Place du Tertre,** where you can watch the amusing street scene from a table in the square. From here you can pick up a taxi to reach the center of Paris.

10.
Rome

The Old City
In Ancient Rome

No visitor can do justice to Rome in a few days, for no other city in the Western world contains so much of historical interest or presents such an extensive view of Western culture.

Yet, unfortunately, your stay in Rome will probably be limited, so these walks have been planned to enable you to visit most of the interesting and important places, as well as to give you some variety. As you are likely to be there during the spring, summer, or early fall, when the weather is warm, the walks have been broken up as much as possible, so that you will not have to cover too much in any single stroll.

Two practical hints: The streets are often very narrow and the drivers speedy, so watch your step; women should be sure to wear low heels, as many of the streets are paved with cobblestones. Luckily, more and more streets in the center are now a haven for pedestrians and are closed to traffic.

You can begin your acquaintance with the Eternal City with three enjoyable and instructive walks: one will introduce you to ancient Rome; the other two—both in the same general vicinity—will take you to some places that are not ordinarily seen by tourists. Since the latter two are relatively short, the three walks can be covered in a single day. However, if you decide on this plan, it is advisable to take a taxi from the point where the second walk ends to the beginning of the third walk.

Begin your walk in ancient Rome at the **Capitol,** set on a hill that has been revered since the days of the Etruscans. In the sixth century B.C. the **Temple of Jupiter** stood here near the site of the Tarpeian Rock.

You should approach the Capitol by climbing the flight of steps from the **Piazza d'Aracoeli** to the **Piazza del Campidoglio,** a few hundred yards from the **Piazza Venezia.** You will be struck by the contrasting effects of the ancient brick **Church of Santa Maria in Aracoeli** (open daily, 7:00–12:00 and 4:00–6:00) above you (built over the **Temple of Juno**) and the ostentatious immensity of the marble **monument to Victor Emmanuel II** towering off to your left. As you ascend the stairs, you pass through a delightful **garden** of oleander, wisteria, palms, and pines. Take the path to the left, below the top, to see the cage containing live wolves—the symbol of Rome. Two large marbles of the **Dioscuri** dominate the entrance to the piazza. You now are facing one of the most beautiful and noblest small squares in the world, designed by Michelangelo. Right in front of you stands the magnificent **equestrian statue of Marcus Aurelius,** an unusually well preserved second-century figure and one of the few large bronzes of imperial Rome to have survived the ages.

The **Capitoline Museum** (open mornings, 9:00–1:30; 1:00 on Sunday; on Tuesday, Thursday, and Saturday, 5:00–8:00) on the left

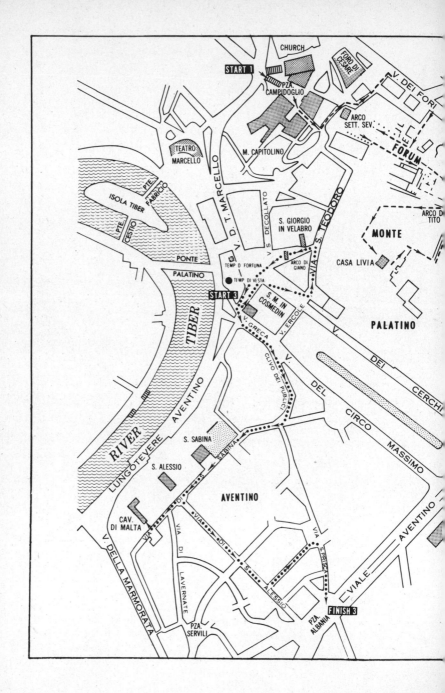

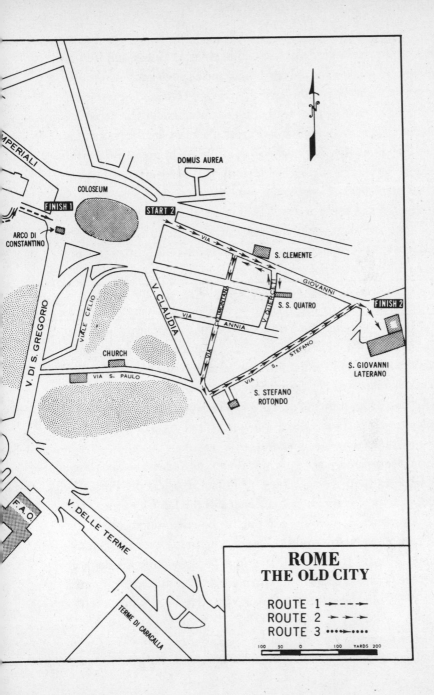

DOMUS AUREA

COLOSEUM

FINISH 1

START 2

ARCO DI
CONSTANTINO

MPERIALI

S. CLEMENTE

VIA

GIOVANNI

S. S. QUATRO

FINISH 2

V. CLAUDIA

VIALE CELIO

V. DI S. GREGORIO

VIA

C. MONTANA

ANNIA

V. QUERCETI

S.

STEFANO

S. GIOVANNI
LATERANO

CHURCH

VIA S. PAULO

VIA

S. STEFANO
ROTONDO

F.A.O.

V. DELLE TERME

TERME DI CARACALLA

ROME
THE OLD CITY

ROUTE 1 ━ ━ ━➤
ROUTE 2 ━➤ ━➤ ━➤
ROUTE 3 •••••➤

100   50   0   100   YARDS 200

contains one of the world's oldest collections of **Greek and Roman statuary.** You will want to return here to see such great sculptures as the *Capitoline Venus,* the *Dying Gaul,* and *Cupid and Psyche.* On your right is another fine museum, the **Palazzo dei Conservatori,** where you will find among many great works of art the statue that more than any other is associated with the founding of Rome, the Etruscan bronze of the *She-Wolf.* Both these museums should be visited, either now or later, when you can spare an hour or so.

Pause for a moment in this magnificently proportioned square to study the lovely ocher-colored façade of the **Palazzo Senatario** with its stately double staircase and graceful campanile. Today it is the mayor of Rome's official residence. It is worth coming here on Saturday evenings, when the square and buildings are illuminated.

Now turn right to the terrace behind the Palazzo Senatario. There before you lies the **Forum,** the center of political and religious life in ancient Roman days. As you gaze over this historic place you will be able to identify several of its better-known monuments—the Arch of Septimius Severus just below to the left, and the Arch of Titus at the far end of the **Via Sacra,** the Forum's major thoroughfare. You will see the Palatine Hill rising just to the right, and the Colosseum in the distance.

From the terrace, make your way down the curving road of huge cobblestones (perhaps the oldest in Rome), the **Via del Foro Romano,** past the colonnade of the **Portico of the Dii Consentes,** dating from the fourth century and one of the last monuments to the pagan religion. Now skirt the Forum (the marvelously decorated column of Trajan is off to your left) until you reach the Via dei Fori Imperiali. Turn right, and you arrive at the Forum's main entrance (open 9:00–one hour before sunset; Tuesday and Sunday, 9:00–1:00).

You can spend as much time in the Forum as will satisfy your thirst for knowledge of ancient Rome. In general only the foundations and several arches and columns have survived the destruction of the ages in their original form, yet the excavated area conveys a sense of the grandeur of ancient Rome. It is a fascinating experience to tread this historic ground and listen to a well-informed guide explain the significance of the ruins that lie all about you. For the purposes of this stroll, several of the more interesting sights will be mentioned here, but for details you should purchase a special guidebook and map of the Forum.

A good place to start your wanderings around the Forum is the great third-century **Triumphal Arch of Septimius Severus.** Not far away is the **Imperial Rostrum** from which orators addressed the populace. Just in front of the arch descend a few steps to the **Lapis Niger.** The tomb of Romulus is said to have been located beneath this black flagstone. The remains of the golden milestone measuring the routes throughout the Empire are to your left as you face the arch.

The **Curia,** where the Senate once met, the square brick building that Julius Caesar began in 44 B.C., is currently closed to the public.

As you stroll along the sanctuary-lined Via Sacra, which was the triumphal route of victorious generals, you will notice to your right three majestic Corinthian columns. They are the remains of the **Temple of Castor and Pollux.** Make your way closer to them so that you can observe the superb capitals of these splendid white marble pillars against the blue sky.

Pause for a moment to admire on the right the beautifully proportioned remains of the **Temple of the Vestal Virgins,** the guardians of the sacred flame that signified the perpetuity of the Roman state. Behind you are the ruins of the **House of the Vestal Virgins.** As you leave them, there is a fine view of the columns of Castor and Pollux.

The high arches farther along on the left as you go up a slight incline on the Via Sacra are the ruins of the huge **Basilica of Maxentius,** which was studied by Bramante and Michelangelo while they were designing St. Peter's. To your right there is a fine view of the umbrella pines, cypresses, palms, and cedars on the crest of the Palatine Hill, the cradle of ancient Rome.

At the end of the Via Sacra you will come to the massive **Arch of Titus,** commemorating the capture of Jerusalem in A.D. 70. Notice the bas-relief under the arch, which depicts the Roman soldiers carrying away the seven-branched candlesticks, the spoils from Solomon's Temple.

After touring the Forum, you should then turn to the right up the hill from the Arch of Titus to the **Palatine Hill** or Monte Palatino, just above you. Settlement of the Palatine is known to date from the ninth century B.C., and it was here that Romulus and Remus are said to have founded Rome.

A stroll on the Palatine among the historic ruins shaded by umbrella pines, palms, and cypresses is one of the most romantic in Rome, so continue up the steps to the terrace of the **Farnese Gardens.** Stop for a few minutes on the main terrace just beyond. You will be enchanted by the striking panorama of the Forum beneath you. As you look out on this fabulous scene, pick out the ruins you found most interesting. In wandering around the picturesque gardens, remember that hereabouts beneath the olive groves were the homes of Cicero, Mark Antony, the orator Crassus, as well as the palaces of several Roman emperors. You should visit the decorative murals in **Casa Livia** ("the House of Livia"), now believed to have belonged to her husband, the Emperor Augustus. A small terrace nearby commands a fine view of St. Peter's dome and the Janiculum. From the House of Livia turn right and walk through the long vaulted underground gallery, known as the **Cryptoporticus,** which connected the palaces on the Palatine to Nero's Domus Aurea. You will see off to your right the remains of the huge **stadium of Domitian** and the **imperial palace,** before descending the hill along the **Barberini vineyard.**

Be sure to see the exciting *Son et Lumière* **performance,** which is presented at the Forum most evenings. This dramatic presentation makes the days of early Rome live again and brings to life the ancient and historic ruins.

You leave the Forum by the gate just beyond the Arch of Titus. Now, you will see to your right the great **Arch of Constantine,** the last of the triumphal arches. Erected in A.D. 315 in honor of the Christian Constantine's victory over the pagan Maxentius, it was built from fragments of earlier Roman buildings. Inspect the reliefs and medallions, which commemorate scenes from the days of Trajan, Hadrian, and Constantine.

Dominating the square is the **Colosseum.** (Open 9:00–3:30 in winter; 9:00–7:00 in summer; closed Monday.) This massive monument has for centuries symbolized the eternity of Roman civilization, for it has survived earthquakes, fires, and vandalism. Even by today's standards the huge stone blocks in the three superimposed colonnades reflect the grandeur and magnificence of the Flavian emperors who built it between A.D. 72 and A.D. 80. To get a good view of the Colosseum, which, incidentally, was named for the colossal **statue of Nero** that once stood near the site, walk up the path on the far side of the pleasant **Oppio Park.** Underneath this park are the remains of Nero's **Domus Aurea,** or "Golden House." (At this writing, closed for extensive restoration.)

Here at the Colosseum is the fitting spot to end this stroll through the greatest monuments of Roman civilization.

Four Churches

The next two walks, each relatively short, will take you to some of the most fascinating **churches** in Rome—ones that many tourists miss. The second walk includes the only church in Rome (San

Clemente) where you can see three centers of religious worship—dating from the second century to the twelfth—superimposed on one another at different levels in the same location. After visiting two other unusual churches, you complete the walk at the great Basilica of St. John in Lateran. The third walk, which you should take in the afternoon, will bring you finally to the **Aventine Hill** at an hour when the soft golden glow adds much to the view you will have over the city.

The first stroll, to St. John in Lateran, can be started at the **Colosseum,** if you have just visited the **Forum** and feel like continuing. If so, take the **Via di San Giovanni in Laterano** to the **Church of San Clemente.** Otherwise go directly (preferably by taxi) to the Church of San Clemente. (Open daily 9:00–12:30 and 3:30–6:30.)

This intensely interesting church of Byzantine design—from the days before the Emperor Nero to the Christian period more than a thousand years later—is unique. Here you can actually see the span of Roman history illustrated by four levels of construction on the same site. (When you go in, ask one of the Irish monks to take you around.)

The twelfth-century upper church, regarded as the finest example of a Christian basilica, was built directly on top of the lower fourth-century church. The discovery of the lower church was made in 1857 by Father Joseph Mullooly. His excavations also revealed the remains of a first-century building at a third and lower level. Later, from 1912 to 1914, it was found that a fourth stratum existed: buildings that were destroyed when Rome burned in A.D. 64 during the rule of Nero. The lowest level is sixty feet below the present entrance to the church.

So today you can descend from the **upper church,** with its decorative twelfth-century mosaic in the apse and its frescoes by Masolino, to the **lower church,** built at the time of Constantine over the **residence of St. Clement,** the third Pope after St. Peter. Fifth-century columns and ninth- and eleventh-century frescoes have survived. Go below to the remains of the second-century **Mithraic temple,** where you will see a bas-relief of the killing of a bull on the altar and also a bust of Apollo, the sun god.

After this exciting experience, turn right just beyond San Clemente into the Via dei Querceti and so on to the Via SS. Quattro; then walk left up the hill and a few steps to the right to reach the entrance of the **Church of the Santi Quattro Coronati.** Go to the far end of the courtyard and ring the bell. A nun will come down and usher you into the lovely thirteenth-century cloister. The graceful arches, the fountain in the center, and the palm trees make this cloister one of the most romantic and beautiful in Rome. The bell tower adds a true feeling of the Middle Ages. Note the thirteenth-century San Silvestro chapel, interesting for its cycle of frescoes depicting Constantine's conversion. (Open in summer, 9:30–12:00 and 3:30–6:00; in winter, 9:30–12:00; closed Sunday.)

Return now to San Clemente and in a few yards turn left on the Via Celimontana. Continue for a few short blocks past a military hospital to a large square. At the end make a sharp left, keeping the hospital on your left, and about fifty yards farther you will come to the church of **S. Stefano Rotondo.** This is reputed to be the largest church in the world built in circular style. It dates from the fifth century. Two concentric circles of columns give its interior a most unusual and interesting architectural appearance. (Open weekdays, 9:00–12:00.)

Turn right when you leave the church and walk along the Via S. Stefano Rotondo until you reach the square dominated by the huge **Basilica of St. John in Lateran,** the Cathedral of Rome, regarded by Catholics as their mother church. The Popes were crowned here until 1870. Although founded in A.D. 315, the church has been rebuilt throughout the centuries; the present building is largely the work of Borromini. The great façade, with the statues of Christ and his Apostles above the Palladian-style portico, dates from the eighteenth century. In Holy Years the **Porta Santa**—the door on the extreme right—is opened. You will want to wander around the impressive interior and the baptistry. But be sure to visit the exquisite thirteenth-century **cloister** on the left of the nave. This is one of the loveliest and most serene corners of Rome. As you walk around this secluded cloister you will be enchanted by the superb twisted and plain columns inlaid with mosaics. A ninth-century wellhead stands in the center of the garden surrounded by green hedges and shrubs. Sit on a ledge in the far corner of the cloister and look above you to the upper cloister and its tiled roof against the great pile of the church. Nowhere in Rome will you find a more perfect spot for repose and meditation. (Open daily, 7:00–7:00; closes at 6:00 in winter.)

At this point, if you wish to continue to the third walk, you should take a taxi to the Church of Santa Maria in Cosmedin.

The Velabrum and the Aventine

Start the third stroll at the **Church of Santa Maria in Cosmedin** in the area known as the **Velabrum,** between the Palatine, the Tiber, and the Aventine. In ancient days this was the marsh where the shepherd Faustulus is supposed to have rescued Romulus and Remus. Later, Byzantines from the Eastern Empire settled in this section of the city.

The church is one of the finest medieval churches in Rome. Its Romanesque **belfry** is particularly beautiful. Just before you enter, be sure to notice on the left of the portico a large **marble mask** in the shape of a human face, known as the *Mouth of Truth*. In medieval times it was believed that when a person suspected of a crime put his hand in its mouth it would close if he swore falsely. The colorful interior of the church, largely the work of the twelfth century, reflects the original Byzantine influence of the eighth-century basilica. The Cosmati mosaic pavement, the varicolored antique columns, and the dark aura make this church particularly enchanting. (Open daily, 9:00–1:00 and 3:00–6:00.)

From the Church of Santa Maria in Cosmedin, go right a few steps, turning right again, into the wide Via dei Cerchi, and in a few yards make a sharp left into the **Via di San Teodoro,** noted for its tall, narrow houses built during the Middle Ages. After two hundred yards, go left into the Via del Velabro to the charming sixth-century **Church of San Giorgio in Velabro,** with its fine Romanesque tower. The rather austere interior is decorated by a beautiful mosaic pavement. Adjoining the church is the third-century arch of the money changers, and almost opposite is the four-sided **Arch of Janus,** built in the fourth century—also a center for money changers. (After the shocking terrorist bombing in 1993, the church has been undergoing reconstruction and will be closed to the public for some time.)

In the large square directly ahead you will see two small, graceful Roman temples, both unusually well preserved. The **Temple of Fortuna Virilis** with its fine Ionic columns is an architectural gem of beautiful proportions. Nearby, the lovely round **Temple of Vesta** was erected in the Greek style at the time of Augustus.

From here turn left past Santa Maria in Cosmedin into the Via della Greca. Then wind your way along the Clivo dei Publici up the quiet, serene **Aventine Hill.** As you walk up the road you will see below you the oblong Circus Maximus at the foot of the **Palatine**

Hill. (If you want to avoid climbing the Aventine Hill, take a taxi to the Piazza of the Knights of Malta and walk down. The shortest way downhill is the small road diagonally across the entrance of the park near Santa Sabina.)

The **Circus Maximus** was the largest arena built during the Roman Empire, 650 yards long and 150 wide, allowing 300,000 spectators to watch shows, races, and even mock battles (in 46 B.C. Julius Caesar staged one with 1,000 infantry, 600 cavalry, and 40 elephants). The rape of the Sabine women, in early Roman days, is believed to have occurred here.

At the top of the hill turn right into a small park. From the terrace at the far side you have a magnificent view over the **Tiber,** of the **Trastevere** section, the hill known as the **Janiculum,** and **St. Peter's,** as well as the domes of Rome's many churches. A little farther along the road you come to the **Church of Santa Sabina,** called the "Pearl of the Aventine." Continue another hundred yards to the **Piazza of the Knights of Malta.** On the wall of this square there are delightful bas-reliefs of musical instruments. The massive **gate of the Maltese villa** affords one of the most extraordinary views in Rome. If you look through the keyhole, you will see an artistically landscaped garden with the white dome of St. Peter's framed in a long avenue of cropped laurel trees.

Retrace your steps a few yards on the Via de Santa Sabina and turn right on the **Via di S. Alessio,** a street lined with stately homes. Oleanders, cypress, and palms in the spacious gardens add much color and beauty to this attractive residential section. Turn left a block of so before the street ends, and then turn right down the Via di Santa Prisca to the **Viale Aventino.** Here you can pick up a taxi or public transport to return to the center of the city.

The Renaissance City
To the Piazza Navona and the Pantheon

These two walks take you through the **heart of Rome.** You will walk some of the narrow old streets, hemmed in by massive palazzi. You will visit a few churches that are exceptional yet often by-passed, a magnificent square, the main shopping district, the Spanish Steps, and the lovely Pincian Gardens. By seeing such varied places, both interesting and beautiful, you will become aware of the many different civilizations Rome has lived through, and in particular, get a feel of Renaissance Rome. You will realize why Rome is indeed the Eternal City.

Start on the Via d. Teatro di Marcello at the foot of the **Capitoline Hill.** The majestic circular tiers of stone of the **Theatre of Marcellus** give you some idea of the huge edifice that the Emperor Augustus erected in 13 B.C. Twenty-two thousand spectators used to crowd it in Roman days. Andrea Palladio, the sixteenth-century Italian architect, modeled his designs on its Doric and Ionic columns. You will notice private apartments built above the arches of the theater.

Wander past the three superb **Columns of Apollo** by the arches of the theater. The remains of the **Portico of Octavia** are now in front of you. Climb the steps from the theater to the Via della Tribuna di Campitelli for an even better view of the Columns of Apollo. Go into the monumental baroque church of **Santa Maria in Campitelli.**

Turn to the right along a narrow street to the tiny Piazza di Campitelli, then go left along the Via dei Funari to the Piazza Mattei. Here is one of the loveliest fountains in Rome, the **Fontana delle Tartarughe** or **"Fountain of the Tortoises."** It's typical of

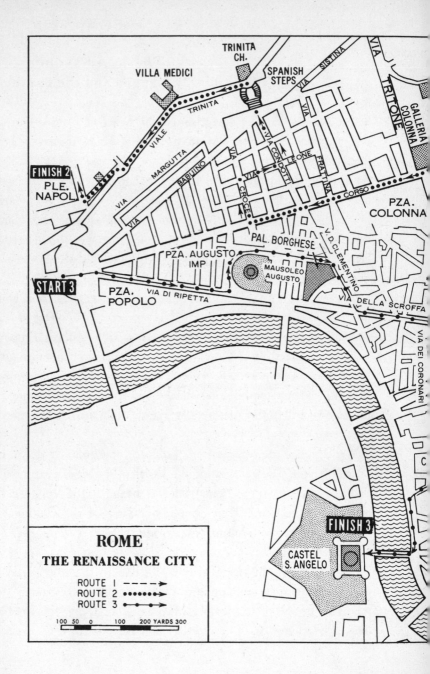

TRINITA
CH.

VILLA MEDICI

SPANISH
STEPS

VIA SISTINA

VIA TRITONE

GALLERIA
COLONNA

TRINITA

VIALE

VIA CONDOTTI

VIA LEONE

FRATTINA

MARGUTTA

VIA BABUINO

VIA CROCE

VIA

CORSO

FINISH 2
PLE.
NAPOL

VIA

PZA.
COLONNA

PAL. BORGHESE

PZA. AUGUSTO
IMP

V. D. CLEMENTINO

START 3

PZA.
POPOLO

VIA DI RIPETTA

MAUSOLEO
AUGUSTO

VIA DELLA SCROFFA

VIA DEI CORONARI

C

FINISH 3

CASTEL
S. ANGELO

ROME
THE RENAISSANCE CITY

ROUTE 1 – – – →
ROUTE 2 ●●●●●●●→
ROUTE 3 ●—●—●→

100 50 0   100   200 YARDS 300

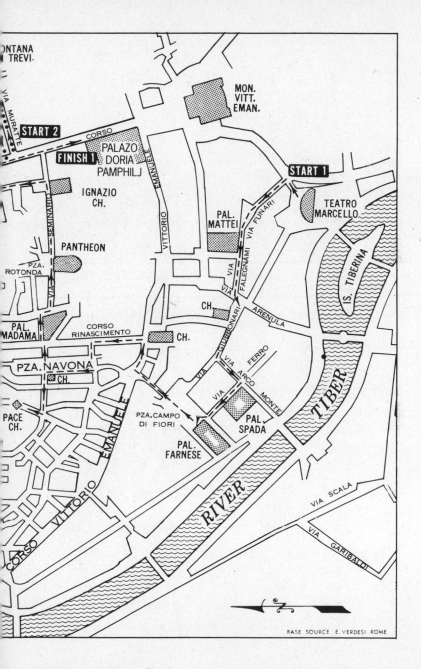

FONTANA
TREVI.

VIA MURATTE

START 2

CORSO

FINISH 1

PALAZO
DORIA
PAMPHILJ

MON.
VITT.
EMAN.

START 1

TEATRO
MARCELLO

IGNAZIO
CH.

EMANUELE

VITTORIO

PAL.
MATTEI

VIA FUNARI

VIA FALEGNAMI

IS. TIBERINA

PANTHEON

PZA.
ROTONDA

VIA

CH.

VIA GIUBBONARI

ARENULA

TIBER

PAL.
MADAMA

CORSO
RINASCIMENTO

CH.

VIA FERRO

VIA ARCO

MONTE

PZA. NAVONA

CH.

VIA

VIA

PZA. CAMPO
DI FIORI

PAL
SPADA

PACE
CH.

EMANUELE

VITTORIO

PAL.
FARNESE

RIVER

VIA SCALA

VIA GARIBALDI

CORSO

BASE SOURCE E. VERDESI. ROME

Rome that in the midst of this rather poor area you should find such an artistic work in the center of a little square. Stand here for a few moments and look at this gem of a fountain with its four youths, each holding a tortoise and each with a foot resting on the head of a dolphin. The figures have been executed so skillfully that one senses a great feeling of life and movement. Diagonally to the left of the fountain is the **Palazzo Costaguti,** with ceilings by Domenichino and Guercino.

On your right just before you reach the fountain is the **Palazzo Mattei,** one of Rome's oldest palaces, now the headquarters of the **Italo-American Association.** Go inside for a closer look at a Renaissance palace. In the first courtyard there are some fine bas-reliefs and friezes, and in the second a series of delightful terraced roof gardens above an ivy-covered wall.

Keep straight ahead on the Via dei Falegnami, cross the wide Via Arenula, and you will come to the **Piazza B. Cairoli,** where you should look in at the **Church of San Carlo ai Catinari** to see the frescoes on the pendentives and in the apse. (Open 7:00–12:00 and 4:00–8:00; closed in May and June.) Follow the colorful and busy Via d. Giubbonari for about fifty yards. Now turn left at the Via dell'Arco del Monte to the Piazza dei Pellegrini. Turning right into the Via Capo di Ferro will bring you to the **Palazzo Spada,** built in 1540 and now occupied by the Council of State. Paintings by Titian, Caravaggio, and Rubens are on display (open 9:00–1:00; closed Sunday and Monday).

Before you enter the palazzo, note Francesco Borromini's façade. The great architect also designed the fine interior staircase and colonnade that connects the two courts. The large statue on the first floor is believed to be the **statue of Pompey** at the base of which Julius Caesar was stabbed to death. (If so, the statue once stood in the Senate house. This is shown in the afternoon and on Sunday morning.)

By tipping the porter, you can see in the courtyard Borromini's unusual and fascinating trick in perspective. When you stand before the barrel-vaulted **collonade** you have the impression that the statue at the end is very large, yet it is actually relatively small. The sense of perspective has been created by designing the length of the columns so that those at the far end of the colonnade are much shorter than those in front. The gardens of the palazzo, shaded by a huge magnolia tree, are most attractive. The courtyard is magnificently decorated.

From the Palazzo Spada you continue another block along the Via Capo di Ferro and Vicolo de' Venti to the imposing **Palazzo Farnese,** begun in 1514 and considered by many to be the finest Renaissance palace in Rome. Michelangelo was the most distinguished of several noted architects who helped design it. Today it is occupied by the **French Embassy** and is closed to the public.

Directly in front of the palace following the Via dei Baullari you will come to the **Campo dei Fiori,** the famous site of executions during the turbulent days of the Counter-Reformation. Today by contrast it is a lively and colorful fruit, vegetable, and flower market. At No. 15 there's a typically Roman wine bar, **Vineria Reggio.** To the left is the Palazzo della Cancelleria where the Cardinal-Vicar resides. Continue on the Via dei Baullari to the Corso Vittorio Emanuele, then turn right for a couple of hundred yards to the **Church of Sant'Andrea della Valle.** As you approach the church on the Via dei Baullari you are passing within yards of the **Roman Theatre of Pompey.** The dome of the church is, outside of St. Peter's, one of the largest in Rome. Opera lovers will be interested to learn that this church is the scene for the first act of *Tosca.* (Open daily, 7:30–12:00 and 4:30–7:30.)

At this point you cross the wide Corso Vittorio Emanuele II to the **Palazzo Massimo alle Colonne** with its interesting courtyard with frescoes above on the loggia. Then walk along the Corso del

Rinascimento a couple of hundred yards, and take the second left on the Via dei Canestrari to enter the splendid **Piazza Navona,** one of the truly glorious sights in Rome.

Your first impression of this elongated square, with its three elegant fountains, its two churches that almost face each other, and its russet-colored buildings, is a sense of restful spaciousness—particularly welcome after wandering around the narrow and dark streets that you have followed since starting this walk.

The site of the oblong piazza is **Domitian's ancient stadium,** which was probably used for horse and chariot races. For centuries it was the location of historic festivals and open-air sports events. From the seventeenth to the nineteenth century it was a popular practice to flood the piazza in the summer, and the aristocrats would then ride around the inundated square in their carriages.

Gian Lorenzo Bernini's **Fountain of the Rivers,** in the center of the piazza, is built around a Roman obelisk from the Circus of Maxentius that rests on grottoes and rocks, with four huge figures, one at each corner, denoting four great rivers from different continents—the Danube, the Ganges, the Nile, and the Plata. The eyes of the figure of the Nile are covered, perhaps either to symbolize the mystery of her source or to obscure from her sight the baroque façade of the **Church of Sant'Agnese in Agone,** the work of Bernini's rival, Borromini.

In the Piazza Navona there are many delightful cafés where you can sit, have a drink or lunch, and watch the fountains in the square. Try the ice cream at No. 28, the café **Tre Scalini.** The scene before you is indeed theatrical and often appears in movies about Rome. Perhaps a street musician will pass to add that extra touch. The Piazza Navona is closed to traffic, which will add to your enjoyment.

Take the Via di S. Agnese in Agone, next to the church and opposite the center of the square, then turn right after about two hundred yards to reach the beautiful **Church of Santa Maria della Pace.** Inside you will find the lovely Sibyls painted by Raphael. The church's cloisters are among Donato Bramante's most beautiful creations. (At this writing the church is closed for restoration.) In the summer, concerts are given in the cloisters.

Now return to the Piazza Navona and leave it on the opposite side by the Corsia Agonale; in a moment cross the Corso del Rinascimento. In front of you is the **Palazzo Madama,** once belonging to the Medici and now the **Italian Senate.** To your right, along the Corso del Rinascimento at No. 40, is the **Palazzo della Sapienza,** now the **National Archives.** Go into the courtyard to see the bizarre, spiral-crowned Chapel of St. Ivo, by Borromini. (Open for Mass Sunday, 10:00–12:00; closed in July and August.) Returning to the Palazzo Madama, you walk by the side of the palazzo and after two blocks along the Via Giustiniani you will come to the **Piazza della Rotonda.** You are now facing the **Pantheon,** the largest and best-preserved building still standing from the days of ancient Rome. (Open Monday–Saturday, 9:00–6:00; in winter, 5:00; Sunday, 9:00–1:00.)

This circular edifice, constructed by Agrippa in 27 B.C., was rebuilt in its present shape by the Emperor Hadrian. It was dedicated as a church in the seventh century. As you pause in the piazza by the Egyptian obelisk brought from the Temple of Isis, you will admire the Pantheon's impressive Corinthian columns.

The Pantheon's interior, still in its original form, is truly majestic and an architectural triumph. Its **rotunda** forms a perfect circle whose diameter is equal to the height from the floor to the ceiling. The only means of interior light is the twenty-nine-foot-wide aperture in the stupendous dome. Standing before the tomb of Raphael, the great genius of the Renaissance, when shafts of sunlight are penetrating this great Roman temple, you are once again reminded of the varied civilizations so characteristic of Rome.

As you leave the Pantheon, take the narrow street to the right, the Via del Seminario, a block to **Sant'Ignazio,** one of the most splendid baroque churches in the city. (Along the way there, about one hundred yards on your right, you pass a simple restaurant, **La Sacrestia,** where you can have the best pizza in Rome.) The curve of faded terra-cotta-colored houses in front of the church seems like a stage set. This is one of the most charming little squares in this part of Rome. One block along the Via de Burro (in front of the church) will bring you to the **Stock Exchange** in the old **Temple of Neptune.** A few yards farther, on the Via dei Bergamaschi, is the **Piazza Colonna.** The great column from which the square takes its name was erected in honor of the Emperor Marcus Aurelius.

You are now at the **Corso,** which, though narrow, is one of Rome's busiest streets. Horse races took place here in the Middle Ages.

If you have taken this stroll in the morning, and you have the time and inclination, walk to the right along the crowded Corso for half a dozen blocks to visit the private collection of paintings— mainly of the sixteenth and seventeenth centuries—in the **Palazzo Doria Pamphilj** (open Saturday, Sunday, Tuesday, and Friday, 10:00–1:00; closed holidays). Turn right into Via Lata, then left in the square to the gallery's entrance. Here is your opportunity to see the inside of a palazzo where the family still lives. To visit the sumptuous apartments, notify the attendant.

Otherwise, cross over the Corso and walk a block or so to the left. You will come to **Alemagna,** a delightful though moderately expensive restaurant which is particularly noted for its exceptional selection of ice creams and *pâtisseries.* Either here, or in one of the modest restaurants nearby, is just the place to end this first walk through the heart of Rome.

To the Spanish Steps

The second walk through the heart of Rome should be taken after lunch, so that you will reach the **Pincian Hill** when the soft light of the late afternoon is at its best.

Take a rest from sight-seeing and have a look at the arcade of shops in the **Galleria Colonna,** opposite the Piazza Colonna. Then wander up and down past the attractive shops along the **Corso.** After this little expedition, walk left from the Galleria one short block on the Corso to the Via delle Muratte, and then left a couple of hundred yards to the **Piazza di Trevi.** You now see before you probably the best-known and most ornate of all the fountains of Rome, the elaborate **Fontana di Trevi,** finished in 1762.

This great group of statues, among which are figures of Triton and Neptune, is brought alive by the tremendous flow of water (17.5 million gallons a day) that pours from many parts of the huge monument. Its construction against the walls of the **Palazzo Poli** gives it the unusual appearance of a theatrical set. Tradition has it that tourists who toss a coin in the fountain are certain to return to Rome.

Now go back to the Corso, turn right, and continue your window-shopping in the direction of the Piazza del Popolo to the Via Condotti. The sidewalks ot the Corso are extremely narrow and crowded but this adds a sense of adventure. Along the **Via Condotti** you will find many of Rome's most fashionable and luxurious stores, including the world-famous jeweler Bulgari and the Italian designer Armani. Other shops specialize in silks, ceramics, leather goods, and men's wear. Stop for an espresso at the historic **Caffè Greco.**

After strolling up and down the Via Condotti, walk a bit farther on the Corso to the **Via della Croce,** where you will be tempted by the high-quality food shops. This entire area is filled with unusual and fascinating stores selling all those Roman specialties that make shopping here so exciting. You will find various kinds of Italian cheese in the food shops and stand-up bars in the wine shops. At No. 39 there's a cozy Roman *trattoria,* **Fiaschetterina Beltramme,** but if you don't feel like lunch, try a glass of chianti at the Rolfi Isabella at No. 75A. So why not wander around for a while. From the Via della Croce you can take the Via Bocca di Leone across the Via Condotti to the Via Frattina.

After this extensive shopping spree, you will probably find yourself back in the Via Condotti in the latter part of the afternoon. This is the best hour to approach the **Piazza di Spagna** at the end of the street. The sun will be getting low in the sky behind you, and its slanting rays will throw an almost unbelievably clear golden light on the glorious **Spanish Steps** and the striking **Church of Trinità dei Monti** which surmounts them. The combination of direct sunlight on the terra-cotta-colored church and the azure sky against which it is silhouetted is without doubt one of the most thrilling and dramatic sights in Rome. Even though it's hard to find a spot along the crowded sidewalk to stand for a few moments, you should do so before you reach the piazza, for when you do you are so close to the steps that the magnificence of the perspective is lost.

Crossing the square to the foot of the steps, you will see Bernini's interesting **Fontana della Barcaccia**—shaped like a boat—in the center.

The glorious sweep of the double flight of steps is artistically divided into well-spaced landings. Here is one of the most popular **flower markets** of Rome, adding a fitting decorative note to the lovely scene.

As you climb the curves of the steps, pause at the first balustrade and look around you at the reddish-yellow baroque houses. The poet John Keats lived and died in a house on the right, now a **Keats-Shelley Memorial House** (open daily, in summer, 9:00–1:00 and 3:00–6:00; in winter, 2:30–5:30, weekdays only; closed holidays). Palm trees, oleander, and hanging vines decorate the different levels of the terraced gardens. From the top balustrade you can see to your right the uneven roofs and skylights of the **Via Margutta,** an interesting street inhabited by artists. There spreads before you one of the finest views over Rome. This is a place to linger for a while, cast your eyes over the panorama, and feel the pulse of Rome.

As you leave the terrace in front of the church and walk along the Viale della Trinità dei Monti, notice the attractive roof gardens on top of the houses below you. The palm, cypress, and olive trees along the road lend a romantic air to the scene.

The large palace on your right is the **Villa Medici,** the French academy for students of the fine arts. Its delightful **gardens,** extending from the lovely interior façade of the palazzo, are currently closed for restoration. Shortly you will come to a circular **overlook,** a favorite spot for artists.

Now cross the road and take the foot ramp to the **Piazzale Napoleone** in the **Pincian Gardens.** In Roman days this was the location of the villa of Lucullus, whose banquets were legendary. Today the gardens are a favorite park of Romans, and Punch-and-Judy shows and other games attract crowds of children. Nearby is the **Casina Valadier,** a delightful café with an outdoor terrace, named for Napoleon's architect, who laid out the Piazza del Popolo below. This is just the spot to enjoy an *aperitivo* while watching the sunset over the city and the Roman hills, with the great **dome of St. Peter's** silhouetted against the sky.

Piazza del Popolo to Castel Sant'Angelo

This is a walk that is right in the center of Rome, that is not very long and includes the Castel Sant'Angelo, the one place of unusual interest where you will want to spend a good deal of time. In addition, this stroll will take you to a street filled with antique shops that you might otherwise miss.

Let's start at the oval-shaped **Piazza del Popolo,** one of Rome's largest squares, just below the **Pincio Hill.** Pause here for a moment and look up at the shell-shaped fountains and the terraces covered with tall cypress, palms, and pointed cedars—those trees that are so characteristic of Rome. When you stand near the massive arch and face the **obelisk** that **Augustus** brought from Egypt, you appreciate the vastness of the square. Water pours from the mouths of four statues of lions at the base of the obelisk. Straight ahead three streets, divided by two symmetrical baroque churches with lovely domes, spread in a fan shape from the square's far side. In the **Church of Santa Maria del Popolo** adjoining the arched gateway there are some outstanding works of art including frescoes by Pinturicchio. The church's **Chigi chapel** was constructed from a design by Raphael; Bramante was responsible for the apse and Bernini for some of the statuary. (Open daily, 7:00–12:15 and 4:00–7:00.)

As you face the twin churches from the Piazza, take the right-hand street, the **Via di Ripetta.** Now you must walk for four or five blocks down this street (you'll want to return for dinner at the wonderful fish restaurant **Porto di Ripetti**) until you reach the **Mausoleo Augusteo.** This huge circular mound covered with cypress trees was the tomb of the Emperor Augustus and his family. Dating from 28 B.C. it was one of the holiest monuments of ancient Rome.

In those days this area was known as the **Campus Martius.** (Admission by written permission only.)

To your right you will find a stairway that leads to a temporary structure housing the reconstructed **Ara Pacis Augustae,** an example of the finest Roman art. This is an altar of peace erected in 13 B.C. and covered with bas-reliefs of ceremonial processions and Roman allegories. It was done in the most classical Greco-Roman style.

Stroll around the tomb of Augustus. On the side away from the Tiber, you will pass one of Rome's most famous restaurants, **Alfredo All'Augusteo.** Here the so-called King of Fettucine holds forth beneath the photographs of celebrities from all over the world, serving personally his own delicious recipe of fettucine with the "gold fork and spoon." Continue past the restaurant and beyond a tiny square. You will cross the Via Tomacelli on the far side of a lively outdoor **food market.** After pausing to enjoy this attractive scene, walk along the **Via di Monte D'Oro,** then turn right at the next street. In a moment you will be in a small piazza, the **Largo della Fontanella di Borghese.**

The **Palazzo Borghese,** one of Rome's Late Renaissance palaces, is on your right. Shaped like a harpsichord, it belonged to Cardinal Borghese, who became Pope Paul V. Walk through the front courtyard to the archway. Long vines hang on the walls from the grape arbor on the loggia above the arch. In the inner court there is a charming scene, typical of Roman palazzi—a fountain, the Bath of Venus, surrounded by a portico of many columns and statuary, plays in the garden beneath the high walls of russet-colored buildings. On top, you'll see delightful roof garden apartments with terraces. (At this writing, the Palazzo is closed to the public.)

When you leave the Palazzo Borghese, stop for a few minutes on your right to browse about the **outdoor market** beneath the curving ocher-colored façade of the palace. Here you will find stalls filled with books, old prints, maps, and bric-a-brac—a fascinating collection of oddities.

Continue to the right on the **Via del Clementino** and at the next corner, the **Via della Scroffa,** turn left. As you stroll along here you'll catch glimpses of fine palazzi, such as the one on the **Via dei Portoghesi** on your right. When the street widens, make a sharp right, turning into the **Via di S. Agostino,** and after passing under an archway into a wide traffic-filled square, go straight across to the **Via dei Coronari.** While crossing the square you'll notice the **Restaurant Passetto,** one of the best dining places in Rome, and thorough a narrow street on your left you'll be able to see the **Piazza Navona.** Don't miss the stone blocks and brick remains of the ancient stadium that occupied this site in Roman days. These are now preserved in the entrance to a modern building on your left.

The Via dei Coronari, lined with Renaissance houses, is just what an antique enthusiast searches for in Rome. A narrow, dingy street, it is crowded with tiny antique shops. Here is one dealing in furniture; there you'll see one specializing in brassware. If you are looking for paintings, glassware, lamps, or china, you'll find them all in one little shop or another. Candelabras, basketwork, and upholstery are also for sale along this street. The Via dei Coronari is closed to traffic, which makes browsing in the shops all the more fun.

Shortly you'll come into the **Piazza di S. Salvatore** in **Lauro.** Turn right into the square. Opposite the church you bear right into the Via della Rondinella to reach the **Via di Tor di Nona,** the broad tree-lined avenue that parallels the Tiber. On the other side of this busy thoroughfare, opposite the **Castel Sant'Angelo,** you have a fine view upstream of the twin towers of the **Villa Medici** outlined against the blue sky, with the bushy cypress trees of the **Pincio** on the horizon.

Turn left and stroll along the promenade under the luxuriant sycamores whose branches hang below the retaining wall. In a minute or two you will reach the **Ponte Sant'Angelo,** three of whose arches were built by the Emperor Hadrian in A.D. 136. The angels' statues from Bernini's studio, which give the bridge such a decorative effect, were added during the seventeenth century.

Pause for a few minutes on the bridge to enjoy the view up- and downstream and the massive circular **Castel Sant'Angelo** surmounted by the statue of a bronze angel after whom the castle was named in the eighteenth century. There is a legend that St. Gregory the Great, praying for a plague to end in A.D. 590, saw an angel sheathing his sword on top of the fortress, thus signaling the termination of the pestilence.

Actually, the Castel Sant'Angelo (open Tuesday–Saturday, 9:00–2:00; Sunday, 9:00–1:00; Monday, 2:00–7:00; closed holidays) was originally the **tomb of Hadrian.** The Emperor built it in A.D. 135. He and succeeding Roman emperors to Septimius Severus were buried in this great mound.

The mausoleum became Rome's fortress when Aurelian defended the city in the third century. Through the barbarian invasions, the citadel was the scene of bitter fighting. In the Middle Ages the castle was used as a prison. During Charles V's sack of Rome in 1527, Pope Clement VII took refuge here through an underground tunnel from the Vatican, which is still in existence. It was a state prison in Renaissance days. You can visit the old cells, from one of which **Benvenuto Cellini** escaped by sliding down a rope of knotted sheets. It has been truly said that the Castel Sant'Angelo encompasses the entire scope of Rome's turbulent history in the dramatic events that have occurred here.

After entering the castle, to reach the museum you walk up a long spiral, tunnel-like **ramp** that dates from the Roman period. On the way up you will pass the **dungeons.** In the **museum** you will find an intensely interesting collection of ancient military weapons, as well as paintings and other art treasures in the apartments of the popes, which are decorated with elaborate frescoes, ceilings, and stuccos.

Stroll around the circular walk on top of the castle. You have a remarkable panorama of Rome. From each embrasure you get a different view over the rooftops, church domes, monuments, and hills of Rome.

Here on the ramparts of the Castel Sant'Angelo, where so much of Rome's exciting history took place, is an excellent place to end this walk in the Eternal City.

To the Via Veneto
The Esquiline and the Quirinal

This walk will introduce you to some parts of Rome that many visitors who have only a few days there aren't likely to explore. It's a walk that you might like to do one afternoon, for it ends up at the **Via Veneto** at a time of day when it's fun to sit at one of the attractive sidewalk cafés. Also, it includes some of the most interesting and beautiful **churches,** as well as pleasant **parks.** As a matter of fact, even if you are particularly interested in seeing churches, it's more sensible to stroll from one to another because you will find that you appreciate them more when you have a chance to see something different in between. Otherwise, by taking a bus or taxi, you will find yourself dashing from one church or museum to another so fast that they all become confused in your mind. This is just one of the advantages of walking, particularly in Rome.

This walk begins on the **Via Nicola Salvi** just above the Colosseum. Follow this street to the Via di Terme di Tito and walk left for a couple of minutes to the square where you will find the **Church of S. Pietro in Vincoli,** founded as a shrine for St. Peter's chains in A.D. 442 (open Monday–Saturday, 7:00–12:30 and 3:30–7:00; in winter, 7:00–12:30 and 3:30–6:00; Sunday, 8:45–11:45). You have come here to see the magnificent **statue of Moses** by Michelangelo, certainly one of the most remarkable and stirring works of the Florentine master. To stand here and study the details of the figure— the majestic posture, the powerful hands and arms, the strength of character shown in the face and eyes, so phenomenally expressed in stone—is indeed an unforgettable experience. You will probably wonder about the prophet's horns, which are explained as either representing rays of light or as a result of some mistranslation from the Hebrew.

Outside the church, turn right into the narrow Via delle Sette Sale, which winds for a short distance over the **Esquiline Hill,** one of the highest of the Seven Hills of Rome. After a couple of hundred yards walk to the right into an attractive **park** with tall evergreens. Shortly you will come to a terrace that offers one of the best views of the Colosseum. Just beyond are the underground ruins of Nero's Domus Aurea, or Golden House.

Returning to the **Via delle Sette Sale,** you walk between the high walls on either side. Olive and eucalyptus trees overhang the road. Continue a few hundred yards to a major traffic intersection where streetcars and buses run. Cross over and keep slightly right on the Via dello Statuto for another block to **Piazza Vittorio Emanuele.** Here is one of Rome's small, attractive parks that is relatively unknown but full of atmosphere. On the edge of the square there is usually a colorful flower-and-vegetable market. Wander around the park under the stately palms rising above ancient ruins. There are several fountains and a pond. You are likely to see a fun fair set up

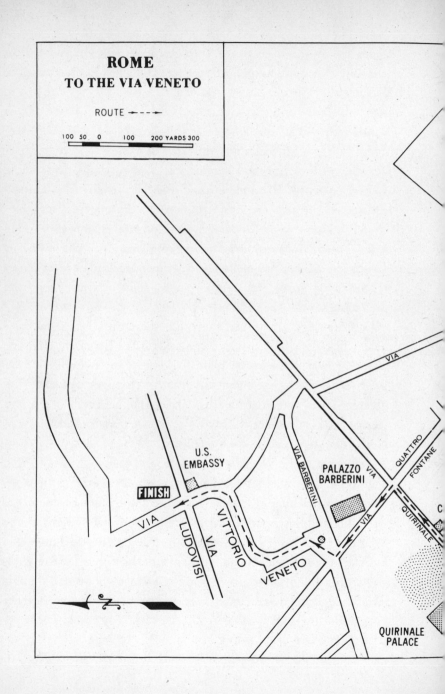

ROME
TO THE VIA VENETO

ROUTE ----→

100 50 0   100   200 YARDS 300

VIA

U.S.
EMBASSY

FINISH

VIA BARBERINI

PALAZZO
BARBERINI

QUATTRO

VIA

FONTANE

VIA

VIA

QUIRINALE

C

VITTORIO

VIA LUDOVISI

VENETO

QUIRINALE
PALACE

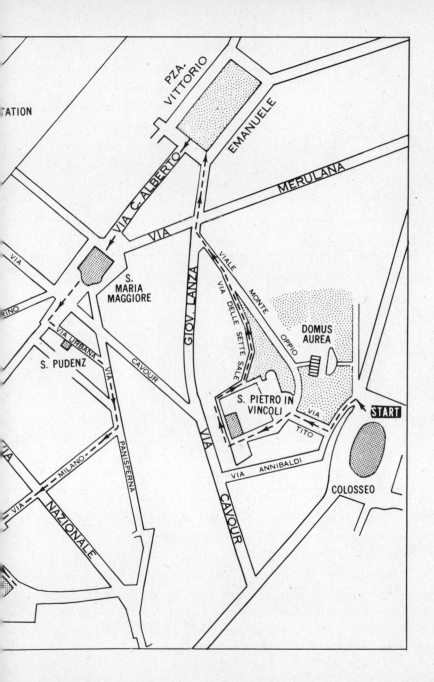

with Ferris wheel, games, and the usual other entertainments. As in so many places in Rome, this park seems to be alive with cats.

You leave the park at the end where you entered and walk along the wide Via Carlo Alberto directly opposite for three blocks to the large **Church of Santa Maria Maggiore,** which you can see ahead.

This vast and impressive basilica, built in the fifth century, is particularly outstanding, not only for its architectural form, but especially for its unusual and fascinating **mosaics.** These extraordinary fifth-century works of art over the triumphal arch represent figures and scenes from the Old and New Testaments. Be sure to request that the special lighting be turned on so you can see the marvelous detail and color. The gold in the **ceiling** supposedly was brought from America by Columbus. The fourteenth-century campanile in front of the church is the tallest in Rome.

Now walk to the rear of the church and through the square, dominated by an obelisk. In a block or so, at the bottom of the hill, turn left on Via Urbana, walk for about fifty yards, and on your right you will see the small and charming **Church of Santa Pudenziana.** On this site below the level of modern Rome, it is said, was **Senator Pudens's** house, where St. Peter is believed to have stayed while in Rome. The church itself, one of the oldest in the city, has in its apse **early mosaics** of the fourth century (open in summer, 8:00–12:00 and 4:00–7:00; in winter, 3:00–6:00 daily).

When you return to Via Urbana turn right and go a block or so on Via Panisperna, then right again on Via Milano. At the corner of Via Nazionale and Via Milano turn left, then right on Via Parma until you reach the large staircase. At the top is a park that you cross to get to the Via del Quirinale. Turn right, and a few yards on the right is the elegant little church of **Sant'Andrea al Quirinale.** Bernini designed this baroque jewel in an elliptical plan. The ornate interior, with tall pink marble columns and angels in the dome, makes it one of the loveliest and most intimate of all the churches in Rome—supreme evidence of Bernini's architectural genius. You are likely to find yourself wanting to drop in again just to absorb more of its exquisite beauty.

Now turn left and walk back along the Via del Quirinale to have a look at the **Quirinal Palace,** the residence of Italy's president, a couple of hundred yards farther on. Stroll over to the balustrade, from which, at this high point on the Quirinal Hill, you have an extensive view over the city, with St. Peter's in the distance. The statues above a beautiful fountain in the center of the square are Roman copies of the Greek figures of Castor and Pollux. The palace, which years ago was the summer residence of the popes, is open on Thursday from 2:00 to 5:00. Submission of your passport is required for entry.

Retrace your steps along the Via Quirinale. When you reach the corner where the **Via dei Giardini** begins, look to your right into a delightful garden. A royal palm above a grape arbor sways in the breeze. Here is one of those amazing sights in the center of this great city that gives Rome such an unusual appeal. A few yards farther along you come to **Via delle Quattro Fontane.** At each corner of the intersection there is a small fountain and in each direction you have a fine view. On your right is Borromini's Church of San Carlino. Don't miss the tiny cloister, a masterpiece of baroque architecture.

Turn left down the hill along the Via delle Quattro Fontane. On your right is the **Palazzo Barberini,** one of Rome's most sumptuous. It is now the **National Art Gallery** (open 9:00–2:00; Sunday and holidays, 9:00–1:00; closed Monday). Its collection of Italian paintings, including excellent examples of the great masters, is the finest in Rome. One of Raphael's marvelous portraits, *La Fornarina,* is here.

At the foot of the hill you will come into the **Piazza Barberini,** a busy traffic junction. Note Bernini's Triton Fountain in the center of the square. At the far end of the square the wide and tree-lined **Via Veneto** winds up the hill. Before you turn into the Via Veneto, look at Bernini's **Fountain of the Bees.** (Bees were depicted on the heraldic device of the Barberini family.) At the top, where the street curves to the left, you will see the stately American Embassy on your right. Now you have reached the smartest couple of blocks in Rome for those who enjoy outdoor café life. Pull up a chair at one of the tables, either at **Doney's** on your right or at the **Café de Paris** across the street, and observe the promenade of people. One of the most entertaining experiences in Rome is to watch the different, and often exotic, types from all over the world as they pass here.

Across the Tiber
Trastevere and the Janiculum

This walk takes you across the **Tiber,** away from the main part of Rome to a section that many tourists don't visit in the daytime— **Trastevere.** (You probably will dine in the evening at one of its many restaurants that have such a colorful air. If you like fish, try **Alberto Ciarla,** piazza **San Cosimato,** in the heart of the quarter.) For generations this has been one of the poorest parts of the city, an area with narrow streets crowded with people. Street vendors shouting their wares, the old houses, and the winding alleys give this section an atmosphere of the Middle Ages. Yet as chic bistros flourish and elegant boutiques proliferate, Trastevere seems somewhat less authentic than it used to be.

Start at the oldest bridge over the Tiber, the **Ponte Fabricio,** near the **Theatre of Marcellus.** Before you cross, wander along the embankment and look at the bridge's high and graceful arches. It's hard to realize that it is believed to date from the days of Julius Caesar. The Ponte Fabricio leads to the **Isola Tiberina,** a small boat-shaped island that has rather a pleasantly quiet atmosphere removed from the traffic that runs along the river. On the island to your right there's a large hospital.

Look to the left toward the gardens on the island with the **Aventine Hill** in the distance. Tall trees stand like sentinels at the tip of the island. Behind you on the embankment you will see the dome of Rome's **main synagogue,** in the old **Ghetto section.**

After crossing the **Ponte Cestio** from the Isola Tibernia to the far bank, turn left and walk along the stream for about fifty yards until you come to the Via dei Vascellari, which you follow to the intensely interesting **Church of Santa Cecilia.** Just before you reach the church be sure to notice on your left a most fascinating **house.** It's a remarkable building because so many different architectural styles are superimposed on one another. When you come in a few yards to the square on your right, you will be entranced by the church's twelfth-century **campanile** leaning slightly above the medieval houses. Opposite is the popular and lively restaurant **Da Meo Patacca,** where you can dine outdoors and listen to strolling singers.

Ask a priest in the church to show you the **crypt** (open daily, 10:00–12:00 and 4:00–6:00). Here you can look around the remains of several rooms of a Roman residence of the first century B.C. In the third century A.D., when St. Cecilia lived here, an attempt was made to kill her by scalding, but she survived, only to be executed later. You can still see the steam pipes of the period. But the **artistic treasures** are the ninth-century mosaics in the apse and the group of thirteenth-century frescoes in the ceiling of the sacristy. Don't miss the lovely statue of the saint below the altar. The fine **cloister** adjoining the church is the oldest in Rome.

Turn right from the front of the church down the Via di San

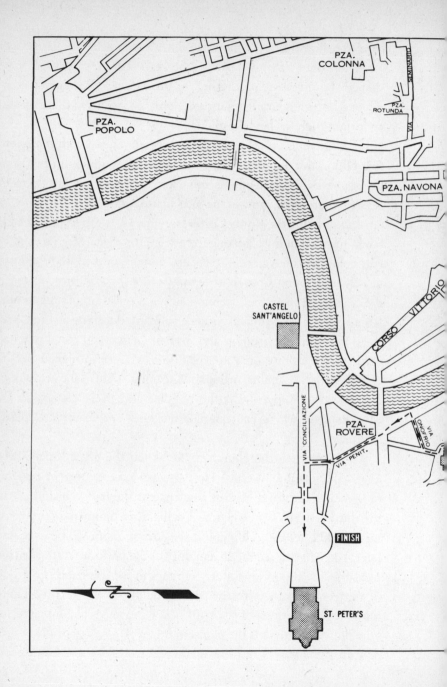

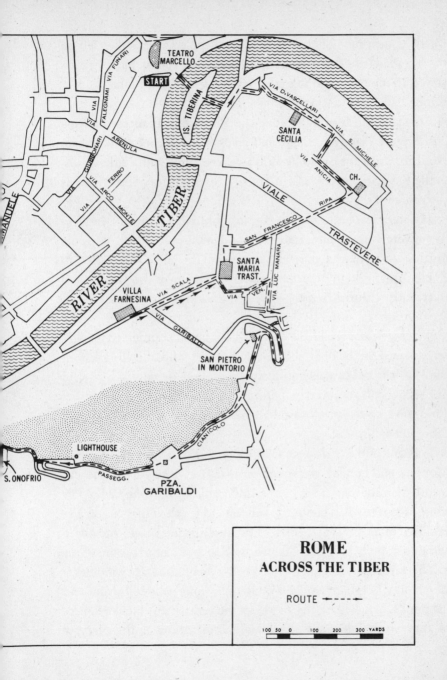

TEATRO
MARCELLO

START

IS. TIBERINA

VIA D. VASCELLARI

SANTA
CECILIA

VIA S. MICHELE

VIA ANICIA

CH.

VIALE

RIPA

TRASTEVERE

SAN FRANCESCO

VIA LUC MANARA

TIBER

SANTA
MARIA
TRAST.

VILLA
FARNESINA

VIA SCALA

VIA

VEN.

RIVER

VIA GARIBALDI

SAN PIETRO
IN MONTORIO

VIA FALEGNAMI

VIA FUNARI

VIA

VIA

ARENULA

VIA GIUBBONARI

VIA FERRO

VIA ARCO MONTE

VIA

ANUELE

GIANICOLO

LIGHTHOUSE

S. ONOFRIO

PASSEGG.

PZA.
GARIBALDI

ROME
ACROSS THE TIBER

ROUTE ·----·

100 50 0   100   200   300 YARDS

Michele, turn right on the Via di Maddalena dell'Orto, then left on the Via Anicia to the **Piazza San Francesco d'Assisi.** Saint Francis stayed in the church in this square when he visited Rome in 1219. (Open daily 7:00–12:00 and 4:00–7:00.)

At this point, turn right along the **Via di San Francesco a Ripa** past typical Trastevere shops and cafés. Have a cool drink at **Ivo,** No. 158. Cross the broad **Viale Trastevere,** filled with market stalls, to the Piazza di Santa Maria in Trastevere. A fine fountain brightens the center of the square.

The façade of the twelfth-century **Church of Santa Maria in Trastevere** (open daily, 7:30–1:00 and 4:00–7:00), with its Ionic portico and colorful mosaics, is one of the most impressive in Rome. You will see other magnificent mosaics of the twelfth and thirteenth centuries over the apse and great arch as you walk about the interior.

When you leave, take the Via della Paglia on your left to the second turning on the right, the Piazza di San Egidio, then fork left on the **Via della Scala,** a delightful old street. You are now in a colorful old section of Trastevere. Continue on the Via della Lungara beyond the arch to visit the **Villa Farnesina** on the right-hand side of the street at **No. 230.**

This graceful Renaissance villa (open 9:00–1:00, except Sunday, Monday, and holidays) was built as a summer residence in the sixteenth century for the art patron and banker, Agostino Chigi. His sumptuous fetes and banquets were famed for their luxury and gaiety. The quiet **gardens** planted with high cypress trees provide a suitable approach to the villa, where Raphael painted some of his loveliest **frescoes.** Here in the long gallery with the large windows is *The Story of Psyche,* designed by Raphael and painted by him and his pupils. You will be entranced by the remarkably lifelike figures of these superb frescoes. In an adjoining room is the graceful

Galatea, another exquisite fresco, which Raphael himself executed in 1514. There is a story—reputedly true—that Michelangelo, curious to see Raphael's work, slipped into the room in disguise and, when the guardian custodian was not looking, drew a lovely black-and-white charcoal head on the wall at the north end. It is clearly visible today on the right-hand corner of the upper wall—one of the most unusual and valuable calling cards ever left. The large windows of the villa brighten the interior, so that these magnificent frescoes can be seen in the radiant colorings that have survived so remarkably for more than four centuries.

Before leaving the villa, you should wander around the delightful gardens with their tall cypresses, oleanders, little fountain, and hedges arching over a walk. Here is an ideal spot to rest for a bit.

After visiting the Villa Farnesina, you can return to the Piazza di Santa Maria in Trastevere to lunch at one of the square's moderately expensive bohemian *trattoria* (informal restaurants), like the **Galeassi.** As you look out over the square, you will see the flamboyant panorama of Trastevere life passing before you.

From here you wind your way out of Trastevere and up to the **Janiculum.** From the Piazza di Santa Maria opposite the Galeassi follow the short street beyond the fountain for a few yards to the Piazza di S. Callisto. Continue straight ahead on Via di S. Cosimato and, after about one hundred yards, turn right on Via Luc. Manara for a few hundred yards to the wide Via Goffredo Mameli. At this point you follow the winding road up the hill. At the fork take a sharp left, cross the road, and go up the flight of steps to the terrace outside the Church of San Pietro in Montorio. It's a ten- or fifteen-minute walk from Piazza di Santa Maria in Trastevere.

Climb the hill and soon you will come to the **Church of San Pietro in Montorio.** Walk to the edge of the terrace for a breathtaking view over Rome. Now go into the small courtyard of the adjoining monastery to see **Donato Bramante's exquisite Tempietto** (open daily, 9:00–12:00 and 4:00–6:00). Ring the bell in the far corner for the English-speaking Franciscan monk to show you around. This tiny domed building of the early sixteenth century rests on sixteen Doric columns. Its circular construction is such a perfect example in miniature of the finest Renaissance architecture that it has been copied in countless churches, including the chapel of the Sacrament in St. Peter's. The dome of the Capitol in Washington was also strongly influenced by Bramante's design. When you go inside, you will appreciate even more its graceful and classic detail, especially Bernini's decoration in the lower chapel.

From this point you continue along the Via Garibaldi to the large Fontana Paola, whose water is carried by the subterranean aqueduct built by the Emperor Trajan. On the right through a gateway you are approaching the crest of the Janiculum ridge. As you stroll along the path, under a double lane of sycamores, the sweep of the **Seven Hills of Rome** unfolds beneath you. Farther along, palm and cypress trees shade the walk. In a few minutes you will reach the statue erected to the Italian patriot, Garibaldi. Here you should pause at the terrace and try to pick out the more prominent features of the landscape—the **Capitol,** the **Pantheon,** the **Quirinal,** the **Villa Medici,** the **Pincian Gardens,** and the **Alban Hills** in the distance. If you happen to take this walk in the late afternoon, the effect of the sun behind you and the soft light falling on the ocher-colored buildings of the city is particularly dramatic. Rome seems more remote from the Janiculum than from the Pincio and perhaps for that reason more alluring. The view is more encompassing and the walk along the ridge more varied. Then, too, the vistas are frequently framed by the swaying branches of palms. The Eternal City seldom seems more artistic and beautiful than from the Janiculum.

Stroll a couple of hundred yards beyond the **Garibaldi Monu-**

ment for the finest view of all, just before you reach the **Lighthouse.** Now you can see to your left the glorious dome of St. Peter's.

If you don't wish to walk any farther, you can pick up a bus at the Garibaldi Monument that will take you to the bottom of the Janiculum.

Otherwise you should continue beyond the Lighthouse and descend the steps on the right. From the terrace below you have a fine view of the **Castel Sant'Angelo** on the Tiber. Turn right into the Salita di San Onofrio, and after about fifty yards go down a long flight of steps on the right, the Via di San Onofrio, to the avenue along the river. Just to the left is the Piazza della Rovere. Cross over to the bridge. Here you have another striking view of the Castel Sant'Angelo. You should inspect it more closely another time, as suggested on page 209.

Return to the square and at the far side go under an archway into the Via S. Penitenzieri, then take a half right into Via Cav. S. Sepulcro to the wide **Via della Conciliazione.** A couple of blocks to the left you will be in the stupendous **Square of St. Peter's**—about a quarter of an hour's walk from the Piazza della Rovere. You will want to pay a special visit to **St. Peter's,** the **Sistine Chapel,** the **rooms of Raphael,** and the **Vatican Museum,** for these are among the greatest treasures in Rome and require at least a half day in themselves. (Open Monday–Saturday, 8:45–1:00; last Sunday in month, July–September and Easter, 8:45–4:00; closed holidays.) Meanwhile, where could you find a more magnificent place to end this stroll than this spot surrounded by Bernini's majestic semicircular **colonnades?**

11.
Florence

JEWEL BOX OF ITALY

To San Miniato

Florence is perfectly suited to the visitor who tours the city on foot.
The old section is small and compact. The major churches, art galleries, and museums are all close by, so you don't have to cover long distances to reach them.

The medieval and Renaissance area of historic and artistic interest is crowded into a relatively tiny area compared, for example, with Rome. Therefore, in Florence it's really essential to walk if you want to appreciate this treasure house of art and culture, for each turning reveals an enchanting church, tower, house, or narrow street.

The walks suggested in Florence are arranged in an organized way so that you can visit its great treasures, for the essence of Florence lies in its marvelous works of art—its buildings, paintings, and sculpture—which are located in many different places throughout the city.

But before you walk through the heart of Florence, you should get a bird's-eye view from a magnificent vantage point overlooking the city, the **Piazzale Michelangelo.** When you stand on this square above the **Arno,** with Florence at your feet, the plain beyond, and the **Apennines** in the distance, you should realize that here below you lies the city that, more than any other, is the birthplace and storehouse of Western art and has been the magnet for art lovers during the past five hundred years. Such an experience will provide you with an overall view of the city before you begin to plunge into the breathtaking, artistic feast that Florence affords.

The walk to the Piazelle Michelangelo will get you into the proper mood to appreciate the masterpieces of painting, sculpture, and architecture, as well as the turbulent history of Florence. Start at the **Church of Santa Croce,** on the Piazza Santa Croce, only a few blocks from the **Duomo,** or cathedral, the center of the city. If possible, take this walk in the afternoon when the soft golden light on the hills above will be especially dramatic.

Santa Croce, often called the city's Pantheon or Westminster Abbey, will, by reminding you of so many of Florence's world-famous figures in art, literature, astronomy, and politics, impress on your mind the magnificent pageant of learning and culture—and the struggles for wordly power—that are wrapped up in its history.

The largest and most beautiful of the Franciscan churches, Santa Croce has been described as the "recognized shrine of Italian genius." (Open 8:00–1:00 and 3:30–6:30.) The striking white façade of this thirteenth-century church is inlaid with dark marble. Inside, you will find the **tombs of Michelangelo, Galileo, and Machiavelli,** three of the world's greatest figures in the fields of art, science, and politics. Here, too, is a memorial to another renowned Florentine, the poet Dante.

The artistic treasures in Santa Croce will whet your appetite for other masterpieces yet to be enjoyed. The series of **frescoes of the**

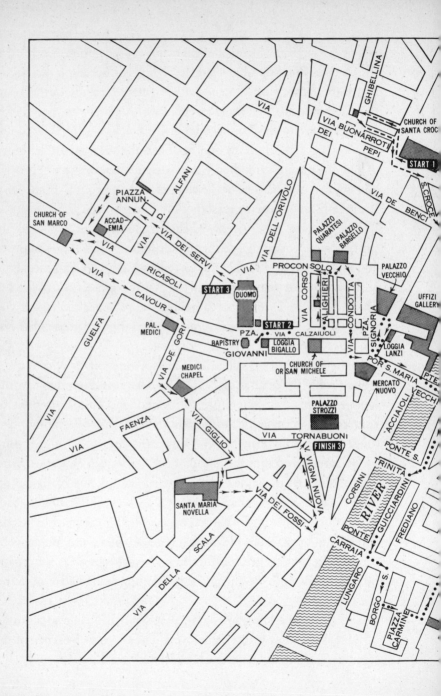

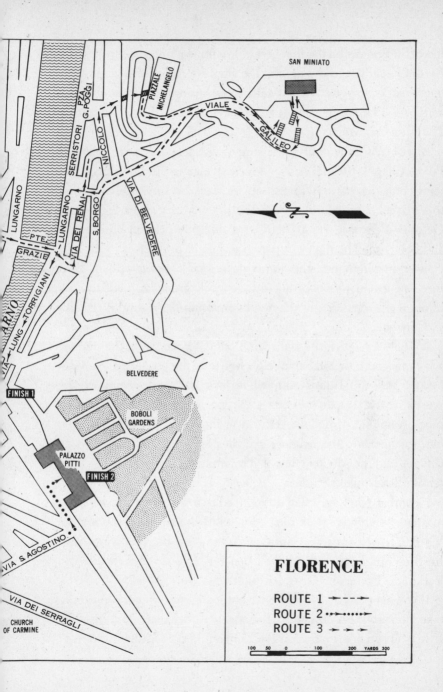

SAN MINIATO

PIAZZALE MICHELANGELO

VIALE

GALILEO

PZA. G. POGGI

SERRISTORI

NICCOLO

LUNGARNO

VIA DEI RENAI

S. BORGO

VIA DI BELVEDERE

LUNGARNO

PTE.

GRAZIE

LUNG.

ARNO

TORRIGIANI

VIA

BELVEDERE

FINISH 1

BOBOLI GARDENS

PALAZZO PITTI

FINISH 2

VIA S. AGOSTINO

VIA DEI SERRAGLI

CHURCH OF CARMINE

FLORENCE

ROUTE 1 ►---►
ROUTE 2 ►•••••►
ROUTE 3 ► ► ►

100 50 0   100   200   YARDS 300

life of St. Francis by the first great Florentine painter, Giotto, in the **Bardi Chapel** just to the right of the altar, are regarded as among his finest works, especially the death scene. Another outstanding example of Florentine genius is Donatello's remarkable sculpture, *The Annunciation.*

After leaving the church, be sure to visit next door the splendid **Pazzi Chapel,** Brunelleschi's lovely Renaissance building, with terra-cotta decorations in the upper walls by Luca della Robbia (open weekdays, March–September, 10:00–12:30 and 2:30–6:30; October–February, 10:00–12:30 and 3:00–5:00; closed Wednesday and holidays). The high campanile and the cypress trees in the first cloister are dramatic. The adjoining second cloister, with its tiled roof, is particularly peaceful, and the lovely green lawn adds to the tranquil air. Incidentally, the nearby **museum** has a superb crucifix by Cimabue.

It's only a step to the right from Santa Croce along the narrow Via Pinzochere to **Michelangelo's house** at the corner of **Via Ghibellina** and **Via Buonarroti,** where you will find several of the artist's works. (Open weekdays except Tuesday, 9:00–1:00.) The room containing Michelangelo's drawings is particularly interesting, for here are the original sketches for St. Peter's, the Sistine Chapel, and the Medici Chapel. This building also houses the Center of Michelangelo Studies.

Now that you have been introduced to many of Florence's great masters, begin your walk to the Piazza Michelangelo by taking the Via B.S. Croce opposite Santa Croce for a few hundred yards past frescoed buildings to the Via de Benci, which, if you turn left, will lead to the **Ponte alle Grazie,** rebuilt after World War II.

If you happen to be in Florence in the summer, you may prefer to take a bus to the **Piazzale Michelangelo** rather than climb the hill. If so, you can get the bus on the **Lungarno** on this side of the river.

It will take you along the curving **Viale Michelangelo** to the Piazza.

However, if you would enjoy the walk in the late afternoon, cross the bridge, and as you do so, look downstream at the ancient Ponte Vecchio to your right.

On the opposite side, you are in the **Piazza de Mozzi.** There are several interesting palazzi here, among them, on the south side, the three thirteenth-century **Mozzi palaces** with overhanging tiled roofs. Just in front of them you turn left into the Via dei Renai and go past the **Serristori Palace,** once part of the city's walls. As you enter the Via d. Giardino note the old bell tower on your right. From here you continue on the Via S. Niccolò to the **Piazza G. Poggi,** where there remains a portico of the old city wall.

From this point, you slowly wind your way up the ramp through the **gardens** above the square and up some steps to the Piazzale Michelangelo. Reproductions of the artist's famous **sculptures,** dominated by a large replica of his statue of David, decorate the square. Stroll leisurely along the balustrade to enjoy the superb panorama of the towers and roofs of Florence, the sweep of the Arno flowing into the distance, and the hills of Fiesole beyond the city. You can pick out **five bridges** over the river, the **tower of the Palazzo Vecchio,** the **campanile,** and the **cathedral,** and to the left you see the remains of the **old city wall** on the cypress-covered hillside opposite. If you are fortunate enough to be at the esplanade in the late afternoon, the dome of the cathedral, the slender campanile, and the russet-colored medieval towers will be bathed in a soft golden light—an unforgettable effect so appropriate for this artistic city. This is just the moment for tea or a drink at the restaurant **La Loggia,** with a lovely terrace and garden, or one of the snack bars in the square.

After this refreshment, you should continue up to the hill along the **Viale Galileo** to one of Italy's most beautiful Romanesque

churches, **San Miniato al Monte.** About 150 yards along the viale
you will come to a wide, double flight of steps that leads to this
eleventh-century church, built in the basilican style (open daily,
8:00–2:00 and 3:00–6:00; Sunday, 8:00–6:00). Both its façade and
interior are decorated with green and white marble in geometric
designs creating a remarkably radiant effect, especially in the late
afternoon sunlight. The beautifully painted ceiling and beams are
most colorful. You should also see the lovely medallions by Luca
della Robbia that adorn the ceiling in the **Chapel of the Cardinal of
Portugal.** On leaving the church, pause on the terrace for another
and even more extensive view over Florence. Don't miss the lovely
old bell tower to your right.

On your way back down along the Viale Galileo, the slanting sun
will throw a dimmer glow over the city and the Apennines will turn
a deeper shade in the background. Turn left just before you reach
the Piazzale Michelangelo and descend a long flight of steps under
rows of cypress trees—the Via S. Salvatore al Monte—to the
fourteenth-century **Porta San Miniato** in the old city wall. Keeping
to the left along the Via S. Niccolò you will return to the Piazza
Mozzi. When you reach the river, finish this stroll by sauntering
along the **Lungarno Torrigiani** to the **Ponte Vecchio.** Across the
Arno, to the right of the low mass of the **Uffizi Gallery,** rises the
tower of the **Palazzo Vecchio,** but there you will visit on your walk
through the heart of Florence.

Cradle of the Renaissance

Your walk through the heart of Florence—which although filled
with historic and artistic interest, will cover perhaps only a mile at
the most—should start at the magnificent cathedral, or Duomo,

and its graceful campanile. This walk will take you to those palazzi and art galleries that all visitors to Florence must see, even if they have only a few hours—the Bargello, Palazzo Vecchio, the Uffizi and Pitti palaces—as well as the Ponte Vecchio. In addition to visiting these wonderful collections, you will be wandering through narrow streets and past medieval buildings that will put you in the mood to appreciate all the more the many great works of art in Florence.

Second only to St. Peter's in size among Italian churches, the **Duomo** was built mostly during the thirteenth century, and is currently closed to the public for extensive repairs. Its correct name is **Santa Maria del Fiore** (Saint Mary of the Flower), which, like the lily in the Florentine coat of arms, is derived from the tradition that the city, "Firenze," was founded in a field of flowers. Before you enter the cathedral, step to one side of the square to view its multicolored marble **façade,** Brunelleschi's large and lovely **dome,** and, next to it, Giotto's graceful **campanile,** an architectural triumph of perfect proportions. Two hundred seventy-eight feet high, this fourteenth-century tower of polychrome marble can be visited only with an appointment obtained from the Italian Tourist Office. Michelangelo considered the dome such an achievement that, more than a century afterward, when designing the dome of St. Peter's in Rome, he remarked that it would be "larger but not more beautiful" than Brunelleschi's in Florence.

You will be impressed by the immensity of the interior of the Duomo, but even more by the masterpieces that fill it—the unfinished *Pietà* by Michelangelo, bas-reliefs by Ghiberti, frescoes by Uccello, and a fresco by Michelino of Dante explaining the *Divine Comedy.* It was here in the Duomo, incidentally, that Savonarola preached. If you climb to the summit of the dome, you will be rewarded by a fine panorama of the city. (The ascent of the campanile, although nearly a hundred feet lower, is a more satisfying experience, for from the stairway you will enjoy superb views of its classic design.)

Opposite the Duomo stands the **Baptistry,** Florence's oldest building, dating from about the year 1000. Octagonal in shape, it is constructed of green and white marble in Romanesque style. Here, indeed, is one of the great artistic treasures of Florence, the world-renowned **bronze doors** with their gilded bas-reliefs. Ghiberti's **East Door,** which Michelangelo called "worthy to be the gate of Paradise," is a marvelous group of panels representing scenes from the Old Testament. This superb piece of sculpture took the artist twenty-seven years to finish (1425–1452). After you have absorbed the details of the Baptistry's unique doors, go inside to see the thirteenth-century pavement and fourteenth-century mosaics in the **cupola.** (Open 8:30–12:30 and 2:30–5:30; closed Sunday.)

Leave the cathedral square by the Via de' Calzaiuoli (named for the sixteenth-century stocking makers). Just before you start along the street, notice the small building with the fourteenth-century Gothic arches and the overhanging tile roof on the corner, the lovely **Loggia del Bigallo,** at one time the home of a Florentine benevolent society for abandoned children. After strolling down this extremely busy street with its elegant shops for about two blocks, you will see on your right the towerlike **Church of Orsan-michele.** Originally built as a grain market, the church is remarkable for the marble statues placed by the different trade guilds in the niches of the outside wall; they include works of such great Florentine sculptors as Donatello, Ghiberti, and Verrocchio. Wander around inside to see the great **Gothic tabernacle** by Orcagna. (Open daily, 7:00–12:00 and 2:00–7:00.)

Enter the narrow Via dei Tavolini almost opposite Orsanmichele and continue along the **Via Dante Alighieri** to the **Houses of the**

Alighieri. At **No. 1,** in the Via S. Margherita, Dante is supposed to have been born, but it is not open to the public. In a moment you will come to the Via del Proconsolo, one of the oldest streets in Florence. At **No. 12** in the Palazzo Nonfinito (it was never finished), where the **Anthropology and Ethnology Museum** is located (open Monday, Friday, and Saturday, 9:00–1:00; closed Sunday except third Sunday each month, open 9:00–1:00). On the other side of the street you will see the **Palazzo Pazzi Quaratesi,** one of Florence's finest fifteenth-century palaces. Now walk in the opposite direction for a short block to the medieval **Palazzo del Bargello** (open weekdays except Monday, 9:00–2:00; Sunday and holidays, 9:00–1:00). Its battlemented thirteenth-century tower rises above an urban fortress, which, successively as prison, execution site, and residence of the city's chief magistrate and later of the chief of police, has witnessed some of the bloodiest scenes in the history of Florence. It is now a national museum, particularly renowned for its unrivaled collection of Tuscan sculpture.

Enter the spacious **courtyard,** enclosed by a colonnade. To your left is a small room filled with the **works of Michelangelo.** Two of them, the young *David* and *Bacchus,* are especially outstanding. As you climb the **grand staircase,** notice the elaborate coats of arms of Florentine chiefs of police on the wall overhead. Giambologna's famous statue of Mercury is on the **Great Balcony.** In the adjoining **Great Hall** you will see some of the finest works of Donatello—especially his wonderful figures of the young David and St. George. On the other floors there are great Florentine **sculptures** by Michelangelo, Cellini, and Verrocchio, **terra-cottas** by the Della Robbias, and **frescoes** by Giotto in the chapel.

After reveling in this artistic feast, turn left into the square, then take a sharp right along the **Via della Condotta** for three blocks. At the corner of the Via dei Cerchi, look left for a fine view of the

Palazzo Vecchio. Now cross the **Via Calzaiuoli,** and walk another block to the **Mercato Nuovo,** the city's main marketplace for flowers, leather goods, linens, lace, costume jewelry, and souvenirs—always a bustling, lively scene. Spend a few minutes wandering around the interesting stalls, then take the Via Vacchereccia to enter the splendid **Piazza della Signoria,** dominated by the fortresslike Palazzo Vecchio, Florence's best-known landmark.

The piazza was the center of the political and social life of medieval and Renaissance Florence. The bitter political struggles between the Guelphs and Ghibellines are associated with this square, and it was here that Savonarola was executed, as you will see from a bronze plaque in front of the **Fountain of Neptune.**

The **Palazzo Vecchio,** now the seat of Florence's municipal government, was the residence of the presiding magistrate during the Florentine republic and later was used by the Medici dukes. The bell in the early fourteenth-century **tower** called citizens to arms or to conclave. As you look at the Palazzo's severe façade, embellished with coats of arms, you will perhaps reflect on the extraordinary contrast between the two great towers of Florence—the warlike Palazzo and the spiritual Campanile.

The great halls and sumptuous apartments, furnished with fine works of art, will give you an idea of the palace as it was in the days of the Medici (open weekdays, 9:00–7:00; Sunday and holidays, 8:00–1:00; closed Saturday). Linger for a few moments in Michelozzo's beautiful **courtyard,** with its decorated ceiling, before you go in. On the upper floor, the huge **Hall of the Five Hundred** is one of the most splendid in all Italy.

Almost next to the Palazzo Vecchio are the three high semicircular arches of the **Loggia dei Lanzi.** Built in the fourteenth century as an assembly place for public meetings, the Loggia contains the greatest outdoor exhibit of **Renaissance sculpture** to be seen anywhere. Cellini's masterpiece *Perseus* and Giambologna's *Rape of the Sabines* are two of the great works that adorn this unusual open-air vaulted arcade.

Between the Loggia and the Palazzo Vecchio you will find the entrance to the narrow **Piazza degli Uffizi.** The **Uffizi Gallery,** containing one of the world's finest collections of paintings, will tempt you, but probably it should be saved until you have had a chance to absorb the rather intensive sight-seeing on this walk. However, do not on any account fail to visit this gallery, with its Botticellis, Leonardos, Raphaels, and many other masterpieces of Italian art (open daily, 11:00–4:00).

Pass the Loggia and turn left into the Via Por S. Maria to the **Ponte Vecchio.** This unique fourteenth-century bridge is the oldest in Florence and the only one to have survived World War II. Silver and jewelry **shops** overhanging the Arno still line it as in the days of Florence's glory. Pause at various points on the bridge for **fine views** in both directions along the river. The **Cellini bust** in the bridge's piazzetta serves as a symbol of the Ponte Vecchio's association with goldsmiths, and in fact, it has always had a goldsmith's shop. The **enclosed passageway** above the shops connects the Uffizi and Pitti palaces.

If you started this stroll in the morning, you will by now be looking for a place for lunch. There are many restaurants in the Piazza Signoria and nearby. Try the **Oliviero,** on the Via delle Terme.

The second part of this walk begins on the far side of the Ponte Vecchio. After crossing the bridge, follow the **Borgo S. Jacopo** to the right to the **Ponte S. Trinità.** From this new bridge, built since the war, you have a good view of the Ponte Vecchio. Now stroll along the **Lungarno Guicciardini** to the next bridge. At the Piazza N. Sauro turn left about fifty yards and right on the Borgo S. Frediano about one hundred yards. A sharp left will bring you into the

Piazza del Carmine. Before you is the **Church of San Maria del Carmine** (open daily, 8:00–12:00 and 3:00–5:30). The purpose of this little excursion is to see the great masterpieces of Masaccio, who, as a forerunner of the Renaissance, revolutionized the art of painting by depicting three-dimensional forms. By this innovation he deeply influenced Raphael and Michelangelo. Masaccio's remarkable series of early fifteenth-century **frescoes of the life of St. Peter,** in the **Brancacci Chapel,** rank among the finest examples of Florentine art. Be prepared to put a coin in the slot to turn on the floodlights so you can see the frescoes properly. The frescoes have recently been cleaned and restored.

When you leave the church, turn right along the Via S. Monaca, cross the Via dei Serragli into the Via S. Agostino, and continue to the end of the street. On your left is the massive **Palazzo Pitti** (open weekdays, except Monday, 9:00–2:00; Sunday, 9:00–1:00). Although it does not have as great a collection as the Uffizi, the Pitti possesses a number of Raphael's works, as well as those of **sixteenth- and seventeenth-century Italian masters,** a gallery of **modern art,** lavish **Royal Apartments,** and a **museum** featuring fine works of silver, ivory, porcelain, and enamel. (Open daily, except Monday, 9:00–2:00; Sunday and holidays, 9:00–1:00.)

Enter a gate to the left of the palace to enjoy the pleasant experience of sauntering leisurely through the famous sixteenth-century **Boboli Gardens** (open 9:00–5:30). Strolling about the hillside, you will discover many splendid fountains, fine statues, grottoes, and secluded nooks, as well as beautiful flower beds, formal terraces, and a profusion of oleander, ilex, tall cypress, and pines. The famous **May Music Festival** takes place here. As you walk to the **amphitheater** beside towering hedges, you have a splendid view over the city. Other alleys of cypress are lined with classical statues and look out on the nearby hillsides. There is a little café in the gardens.

Here, while enjoying a cooling drink, you have a fine view of the cathedral, its campanile, the Palazzo Vecchio, and the **hills of Fiesole.** This delightful park, with the artistic glories of Florence spread out before you, is an appropriate place to end your stroll.

In the Footsteps of the Medici

Florence is crowded with so many remarkable works of art that it would be foolish to attempt to see too much on any one walk. This stroll includes additional masterpieces of painting and sculpture that you should not miss while visiting the city; furthermore, it provides a pleasant change by taking you through the fashionable **shopping district.**

Start on the opposite side of the **Duomo** this time and stroll along the **Via dei Servi**—a business and shopping street—for two long blocks to the **Piazza della Santissima Annunziata,** often considered the most beautiful square in the city. As you walk along, glance now and again into the courtyards that you pass.

When you arrive at the square, you will see two graceful arcades facing the piazza and its decorative fountains. But it is Brunelleschi's portico of the fifteenth-century **Hospital of the Innocent** (the first foundling hospital in Europe), on your right, that merits the closest inspection (open weekdays, 9:00–2:00; Sunday and holidays, 9:00–1:00; closed Wednesday). Above the arches of the colonnade are Andrea della Robbia's lovely enameled **terra-cotta medallions.** The small cream-colored figures of babies in swaddling clothes against the exquisite light blue background are surely among the artistic gems of Florence.

Next, cross the square, and at the opposite corner take the Via Cesare Battisti to the **Piazza San Marco,** where you turn sharply to the left along the via Ricasoli for a few yards to visit the **Galleria dell'Accademia** (open weekdays, 9:00–2:00; Sunday and holidays, 9:00–1:00; closed Monday). Although this gallery houses a collection of thirteenth- and fourteenth-century Tuscan **paintings,** as well as several remarkable pieces of **sculpture** by Michelangelo, the masterpiece that you have come to see is Michelangelo's gigantic statue of David, fashioned when the artist was only twenty-five years old.

Leaving the Accademia, you turn right to the Piazza San Marco and cross to the far side. Next to the Church of San Marco, in the monastery, is the **Museo dell'Angelico** (open weekdays, 9:00–2:00; Sunday and holidays, 9:00–1:00; closed Monday). Enter the delightful cloister with its red-tiled roof, shaded by a tall cedar tree. Upstairs, above the cloisters, Fra Angelico painted on the walls of the monastery's small cells his superb and incomparable **frescoes,** of which *The Annunciation* (at the top of the stairs) is generally considered the loveliest. Be sure to ask the attendant to lend you a magnifying glass so you can study the details of the paintings. The artist-monk passed nine years of his life here. Here too, Savonarola occupied a cell (the last one on the right at the end of the corridor), and in it you will see some of the Florentine reformer's personal belongings. Stop in also at the **Chapter House** off the courtyard to see Fra Angelico's large fresco of the Crucifixion.

After leaving San Marco, cross the square and walk down the Via Cavour. At the end of the second block on your right you will come to the **Palazzo Medici-Riccardi** (open weekdays except Wednesday, 9:00–12:30 and 3:00–5:00; Sunday and holidays, 9:00–12:00).

This forbidding palace, so reminiscent of the turbulent era of the Medicis, was built by Michelozzo in the fifteenth century for Cosimo the Elder and was later the scene of Lorenzo the Magnificent's brilliant court. Inside you will find many **relics** of Florence's great rulers, including Lorenzo's death mask, in the Medici Museum, as well as Gozzoli's admirable **frescoes** in the chapel.

But the Medici are remembered in the world of art more for their burial place than for their residence because Michelangelo adorned the tombs of the Medici with some of his greatest sculptures. To visit these extraordinarily expressive marble statues you turn right at the corner of the Medici Palace, go past an **outdoor market,** then turn left on the Via del Canto de' Nelli, and walk around the **Church of San Lorenzo** for one hundred yards to the entrance of the **Medici Chapel** in the **Piazza Madonna** (open weekdays, 9:00–2:00; Sunday and holidays, 9:00–11:00; closed Monday). Don't linger in the ornate chapel, but go on to the **new sacristy.** Here you will stand in awe before the remarkable male and female figures of *Day* and *Night,* as well as those of *Twilight* and *Dawn.* These amazing pieces of sculpture—and that of Lorenzo in the posture of meditation—represent the height of Michelangelo's genius in portraying life in stone. On leaving you may wish to stop at the grandiose **Chapel of the Princes,** lavishly decorated in semiprecious stones.

From the Piazza Madonna, cross to the Via del Giglio directly opposite. Then turn right on Via Panzani and immediately left again to the Piazza Santa Maria Novella. Across the square is the splendid green and white marble façade of the **Church of Santa Maria Novella** (open daily, 9:00–2:00; Sunday, 8:00–1:00; closed holidays).

This church of the Dominican order, begun in 1278, possesses some of the finest **frescoes and paintings** by Cimabue, Masaccio, Giotto, and Filippino Lippi, but it is especially noted for the wonderful Ghirlandaio frescoes in the **choir chapel.** After you have explored this art gallery in a church, stroll around the fourteenth-century green **cloisters** just to the right of the church's main entrance. The faded frescoes on the walls, the green and white vaulting in the roof, the tall cypresses, and the lofty campanile towering above combine to create an extraordinarily beautiful effect. As you wander around the cloisters, you can also see, on request, the remains of frescoes by Paolo Uccello in the refectory. (Opening hours are the same as for the church.)

At this point you may want a rest from sight-seeing, so why not cross the little park in the square in front of Santa Maria Novella and follow the **Via dei Fossi** on the opposite side for a shopping tour. This street is crowded with shops selling antiques, furniture, statuary, and so forth, where you can browse for a while.

At the far end of the Via dei Fossi you will come to the **Piazza Goldoni.** Turn left and stroll along one of Florence's leading shopping streets, the **Via della Vigna Nuova,** where **elegant stores** feature such Florentine specialties as hand-bags, shoes, silk, jewelry, and leather handcrafts. (It's worth keeping in mind that shops in Florence, as in other Italian cities, close for the siesta between 12:30 and 3:30 but stay open late, often until 7:30 or so.)

The Via della Vigna Nuova will lead you into the **Via de' Tornabuoni,** Florence's most fashionable shopping center. Directly across is the **Palazzo Strozzi,** a huge Renaissance mansion famous for its fine cornice and wrought-iron torch holders. Its forbidding exterior reminds you that fifteenth-century palaces were also fortresses. Now you should saunter along to the famous **Café Giacosa,** the rendezvous of the leading Florentine families. Giacosa is just the place to relax for a while and enjoy coffee or a drink, while you try to decide which of Florence's many artistic glories you want to revisit during your stay.

12.
Venice

BEWITCHING BYWAYS

In the Shadow of the Campanile

Every visitor looks forward to touring **Venice,** the fabulous city of canals, by gondola. By all means enjoy the unique and delightful experience of gliding in a gondola through the labyrinth of the canals. The budget-minded should try the *vaporetti.*

But to explore the many bewitching byways of Venice, and feel a part of this extraordinary and little-changed community built on more than one hundred islands, one must go on foot. Venice, unlike any other city, in truly a world for the pedestrian, because all the streets are reserved for the walker.

Wandering along the alleys or lingering by a bridge over a back canal away from the crowds, you will discover fascinating bits of the old city. Wander where you wish, take your time, lose yourself in the spirit of Venice. You will not be harassed by traffic noises as in almost every other city; in Venice the sounds you hear are mostly those of the padding of feet on the flagstone pavements, voices

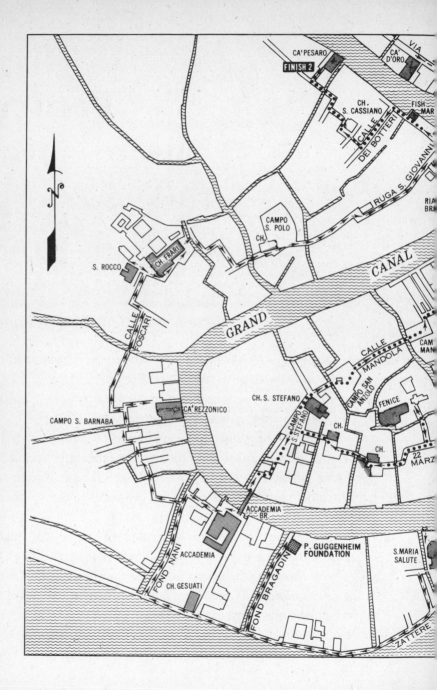

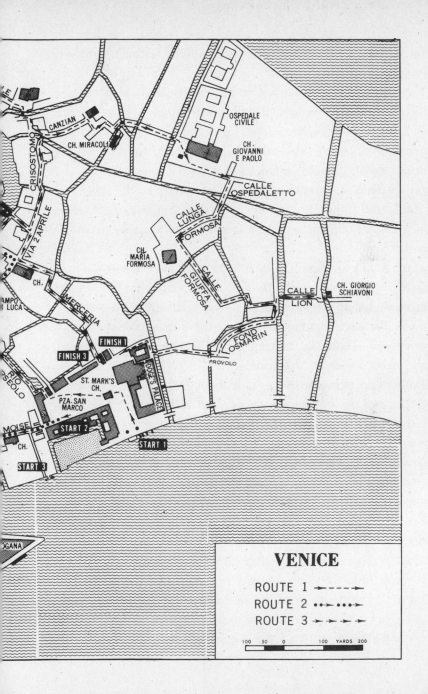

OSPEDALE
CIVILE

CANZIAN

CRISOSTOMO

CH. MIRACOLI

CH.
GIOVANNI
E PAOLO

CALLE
OSPEDALETTO

VIA 2 APRILE

CALLE
LUNGA

FORMOSA

CH.
MARIA
FORMOSA

CALLE
GIUFFA
FORMOSA

CH. GIORGIO
SCHIAVONI

CALLE
LION

CH.
MERCERIA

CAMPO
LUCA

FOND
OSMARIN

FINISH 1

FINISH 3

PROVOLO

RIO
OSEOLO

ST. MARK'S
CH.

DOGE'S PALACE

PZA. SAN
MARCO

MOISE

START 2

START 1

CH.

START 3

OGANA

VENICE

ROUTE 1 ➤ - - - - ➤
ROUTE 2 •➤••••➤
ROUTE 3 ➤ ➤ ➤ ➤ ➤

100 50 0 100 YARDS 200

from an upper balcony, the lapping of water against the stone buildings.

Here are three separate walks, none particularly long because Venice is compact. The first will take you through **"classic" Venice,** with its splendid historic monuments and churches as a background for its present workaday life. The second supplements the first and leads to Venice's famous **fish market** across the Rialto and to its **museum of contemporary art.** The third is on the **other side of the Grand Canal,** where lovely baroque churches, the **Accademia,** Venice's famed art gallery, and sumptuous palazzi express the mood of Venice.

Just strolling about this fascinating city for a few hours is a pure delight. Even in midsummer the weather is not too hot for walking. The strong Italian sun beats down only in relatively few piazzas and campos; the streets and alleys are so narrow that most of the time you are in the shade. In the winter, the Piazza is apt to be flooded, and rainproof boots are recommended!

Perhaps the best time to set out is about 4:00, when life in Venice resumes after the long midday siesta. Start at the center of Venetian life, the **Piazza San Marco,** but before commencing your walk, look around the renowned square. The sparkling mosaics above the doorways of **St. Mark's Church,** together with its bulbous domes, cast an Oriental atmosphere over the square, recalling Venice's traditional ties with the East. This lavishly decorated basilica, embellished with more than five hundred columns of marble—mostly Oriental—was designed in the form of a Greek cross and rebuilt during the eleventh century on the site of a former church. Perhaps it is the unusual combination of Oriental and Gothic styles—the colorful Oriental domes and mosaics and the Gothic pinnacles adorned with stone figures—that makes St. Mark's so enchanting.

Over the **main entrance** stand copies of the famous **four gilt-**

bronze horses (the originals have been brought indoors to prevent further deterioration), Greek workmanship of the period of Alexander the Great. To study these lovely pieces of sculpture, climb up to the porch by the stairs inside the church. From here you also have a striking view of the square.

The **interior** of St. Mark's is so filled with marvelous early Byzantine mosaics and rare marble that it defies description. The magnificent golden **altar screen,** parts of which date back to the fifth century, with its six thousand jewels, is merely one of many dazzling works of art. (Open weekdays, 9:00–12:00 and 3:00–5:00; Sunday and holidays, 9:00–12:00.)

A few yards from the square, on the **Piazzetta** beyond the campanile, is the **Doges' Palace,** one of the finest and most beautiful secular buildings in the world. The creamy, pink and white marble façade, above the graceful upper and lower Gothic arcades, presents a remarkably harmonious, massive yet delicate architectural picture. It was originally built in the twelfth century and rebuilt in its present style almost two hundred years later. The sumptuous **ducal apartments** and **council chambers,** decorated with lavish paintings by the great Venetian artists, should be visited when you have an hour or more at your disposal (open in winter, 9:00–4:00; rest of year, 9:00–7:00).

The **two columns** in the Piazzetta, close to the water, are noted Venetian landmarks and were brought from Constantinople. The symbol of Venice, the Lion of St. Mark, surmounts one, and on the other you see Saint Theodore and his crocodile.

Opposite the Doges' Palace in the Piazzetta is Sansovino's sixteenth-century **library,** which contains an archeological museum. Next to the library is the Marciana collection of rare books and manuscripts.

Returning to St. Mark's Square, you see, directly opposite, the

Renaissance **Torre dell'Orologio**—the clock tower over an arch beneath which runs the **Merceria,** Venice's main shopping street. This tower is one of the loveliest sights in the square. Its great clock face in gold and enamel bears the Signs of the Zodiac and shows the phases of the moon. Above the dial, and below the golden **Lion of St. Mark**—resplendent against a decorated blue field—Roman and Arabic numerals show the hour. On top, the famous two bronze Moors have been striking the hours with heavy hammers for five hundred years.

Now pass beneath the towering **campanile.** (An elevator will take you to the top for a panoramic view of **Venice,** the **Lido,** and adjacent **islands.**) On either side of the square are arcades, beneath the old **Law Courts** on the right and beneath the **Correr Civic Museum** on the left (open daily, except Tuesday and holidays, 10:00–4:00; Sunday, 9:00–12:30). Napoleon's **Fabbrica Nuova** (New Building) at the end completes the magnificent piazza.

At the northwest corner of the square a passageway leads to the **Bacino Orseolo.** This small open space of water, opposite the **Albergo Cavalletto,** is often filled with gondolas bobbing up and down in silence while the gaily dressed gondoliers await customers.

Follow the crowded street alongside the **Rio Orseolo.** You will brush past porters with crates of tomatoes on their heads. Cross the bridge (there are about four hundred in Venice) and walk down the Calle Goldoni to the **Campo San Luca.** Cross the square and take the last turn on the right—the Calle San Luca. Turn left on the Calle dei Fabbri (at No. 909 is a gastronomic restaurant, **Noémi,** where you may want to return for dinner), continuing on the Calle de la Bembo, to reach the Grand Canal. From the quay you have perhaps the best view of the Rialto Bridge on your right and down the canal to your left. Make your way to the famous **Ponte de Rialto.** Designed by Giovanni da Ponte in 1588, the approaches to this great stone landmark spanning the Grand Canal rest on some twelve thousand poles. Its high arch was designed to permit clearance of an armed galley. Twin rows of little shops crowd the sides of the center walk.

Pause for a moment while crossing the Rialto and look down the **Grand Canal,** teeming with ferries, launches, motorboats, and gondolas. The spectacle is diversified and exciting. On either side of the canal stretch the lines of great palazzi, those ornate private palaces of Venetian nobility and wealth.

From the Rialto, staying on the same side of the Grand Canal as before, walk about fifty yards or so straight ahead, then turn right on the Calle del Fontego dei Tedeschi to the Campo S. Bartolomeo. Turn left along the busy **Salizzada del Fontego dei Tedeschi** alongside the central post office.

You now keep straight ahead on the Salizzada S. Zuane over two bridges, and shortly you will be in a square opposite the Church of the Apostoli. Now turn left into the wide Via 28 Aprile. A few hundred yards farther on, you turn left on the Calle d'Oro to the **Ca' d'Oro,** an exceptionally splendid old brick palace of a Venetian nobleman which contains Franchetti's art collection, including Titian's noted *Venus with the Mirror* and, in the chapel, Mantegna's *San Sebastian.* (The palace has been restored and is open daily, July–September, 9:00–4:00; October–June, 9:00–2:00.) Now retrace your steps to the Church of the Apostoli and cross the little bridge.

You will have noticed that all the Venetian bridges have steps leading up and down, for they have all been constructed to clear large barges. Pushcarts are specially designed with a set of small front wheels to negotiate the steps.

A hundred yards or so on the Calle Dolfin will bring you back to the Salizzada. Here in the Campiello Flaminio Corner by an open market you turn left on the Salizzada S. Canzian to the **Church of**

S. Canziano, then right and left into the Campo Santa Maria Nova. Immediately over the bridge before you is the **Church of Santa Maria dei Miracoli,** a gem of Venetian Renaissance architecture built at the end of the fifteenth century (open 9:00–12:00, 3:00–6:00). This little building standing off by itself (one side washed by the canal) is an example of perfect design and exquisite ornamentation. Porphyry and serpentine (the first a dark red and purple stone, the second a mottled green) highlight its outside decoration of white and colored marble. Inside, the walls of the nave are covered with precious marbles; the beautiful sixteenth-century carving at the base of the columns by the altar and the vaulted ceiling of painted wood are equally fine. No other Venetian church is like this one. Ask the attendant for a mirror, so that, without straining your neck, you can study the **painting of St. Francis** in the ceiling to the left of the entrance.

Return over the bridge you crossed from the **Campo Santa Maria Nova** and immediately beyond, to the right, you will come to a graceful iron-railed bridge. This is one of those inimitable corners in which the city abounds and which gives Venice its paintinglike quality. It is characterized by russet-brownish houses and ivy-covered terraces. To your left, red awnings overhang a tiny tree-lined garden. Behind you is a stone bridge and the Church of the Miracoli. Below in the canal lie barges filled with freight. A lavishly decorated gondola with a happy wedding party may slip by.

A few minutes' walk over two bridges brings you to the **Church of SS. Giovanni and Paolo,** before which stands the famous **equestrian statue of Bartolomeo Colleoni** by Verrocchio, considered by some critics to be the greatest of its kind. The dynamic figure of the fifteenth-century *condottiere* on his battle charger, apparently about to prance from the pedestal, expresses arrogant defiance. As you stand at the base of the statue, look at the stone trompe l'oeil bas-reliefs at the entrance to the **Ospedale Civile** next to the church. There's a striking view of the statue against the sky from the front of the Ospedale.

This is a good time to sit down at the café on the square, have a cooling drink, and study the details of the militant and arresting statue. Also notice in the square the sixteenth-century well, one of the finest in Venice.

Now stroll alongside the large Church of SS. Giovanni and Paolo, known as Venice's Pantheon because so many doges are buried there. Just beyond the end of the square, turn right along the Calle dell'Ospedaletto, then veer right into the shopping street of the Calle Lunga S. Maria Formosa to the large **Campo S. Maria Formosa.** The church and its campanile provide a dramatic backdrop for the lively and colorful **fruit and vegetable market** in the spacious square.

Walking down the Ruga Giuffa Santa Maria Formosa at the left end of the square, turn left on the Salizzada Zorzi, cross the bridge, and you are on your way to the little **Scuola di San Giorgio degli Schiavoni** to see the marvelous paintings by the late fifteenth-century Venetian painter Carpaccio. (This is one of those frequent occasions in Venice when you can easily take the wrong turn. But, even if you do, you may well come upon a fascinating scene that you probably could not find if you tried. The safest rule to follow when you are uncertain is to go with the crowd.) Walk to the end of the street, and keeping to the left, cross a bridge to the Calle dei Preti, then another to reach the Calle de Ca' Lion, which leads to the Scuola. (Open weekdays except Monday, 10:00–12:30 and 3:30–6:00; Sunday and holidays, 10:30–12:30.) Stop for a moment on one of the bridges and watch how a city that moves by water carries on its daily life. The **Carpaccio masterpieces** were painted in panels fixed to the walls of this small building, originally an institution for Dalmatian seamen. The series on Saint George is particularly famous; it is entertaining and colorful and, with superb artistry, presents the detailed life of the period.

After enjoying the Saint George and the other series Carpaccio painted here, return by the Calle Lion. Cross the next bridge, then turn left along the canal (on your left you see the Church dei Greghi, the Greek Orthodox Church, surrounded by trees) to the Fondamenta dell'Osmarin. At the Campo S. Provolo make a turn to the right and follow the Salizzada S. Provolo to the **Campo S. Filippo Giacomo.** This is one of those charming little squares crowded with open market stalls, selling fruit, clothing, and souvenirs, that make Venice so appealing and vivacious. Just before you reach the Piazza San Marco you will cross the canal behind the Ducal Palace, from which you have a fine view of the **Bridge of Sighs.**

A turn to the left will bring you to **Jeshurun,** the fine lace and embroidery establishment, where you can see the work in process.

Late in the afternoon is the perfect time to relax at **Quadri's** or **Florian's,** the liveliest cafés in the piazza. Listen to the music as you watch the golden sunlight illuminating the brilliant multicolored mosaics over the **portals of St. Mark's** and bathing the entire Byzantine façade in its soft glow.

Along the Back Canals

This walk in Venice will take you through another section of the city to charming squares, past leaning campaniles, over the Rialto to Venice's fabulous markets, and finally to its outstanding gallery of modern art. And, of course, you will constantly be crossing the myriad of bridges over the network of canals—a never-ceasing source of fascination, interest, and amusement.

Start at the **Piazza San Marco** and wander along the arcades to the far end—the side closest to the **Grand Canal.** Go under the archway and follow the Calle dell'Ascensione and the **Salizzada S. Moisé** past attractive shops until you find on your left the dramatic baroque façade of the **Church of S. Moisé,** containing a late painting by Tintoretto. Cross the wide bridge and shortly you will see on the Calle Larga 22 Marzo a very "in" bistro with Venetian cuisine, **La Caravella.** Turn right along the Calle del Sartor da Veste for a few hundred yards and over a couple of bridges until you reach **La Fenice Theatre** on your left in a small square. La Fenice is one of the most exquisite opera houses in the world. It was the scene of the young composer Verdi's most spectacular triumphs. You will want to return to **Antico Martini,** one of Venice's finest restaurants, to enjoy your favorite Italian specialties. The Renaissance church on the square, San Fantin, has paintings by Palma el Viovane.

Return to the Calle 22 Marzo and continue, via the Calle de la Ostreghe, to the **Campo S. Maria Zobenigo.** Notice the Tintorettos and two beautiful pictures attributed to Rubens inside. The façade of the seventeenth-century church gives the square a distinguished air. But, as so often in Venice, there is also a touch of simpler forms of beauty. Look at the colorful flowers on the roof of a nearby shop.

From here you follow the signs on the buildings pointing to the Accademia. They will lead you through another square and then, in a few moments, to the large **Campo San Stefano.** Keep to the left to the Campo S. Vidal and pause just in front of the **Accademia Bridge.** On your right are two of the most charming small houses that you will see in Venice. Not only are the russet and gray houses themselves attractive, but they are set back in a lovely garden full of oleander bushes. Just opposite is the **Palazzo Cavalli,** now a bank. Go in for a minute for an interesting view of the Grand Canal.

Now return to the large square—the Campo San Stefano—and straight ahead you will see the Gothic **Church of S. Stefano,** with its fourteenth-century façade (open daily, 7:00–12:00 and 4:30–7:30). Notice the **Renaissance campanile** to the right of the church. It leans more than any other in Venice. Beyond the church you keep straight ahead through the Campo S. Anzolo and enter the **Calle de la Mandola,** a narrow street filled with enticing market shops. Over the next bridge is the Campo Manin. Just a bit farther, when you reach the Campo San Luca, you turn left down one of Venice's many narrow alleys to the Grand Canal. As you wander along here you have a fine view of the Rialto Bridge. Perhaps this is a good moment to sit at an outdoor table facing the canal, have a refreshment, and gaze at the passing crowd.

Now you are about to plunge into one of the most exciting corners of Venice—the site of the main **food markets.** Cross the Rialto and on the other side you will find yourself in a street crowded with shoppers. Any weekday morning you will see people gathered before one open stall after another, selecting from the fascinating displays of fruit, flowers, vegetables, meat, chicken, and every conceivable variety of Italian cheese. You will have lots of fun just wandering from one shop to the next, inspecting the food, checking over the prices, and watching the excitement—so typical of Italy—generated both by vendors and customers.

But the most colorful scene is yet to come. Turn right under the arcade, and after zigzagging for a hundred yards or so (in fact, go left, then right, and left again), you'll reach the city's **fish market.** On the way, more street merchants will be shouting, even singing, their wares. Under the building's high arches are countless open tables, each with a different kind of seafood. You will find mussels, snails, shellfish (**scampi**), octopus, squid, and all the local fish. It is certainly one of the most amusing and colorful scenes in Venice. As James Morris graphically describes it in his excellent book, *The World of Venice* (which, incidentally, you should read while you are there): " . . . a glorious, wet, colorful, high-smelling concourse of the sea . . . its stalls are lined deliciously with green fronds, damp and cool; and upon them are laid in a delicately-tinted, slobbering, writhing, glistening mass, the sea-creatures of the lagoon."

From the fish market, walk along the Grand Canal to the end of the quay, cross the bridge, turn left into the Calle dei Botteri, right at the Calle dei Cristi, and then into the Calle dei Morti. After about one hundred yards look for the sign pointing the way to the **Ca' Pesaro,** the **Galleria Internazionale d'Arte Moderna.** Finally, you approach the palace that houses it along a small canal.

The home of the international gallery of modern art exhibits works by nineteenth- and twentieth-century artists of Europe and America (open weekdays, 10:00–4:00; Sunday and holidays, 9:30–12:30). You also will find here many works that have been shown in the **Venice Biennale exhibits.** If you are interested in contemporary painting and sculpture, you will find the exhibit at the Ca' Pesaro stimulating and perhaps a welcome change from the old masters shown in the other Venetian galleries. The Oriental Museum is on the third floor (open daily, except Monday, 9:00–2:00; Sunday and holidays, 9:00–1:00).

When you leave the palace, why not return to San Marco on a *vaporetto* (Venice's **water bus**)? To reach the dock, cross the bridge outside the palace and turn right to the Grand Canal.

Across the Grand Canal

Although the part of Venice that lies across the **Grand Canal** from San Marco is a lesser-known section, it is intensely interesting. On it is one of the city's great landmarks, the Church of Santa Maria della Salute; as well as the famous Accademia art gallery, the Palazzo

Rezzonico; the Scuola San Rocco, noted for its wonderful paintings by Tintoretto; and the Church of the Frari with its great painting by Titian.

Start at **San Marco,** but instead of taking a *vaporetto* from the dock just below the gardens that face the lagoon, step aboard a *traghetto,* a **public gondola** that ferries Venetians across the Grand Canal from the **foot of the Calle Vallaresso.**

When you land, walk past the **Church of the Salute,** which dominates this end of the Grand Canal, to the **Dogana,** or Customs House, at the end of the quay. This seventeenth-century building is rather fine itself, and its position at the juncture of the two canals overlooking the lagoon is quite exceptional. From this point you have a marvelous view of the **Doges' Palace,** the **campanile,** the **harbor,** and the **Island of S. Giorgio Maggiore** to the east.

Returning to the Church of the Salute, which Longhena designed in the baroque style during the seventeenth century, go up its stately steps and inside to see the paintings by Titian (especially the three on the ceiling, which are examples of his mature period), as well as a fine work of Tintoretto. This church has been restored with the help of the French Association for the Preservation of Venice. (Open daily, 8:00–12:00 and 3:00–5:00.)

Walk along the side of the church and the old abbey opposite to the **Ponte della Salute.** After crossing this bridge, you turn sharply left down a narrow alley, the Calle del Squero, to the **Zattere,** the embankment along the Canal della Giudecca. Ruskin lived at **No. 780.** As you walk along, you will notice Andrea Palladio's **Church of the Redentore** across the canal in **La Giudecca,** the old "Ghetto" of Venice. Continue to the baroque **Church of Santa Maria dei Gesuati,** where there is a fine ceiling by Giovanni Battista Tiepolo.

Turn into the Fondamenta Bragadin until you reach the Calle

S. Cristoforo, to discover the **Peggy Guggenheim Foundation.** This ancient Venetian palazzo is covered with luxuriant vegetation, contrasting dramatically with the white stone building. Ms. Guggenheim, "the surrealists' muse," who was once married to Max Ernst, during her lifetime assembled a striking collection of twentieth-century painting and sculpture, including major works by Magritte, Dali, and de Chirico (open April–October, daily, exept Tuesday, 12:00–6:00).

Retrace your steps to the **Fondamenta Nani,** just beyond the Church of Santa Maria dei Gesuati, and turn right along a small canal. If you walk down the near side of this canal to the last bridge, you will get an unusual glimpse of one of the large palaces, with the Grand Canal beyond. A little farther on, turn right into the **Calle Gambara** to reach the **Accademia,** one of the leading art galleries in Italy and certainly the finest in Venice (open weekdays, 9:00–2:00; Sunday and holidays, 9:00–1:00; closed Mondays). Naturally, most of its paintings are of the Venetian school; they range from the earliest period to the eighteenth century. The Bellinis, Carpaccio, Piero della Francesca, and Giorgione, as well as Titian, Tintoretto, and Tiepolo, are some of the masters whose great works are on exhibit in this remarkable collection. Be especially sure to see such treasures as Giorgione's *Tempest* and Carpaccio's *Legend of St. Ursula,* but don't overlook Gentile Bellini's fascinating scenes of Venetian life about 1500.

From the Accademia turn left on the Campiello Gambara and watch for the blue signs marked "Ca' Rezzonico." These will lead you to the **Campo S. Barnaba.** Cross the next bridge and turn right along the **Fond. Rezzonico** to Longhena's majestic late-baroque palace, built in the seventeenth century (open weekdays except Friday, 10:00–4:00; Sunday and holidays, 9:30–12:30). Considered by many to be the most splendid patrician residence in Venice, the recently restored **Ca' Rezzonico** contains an exceptional collection of eighteenth-century paintings, furniture, and tapestries. On the second floor is a series of colorful and amusing **frescoes by Giovanni Domenico Tiepolo,** moved from his own villa. The English poet Robert Browning died in his apartment in this palace. The extensive exhibitions of costumes, porcelain, curios, and an old chemist's shop will give you an idea of eighteenth-century Venetian life.

From the Ca' Rezzonico to the Scuola di San Rocco you will wander through some of Venice's charming byways, over little bridges with views, down sleepy canals, through local markets, and past neighborhood cafés. This is an area where you encounter few tourists. But just when you feel you have been transplanted to the Venice of centuries ago, you will suddenly encounter a modern shop in an old building displaying the latest computers—a reminder that the electronic age is encroaching even in the most ancient parts of Venice. Still, Venice has been spared the noise of motor traffic, and it is this fact, perhaps more than any other, that enables you to sense in the byways and corners of this city the spirit of its old civilization.

Walk along the canal from the Ca' Rezzonico to the Calle de le Boteghe, then turn right to the Calle del Capeler and across a small square to the Calle Foscari. After crossing the bridge, the street widens. Go straight ahead, then down a narrow alley, Calle de Dona Onesta, then cross another bridge, turn left, then right in Calle Ca' Lipoli to the **Campo dei Frari.** (If these directions seem too complicated, simply ask a shopkeeper for Chiesa dei Frari.)

On reaching the back of the large **Church of the Frari,** go left a few yards to the entrance of the **Sculoa di San Rocco** (open April–October, daily, 9:00–1:00 and 3:30–6:30; November–March, weekdays, 10:00–1:00; weekends and holidays, 10:00–4:00). This Renaissance building, formerly one of Venice's six great schools for the education of poor girls, contains a large number of **paintings by**

Tintoretto. The great sixteenth-century artist's huge canvases on the walls and ceilings, depicting scenes from the Old and New Testaments, are one of the most extraordinarily dramatic and imaginative series of paintings in Venice.

Across from San Rocco is the tall brick campanile of the Church of the Frari (open 9:00–12:00 and 2:30–5:30). Go around to the front of the Gothic church, the largest in Venice, and inside you will find Titian's *Assumption* over the altar, a lovely Donatello of St. John the Baptist, and, in the sacristy, a fine triptych by Giovanni Bellini. Also look around the **cloisters** with their white-stone arches and russet-colored walls.

When you leave the church, you should walk to the **Rialto,** less than fifteen minutes away. To do so, you simply follow the red signs marked "Rialto," which you will notice just after crossing the bridge on the other side of the square from the Frari. As is common in Venice, the route will wind in and out of narrow streets and alleys, but wherever it leads, you will discover some new phase of this lively and fascinating city. The last part of the route before you turn right to the Rialto is along the **Ruga S. Giovanni.**

On reaching the Rialto, you can take a *vaporetto* back to San Marco. Or, if you wish to do some shopping, return to San Marco by the **Merceria,** Venice's leading shopping street, specializing in silks, leather goods, and glassware. To get to the Merceria from the Rialto, you turn right into the Via 2 Aprile and in a hundred yards or so, by the **Church of S. Salvatore,** you turn left. At the end of this crowded street, you will pass under the famous clock tower into the square of San Marco.

Now, having discovered the enchantment of Venice, it is time to take a gondola and, as you slip through the narrow canals, ruminate upon the ages-old fascination of this unique city, less changed since its days of glory than almost any other you will visit in Europe.

However, today Venice is in danger. Ocean humidity is slowly but surely damaging its historic splendor, and the very foundations of the city are threatened. Fortunately, UNESCO, the Council of Europe, and other international organizations are developing an energetic program for saving Venice. Even the Italian National Lottery is contributing to the effort of saving Venice!

13.
Vienna

BAROQUE BEAUTY ON THE DANUBE

In Alt Wien

Your first walk in **Vienna** should be in the oldest part, the **inner town.** Here, you will find winding streets and obscure little squares; you will peek into bewitching courtyards and old baroque palaces; and you will see the rooms where Mozart composed. Not only will you visit famous St. Stephen's Cathedral, which dominates the old quarter, but you will also explore lesser-known but still fascinating old churches. In this way you will absorb the spirit of *"Alt Wien."*

Start at the world-renowned Vienna **State Opera House,** the center of the city's cultural life. You can tour this magnificent and modern (reconstructed between 1945 and 1955) opera house—a most worthwhile experience—with a guide from mid-April–June, September, October, and December 26–January 3 at 10:00, 11:00, 1:00, 2:00, and 3:00; in July and August at 9:00, 10:00, 11:00, 1:00, 2:00, and 3:00; and during the rest of the year at 2:00 and 3:00. The Opera House is located on the **Opern Ring,** a section of the wide

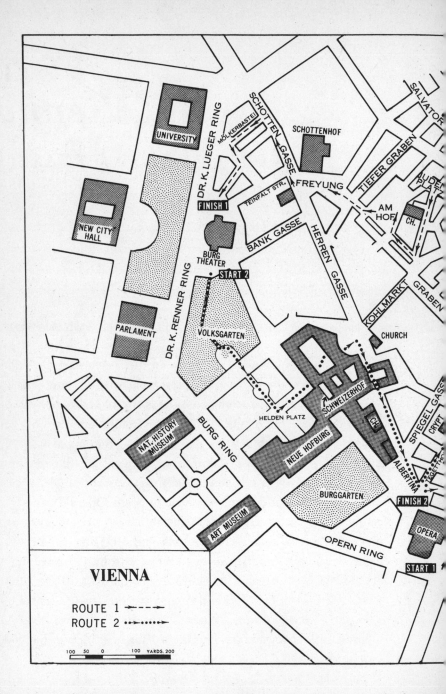

UNIVERSITY

SCHOTTENHOF

DR. K. LUEGER RING

SCHOTTEN GASSE

MÖLKERBASTEI

SALVATOR

TIEFER GRABEN

JUDEN PLATZ

AM HOF

CH.

FINISH 1

TEINFALT STR.

FREYUNG

NEW CITY HALL

BANK GASSE

HERREN GASSE

GRABEN

BURG THEATER

KOHLMARKT

START 2

PARLAMENT

VOLKSGARTEN

CHURCH

DR. K. RENNER RING

SCHWEIZERHOF

SPIEGEL GASSE

HELDEN PLATZ

CRYPT

NAT. HISTORY MUSEUM

BURG RING

CH.

NEUE HOFBURG

ALBERTIN

FINISH 2

BURGGARTEN

ART MUSEUM

OPERN RING

OPERA

START 1

VIENNA

ROUTE 1 ->-- -->
ROUTE 2 •••••••••>

100 50 0   100 YARDS. 200

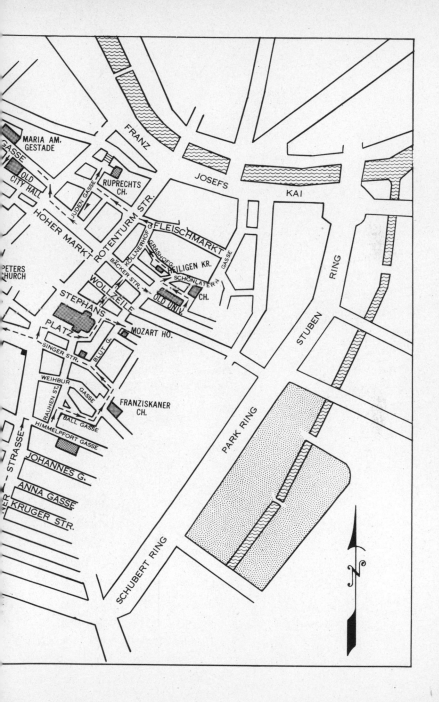

boulevard that circles the inner city on the site where its ancient walls once stood.

Saunter along **Kärtner Strasse,** Vienna's main shopping street. Join the crowd now gazing at the tempting windows, now browsing in and out of the stores. But in a moment or two you will leave this bustling scene of present-day Vienna and immerse yourself in the atmosphere of two hundred years ago by simply turning right off this up-to-date thoroughfare, a few hundred yards from the Opera House into **Himmelpfort Gasse.** Down on the right at **No. 8** you will come to the majestic **town palace of Prince Eugene of Savoy,** one of the greatest military leaders of the eighteenth century, who helped save Vienna from the Turks and later became Marlborough's ally against Louis XIV. This baroque building, now the **Ministry of Finance,** was designed at the end of the seventeenth century by the great architect Fischer von Erlach. Before entering, inspect its impressive façade. (Open Saturday and Sunday, 3:00–5:00. On other days, you will probably be allowed to look around the entrance hall and stairway.) The ceiling painting over the stairs, the rococo plaster figures, and the ornamental balustrading will give you some idea of its elaborate interior.

Retrace your steps a few yards and turn right on the Rauhenstein Gasse and again right on winding Ball Gasse until you reach little **Franziskaner Platz.** Here you can stop for coffee Viennese style at **Das Café,** a student favorite. This old square with its little fountain faces the white walls of the **Franciscan monastery and church,** built in the early seventeenth century. Be sure to see its sumptuous baroque interior. Notice the lovely, baroque houses around the square. Upon leaving the church, turn right into the curving Singer Strasse. Then turn left and just beyond Blut Gasse on the right you will come to the **Hall and Chapel of the Teutonic Knights** (open May 1–October 31: Monday, Thursday, Friday, Saturday, and Sunday, 10:00–12:00; Tuesday, Friday, and Saturday, 3:00–5:00; November 1–April 30, closed Friday and Sunday mornings). The church, dating from the fourteenth century, contains flags and coats of arms of the Knights of the Holy Roman Empire. On the second floor, you will find a most interesting collection of religious plate and armor. Notice the splendid sixteenth-century Flemish altarpiece. On leaving the church, turn right along Singer Strasse a short distance until you return to Kärtner Strasse.

Cross over to see the **Stock im Eisen,** a strange relic rather inconspicuously attached to the corner of a large building. During the fifteenth century, locksmiths, inspired by an old legend, used to drive a nail into this old stock or stump for good luck. Now, some five hundred years later, you see the remains of the tree trunk covered with nails.

You are now facing **St. Stephen's Cathedral,** one of the great Gothic cathedrals of Europe and the spiritual center of Viennese life. Its slender spire against the sky is an inspiring sight. Before crossing the Stefans Platz to visit the cathedral, saunter along the **Graben,** one of the city's main shopping streets. Perhaps this is the moment to stop in for Viennese coffee *mit schlag* (with whipped cream) at one of the attractive cafés on the Graben. Notice the interesting Black Plague Column in the center. You can take a guided tour of the Cathedral at 10:30 and 3:30 (open evenings from July–September).

Turn off to the Petersplatz to visit **St. Peter's Church,** built in 1702. Its magnificent interior with its multicolored marble is a fine example of the Austrian late baroque. **Stefans Platz,** in front of the cathedral, used to be the scene of the **Passion Play** centuries ago. When you enter the cathedral, notice the giant door dating from 1230 and built in the Romanesque style. The Romanesque and Gothic parts of the cathedral were built between 1147 and 1511. It was reconstructed in 1945. After you have spent a while wandering about this historic shrine and looking at its artistic treasures, take the elevator to the bell tower (open April–September, 9:00–6:00; October–March, 8:00–5:40). The **view over the city** from this high vantage point is quite exceptional. Here you will see the huge new bell, or **Pummerin.** The new Pummerin was made from metal taken from the famous old Pummerin, which had been fashioned from Turkish cannon captured at the liberation of Vienna, but which was damaged during World War II.

At the back of the cathedral you will discover a little passage under an arch (5 Stefans Platz) that leads into **Dom Gasse.** Here, at No. 5, is **Figarohaus,** Mozart's home from 1784 to 1787 (open weekdays, except Monday and holidays, 9:00–12:15, and 1:00–4:30; Sunday, 9:00–1:00). You should climb the steps in this old building to visit the rooms where the great composer wrote *The Marriage of Figaro.* It's exciting to realize that Mozart played chamber music with Haydn and Beethoven in this apartment. The little museum has many Mozart souvenirs and manuscripts on display.

Retrace your steps through the archway, and on your right you will find another little passageway at No. 6 Stefans Platz, opposite the cathedral. This will lead into Wollzeile. Cross over and continue through a similar alley at No. 5. The alley is called a *Durchhaus,* and was standing in the days when Turkish cannon balls were raining on the city. You might like to stop in at a little *Weinstube* here for a refreshing glass of Heurige, the famous Viennese wine.

At the end of the passage you will come out in **Bäcker Strasse,** right in the heart of medieval Vienna. Look into the picturesque, ivy-covered courtyard at No. 7, then turn right and go to the square at the end of the street—Dr. Ignaz Seipel Platz. This is the **old university quarter;** the large building on the left in French classic style was formerly the Aula, or Assembly Hall, of the old university. It is now the Academy of Science. Go in the recently restored Jesuit church built in baroque style to see the ceiling paintings and fine marble columns. A few yards along Sonnenfels Gasse turn right into the narrow and winding **Schönlatern Gasse,** typical of old Vienna. Notice the **Basilisk House,** No. 7.

Just to the left of this house you encounter one of those surprising retreats in the middle of the city. On your left is the **Heiligenkreuzerhof,** the winter residence of the monks from the Holy Cross Monastery in the Vienna Woods. This large building facing an oblong courtyard has been in the possession of the abbey since 1206. Take a look at the small baroque chapel. Leave by the archway at the far side, walk along the Grashof Gasse, then turn right on Köllnerhof Gasse, and go to the **Fleishmarkt.** One of the most ancient streets in Vienna, this street of the Butchers Guild—the center of the Greek and Armenian trading community—was called by its Roman name, the Via Carnorum, until about a century ago. Next to the **Greek Orthodox Church** is **Griechenbeisl,** one of the oldest Viennese restaurants with a reputation for the best beer in Vienna. It is said that the ballad "Ach, du lieber Augustin" was written here. The balconies over the tiny courtyard give it a delightful air. If you started this stroll in the morning, by now you will probably feel ready for lunch, so why not stop either in here or in the restaurant **Zur Linde,** a famous guest house founded in 1435 and a favorite of the composer Johannes Brahms. It is just around the corner from the Fleischmarkt on the **Rotenturm Strasse.** Here you can enjoy your favorite Viennese dish in a pleasant garden.

After a leisurely lunch, cross the Rotenturm Strasse and continue along the Fleischmarkt up a flight of steps to **Juden Gasse.** This section, the old **Ghetto,** still retains some of its former character. Turn right and go about twenty-five yards to the **Ruprechtskirche,** built on the old walls above the **Danube Canal.** This is the city's oldest church and dates from the eleventh century. The church is open only for religious services from Easter–October 1, Monday–Friday, 10:00–1:00. Just to the right of the little square you will find the **synagogue** at No. 4 Seitenstetten Gasse.

Return along Juden Gasse, past the street merchants selling old clothing, into the **Hoher Markt.** Notice the so-called Marriage Fountain, with its canopy shielding the young couple. This is the oldest section of the city and was the center of the medieval town. Underneath the present busy square are the ruins of the Roman settlement, **Vindobona.** You can visit these excavations at No. 2 Hoher Markt. (Open 10:00–12:15, and 1:00–4:30; closed Monday and holidays.) At one end of the square you will notice a colorful clock, the **Ankeruhr.** Historical figures associated with Vienna parade across its face when the noon hour strikes.

Leaving the Hoher Markt at the far end, turn right into **Marc Aurel Strasse** (the great Roman emperor died in Vienna), and then left along Salvator Gasse. On your left, at No. 5, is the Early Renaissance portal of the old Salvator Chapel. Just a few yards farther along, you will come to the lovely late fourteenth-century **Maria am Gestade,** the Church of St. Mary, which overlooks the Danube Canal. As it was so close to the river, fishermen and boatmen used to worship here during the Middle Ages. To get a good view of the church and its high tower, it's worthwhile descending some of the steps below to the place where in the earlier days boats were moored.

Return past the back of the church a block to **Stoss in Himmel Gasse** (literally translated "thrust in Heaven Lane," the name is associated with a Viennese legend) on your right to **No. 3,** a beautiful baroque house. About fifty yards farther on the left on Wipplinger Strasse the **old City Hall** faces the former Bohemian chancellery, now the **Law Courts,** a building also designed in the manner of Fischer von Erlach, at the beginning of the eighteenth century. Cross the street and walk along the short Fütterer Gasse to Juden Platz. On the opposite side of this square wander down the curving Pariser Gasse into the **Schulhof,** a little square where you will find, at No. 2, Vienna's **Clock Museum** (open daily, 9:00–4:30; closed Monday and holidays), where thousands of clocks made during the past eight hundred years are on display.

You are now in one of the most enchanting corners of Vienna. Just ahead is the rounded back of the **Church of the Nine Choirs of Angels.** A tiny boutique has been built right in between the buttresses. Here one can sense the characteristics of old Vienna: the juncture of four streets so narrow that only one car can go down them, the cobblestone paving, an old house (the **Pfarrhof,** dating from the sixteenth century) on the corner of **Steindl Gasse,** and the high walls of the church. Pause for a few minutes, look in at the shop, and just stroll around this secluded spot. Then walk along Seitzer Gasse beyond the church and turn right on Bogner Gasse to **Am Hof,** a wide square that was the site of medieval tournaments. As you walk around the square, you will find fine baroque façades at No. 7 and No. 12. No. 10, a good example of an eighteenth-century building, used to be Vienna's arsenal. A Turkish cannon ball, a souvenir of Vienna's critical years, is lodged over the doorway of No. 11.

Leaving the square by the Heidenschuss, directly across from Bogner Gasse, you come into the Freyung, an area so named because fugitives could find sanctuary here. No. 4, on the left, is the handsome late-baroque **Kinsky Palace.** Just across stands the massive **Schottenhof.** Its tree-shaded courtyard, which you enter by **Schotten Gasse,** is another good place for some refreshment. The first monks in the twelfth century were Scots (hence the name) and Irish, but their addiction to sports and dances, in addition to their habit of selling religious objects for profit, led to their replacement in the fifteenth century by the more suitable German Benedictines. On the opposite side of this street, No. 3, you can walk through a small courtyard to visit the deep cellars of the **Abbey of Melk** (Melkerhof).

Proceed a few yards farther on the Schotten Gasse, turn left, and climb the steps to the Mölkerbastei, built on the old fortifications. Go around to the outside, where on the corner of the Schoenvogel Gasse is a delightful rococo house known as the **Drei Mäderlhaus** (named for the three girls in the musical about Schubert, *Lilac Time*). Around the corner, to the right, at **No. 8** on the **Mölkerbastei,** is the lovely house where Beethoven lived on the fourth floor. (Open daily, 10:00–12:15, and 1:00–4:30; closed holidays.) At the foot of the ramp turn right a few yards to the Oppolzer Gasse, which will bring you out on the **Ring**—the end of this walk through old Vienna. From here you can take a streetcar or taxi back to the Opera.

The Grandeur of Imperial Days

The second walk in Vienna includes many of the city's sights that are most interesting from a historical and artistic point of view. The places you will visit are largely associated with the Hapsburgs, and the Holy Roman and Austro-Hungarian Empires, which they ruled successively until the end of World War I.

Start at the **Burgtheater,** or national theater, on the **Ring** just opposite Vienna's large **City Hall,** built in the Gothic style during the nineteenth century. Just across from the theater, on the same side of the Ring, you enter the beautifully landscaped **Volksgarten,** a park laid out on the site of the old fortifications. In summer the formal rose garden and semicircular rose beds throughout the garden are particularly attractive. Just to your right, across the Ring, you will see the **Austrian Parliament** building, designed in the classic style nearly one hundred years ago. Under the trees in the park are two delightful outdoor cafés, providing an enjoyable spot for a drink or a light lunch.

When you leave the Volksgarten you will face a large open square, the **Helden Platz.** Directly beyond stands the massive **Neue Hofburg,** the newer section (late nineteenth century) of the **Imperial Palace.** The great sprawling block of buildings to the left is the **Alte Hofburg,** the main part of the Hapsburgs' royal residence. Tragically, in November 1992, a fire broke out and seriously damaged parts of the Hofburg. The sixteenth-century dance and concert hall, where Beethoven had given concerts and the Vienna Opera sometimes performed, was totally destroyed. The fire came close to damaging the Spanish Court Riding School, and the sixty-nine white Lipizzaner horses had to be evacuated. Luckily the Library, containing over two million precious books, was not affected, but some of the oldest books and manuscripts had to be removed. The Hofburg is quite a mixture of styles and shapes, because throughout nearly five hundred years of the Hapsburg reign in Vienna there were frequent alterations, reconstructions, and extensions.

Go through the entrance on the left of the Helden Platz, into the great central court. There are many parts of the palace you can visit, especially the state rooms, including the **apartments of the Emperor Franz Joseph I.** (Open weekdays, 8:30–4:30; Sunday and holidays, 8:30–1:00.) But the most interesting section is the **Schatzkammer,** the collection of religious and lay treasures that you reach by entering the oldest section of the palace, the Schweizerhof, which dates from the thirteenth century (open Tuesday and

Friday, 10:00–6:00; Saturday, Sunday, and holidays, 9:00–6:00; closed Monday). Here you will be fascinated to find the **Hapsburg crown jewels,** especially the crown of the Holy Roman Empire, set with precious stones. It is believed to be nearly a thousand years old. You will be excited to see **Charlemagne's own prayer book,** as well as ancient swords, orbs, and scepters of the Holy Roman Empire and the Hapsburg dynasty. The crown jewels, coronation garments, vestments, and insignia comprise an unusual display.

Right nearby is the entrance to the **Burgkapelle,** or Imperial Chapel, where the noted **Viennese Choir Boys** sing on Sunday morning at 9:30 Mass (from mid-September to the end of June) as their predecessors, including such great musicians as Haydn, Mozart, and Schubert, have done for 450 years.

Returning to the central courtyard, take the passage on your right to Michaeler Platz. Just across the small square is the **Michaelerkirche,** one of Vienna's oldest churches, a combination of Romanesque and Gothic architecture.

From the church turn left along Reitschul Gasse, and in a moment, on the right, you reach the famous winter riding school and its majestic riding hall. No visitor to Vienna should miss the magnificent spectacle of the **Spanish Court Riding School's** white Lipizzaner stallions being put through their paces by their trainers with balletlike precision, just as has been done for nearly three hundred years. Even today the riders never begin a performance without saluting the Royal Box with its picture of Emperor Charles VI—an illustration of the Austrians' ingrained respect for the imperial tradition. (The school is closed during July and August. During the rest of the year inquire for tickets from the concierge of your hotel.) Across the street from the school is the Stallburg, the stables.

Walk under a passageway on this street and you will come into the **Josefs Platz,** an impressive baroque square. The **National Li-**

brary, which possesses an outstanding collection of books, maps, and manuscripts, occupies one side of the square. Just a few steps beyond the square on Augustiner Strasse you will find on your right the noble **Augustinerkirche** where Napoleon was married to Marie Louise in 1810.

At the end of the street, on your right, is one of Vienna's finest art collections, the **Albertina,** including a remarkable group of **drawings by Albrecht Dürer.** (Open Monday, Tuesday, and Thursday, 10:00–4:00; Wednesday, 10:00–6:00; Friday, 10:00–2:00; Saturday and Sunday 10:00–1:00. During July and August, closed on Sunday and holidays.) The **Music Collection** of the National Library is also here.

Now turn left, on the other side of a small square, along Tegetthoff Strasse to visit the **Imperial Crypt,** the burial place of the Hapsburgs beneath the Kapuzinerkirche. It's an extraordinary experience to descend into the vaults and find lead or copper coffins of the 141 Hapsburgs laid out in rows. At the end is the decorative double sarcophagus of Empress Maria Theresa and her consort. (Open daily, 9:30–4:30.)

Retrace your steps along Tegetthoff Strasse to the **Opera House.** This may be just the moment to drop in at **Sacher's,** Vienna's most famous hotel, and try the delicious Sachertorte at one of the outdoor tables. After leaving Sacher's, walk a block past the front of the **Opera** to the **Ring.** Now go down the stairs to see how excellently, in recent years, the Viennese have developed pedestrian underpasses below major traffic centers. You will find snack bars and shops attractively planned with many stairs and escalators leading to the different streets and bus and train stops.

There is one art collection that you must visit—at the **Museum of Fine Arts**—undoubtedly one of the finest in Europe and the fourth largest anywhere (open weekdays except Monday and holidays,

April–October, 10:00–6:00; Saturday and Sunday, 9:00–6:00; November–March, 10:00–4:00. The art gallery is also open Tuesday and Friday, 7:00–9:00). Just walk right, along the Opern Ring, for four blocks. On your right you pass the attractively landscaped **Burggarten,** in case you feel like strolling through another of Vienna's parks. When you reach the museum on the left, go to the first floor to see the paintings. In the extensive collection are outstanding examples of such **Italian masters** as Raphael, Giorgione, Titian, and Tintoretto, great **Dutch artists** like Rembrandt, leading **Flemish painters** like Van der Weyden and Pieter Bruegel and Rubens and the **Spanish school** including Velasquez. The museum possesses the greatest collection of Dürer's paintings anywhere in the world. It's fitting to end your walks through this city, renowned for its culture, among such superb works of art.

Some of the most important sights in Vienna are not accessible on foot, but since taxis are cheap, this is no problem. No visitor to Vienna should miss **Schönbrunn Palace** (the Versailles of Vienna), of historic and artistic interest. **Belvedere Palace,** built for Prince Eugene of Savoy by L. von Hildebrand, has important museums. It is worth taking a trip to the **Kahlenberg,** a hill outside Vienna, where you have a splendid view over the city. There is a good restaurant on the **Kahlenberg,** and this spot is perhaps the most beautiful on a warm summer day.

14.
Prague

GOLDEN CITY OF BOHEMIA

The Old Town

The capital of the Czech Republic can be considered the geographic crossroads of Europe, where many paths and cultures merge. **Prague's** architecture, ranging from early Gothic to late baroque, includes French, Spanish, Italian, and German influences, yet the end result is unique. Here, the Renaissance is not Italian, classicism not quite German, the rococo period not really French. With an alchemy all its own, the city transforms foreign contributions into a harmonious whole.

The first-time visitor to Prague is struck by its haunting, enigmatic quality. Wandering through its serpentine cobblestoned alleys, crossing the noble Karlův Most (Charles Bridge) with its thirty sculpted saints, strolling amid ancient graves in the extraordinary Jewish Cemetery—the oldest in Europe—you feel that you are immersed in a magical past, traveling back through the centuries as if you were in a time capsule. The 1989 "Velvet Revolution" and the subsequent return of private enterprise is slowly bringing about

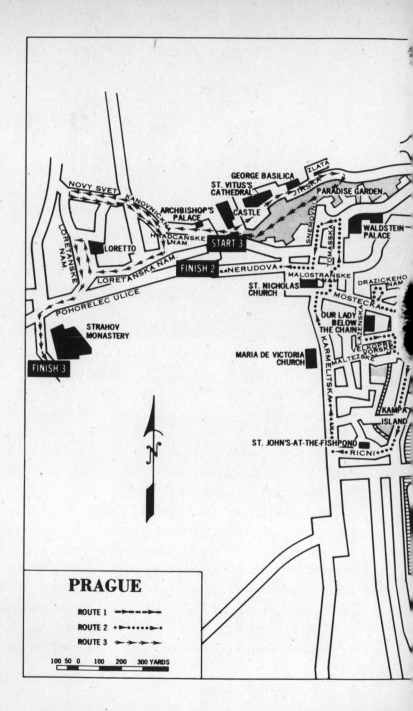

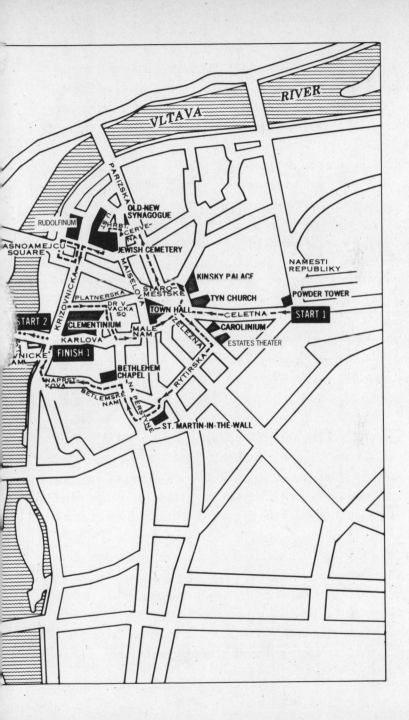

changes. Palaces and museums are being renovated, and restaurants and boutiques seem to spring from the ground, as Prague, once a "sleeping beauty," awakens to embrace the twentieth century. Fortunately, the romantic, mysterious mood of the city remains unchanged.

Much of the pleasure of exploring Prague stems from the unexpected discovery: an unusual statue in a courtyard; the little wine cellar nestled amid nineteenth-century street lanterns, still lit at sundown by wizened women; the pastel-colored cottages on Golden Lane. And the only way to visit Prague is indeed on foot. While the city is most enchanting in late spring (when you'll want to attend some of the fine concerts given during the Prague Music Festival), Prague is in fact a city of all seasons. Autumn fog shrouds it in mystery; its snow-covered winter rooftops have a peculiar charm all their own; and the summer sun brilliantly illuminates the city known locally as "Zlatá Praha" ("Golden Prague").

Your walk through the Old Town begins near Náměsti Republiky (Republic Square) at the **Powder Tower (Prašná brána).** Built in 1475, it was used to store gunpowder back in the eighteenth century. Prussian bombardments caused heavy damage in 1757; in the nineteenth century the tower underwent extensive reconstruction and acquired its Neo-Gothic façade. Further renovations were undertaken in the 1960s. Climb the 186 stone steps to the top for a splendid panoramic view of the city. (At this writing, it is closed for restoration.)

Saunter along the Celetná ulice, a charming street lined with baroque and Gothic buildings. It was once the so-called Coronation Road that lead to the Charles Bridge and through today's Nerudova Street to the Prague Castle. On your way to Staroměstské náměsti (Old Town Square), take a peek at the **Pachta Palace,** built in the fifteenth century when it was part of the royal court; a century later, it became a mint and acquired its baroque façade in the 1780s. Today it is a court of law. At No. 34 Celetná ulice, note the "Black Virgin" house, and impressive modern building in the cubist style, built by the Czech architect Josef Gočár. The most remarkable building on this street is the **Hrzán Palace** (at No. 12). Its graceful baroque lines are characteristic of Prague's architecture. The remains of a Roman house were found in the basement. And at No. 2, stop to glance at the beautifully restored **U Sixtů,** with its luxurious **Café Kisch** and an elegant wine cellar where you can dine in style. Decorated with baroque busts of emperors, the house once belonged to the Sixt von Ottersdorf family, who collected an impressive variety of books and paintings. At No. 8, wander into one of Prague's famous record shops, offering high-quality records and compact discs at moderate prices. You will surely want to purchase Czech folk music and classics by Dvořák, Smetana, and Jánaček.

Staroměstské náměsti, or **Old Town Square,** one of the most delightful corners of Old Prague, played a major role in Czech history. In 1621, twenty-seven Bohemian lords were executed here in a bloody massacre for having rebelled against harsh Hapsburg rule. The square boasts Renaissance, baroque, and rococo façades that were constructed upon Roman and Gothic ruins. The **Town Hall** has been rebuilt and remodeled from the fourteenth century on. Its south façade is famous for the **Apostle's Clock.** Tourists and citizens of Prague alike crowd around this city landmark to hear the hour sound. A polychrome fifteenth-century clock, it shelters tiny symbolic figures that appear just before the hour strikes. One of them, the "Bone Man," tolls a death bell. Then the apostles emerge, one by one, facing the audience as if awaiting applause, and finally the cock crows, on the hour.

Cross over to the **Kinsky Palace,** the most impressive rococo building in Prague, which once housed the school where Franz Kafka, the great Czech writer, attended classes. This eighteenth-century palace, built by Anselmo Lurago, contains drawings from the Prague National Gallery collection. (At this writing, the palace is closed to the public.)

Stroll to the center of the square for a look at the **Jan Hus Memorial Statue.** It dates from 1915, the five-hundredth anniversary of the great Czech reformer's death. If nothing else, the statue is imposing, although its jarringly modern lines contrast incongruously with the harmony of the square's architecture.

The most unusual building on Old Town Square is the **Týn Church,** hidden among the arcades. Enter No. 14 and go through a rather ordinary dim hallway past the mailboxes to reach this small, splendid Late Gothic church. Its superb Gothic pulpit, the Madonna, and, at the altar, the fifteenth-century scene depicting Calvary, are among its treasures. This animated square is today the heart of Prague. Students and tourists mingle on the grass behind the Town Hall; you can listen to an improvised concert by strolling musicians as you sip a *pivo* (Czech beer, world-famous) in one of the several terrace cafés.

If you want to do some shopping before continuing on your walk, stop in at No. 6, **Bohemia,** which offers a vast sampling of crystal objects and glassware.

When you leave Old Town Square, take the wide boulevard Pařižská (Paris Street) until you reach Červená ulice. Turn left: now you are in **Josefov,** the Jewish quarter. Stop to visit the thirteenth-century **Old–New Synagogue,** the oldest in Europe and one of the oldest Gothic houses of worship in Prague (open daily except Saturday 9:00–5:00; November–March, 9:00–4:30; Friday, 9:00–2:00). The interior is richly decorated and has unusual five-sided vaults. Note the Torah (the five books of Moses) on the altar. Farther along the Červená ulice, at No. 4, is the **Town Hall Synagogue,** whose unassuming exterior contrasts with the unexpectedly sumptuous Renaissance room on the first floor. Today it's the State Jewish Museum. Here you can see the permanent exhibit, "A Thousand Years of Jewish Culture in Bohemia." (Open daily except Saturday, 9:00–4:30.)

Now turn left on Červená ulice until you reach Maiselova. At No. 18 is the **Jewish Town Hall,** which despite its rococo appearance, is a Renaissance building. Here you'll discover Prague's only kosher restaurant, where the cuisine is excellent. Then turn left on U Starého hřbitova. At No. 5, stop to see the **Klaus Synagogue.** Once the temple where Rabbi Loew taught—he was a noted scholar and teacher of the Talmud—it is today a museum devoted to Jewish culture and contains old furniture, Hebraic manuscripts, china, and clothing (open daily except Saturday, 9:00–5:00).

Now continue until you arrive at one of the most moving sites in Prague, the **Jewish Cemetery** (open daily except Saturday, 9:00–4:00). The oldest cemetery in Europe, it managed to survive Nazi pillage. This symbol of Prague's ghetto originated in the mid-fifteenth century and ceased to be used for burial purposes in 1787. Ancient gravestones are crammed together, leaning toward each other, and give the impression of quiet irregularity. Trees grow as if by chance amid graves. The first known grave dates back to the 1300s; in some places as many as twelve separate tomb layers exist. The ancient Hebraic inscriptions frequently represent the profession of the deceased. Names are sometimes disguised as animals (stags or foxes). The best-known grave is that of the High Rabbi Loew. A famous ghetto legend grew up around him, that of the Golem, which he allegedly created from a lump of clay with the help of cabalistic magic. You will want to rest here on one of the benches and contemplate the peaceful yet eerie atmosphere.

When you leave the cemetery through a little iron gate, pause a moment at the right of the entrance, where there is a very moving exhibit of drawings by children who perished in the Theresianstadt concentration camp. Take the Široká ulice just behind it to the **Pinkas Synagogue,** of which the Romanesque walls are still preserved. Somewhat damaged by centuries of humidity, the Synagogue has recently been restored. Inside, you will be moved to tears by the stark, dignified lists of Czech Jews who perished in the concentration camps during World War II. (Open daily except Saturday, 9:00–5:00.)

Then turn right on Široká ulice until you reach Krasnoamějců Square, where you can enjoy a magnificent view of the **Hradčin Hill** and the castle overlooking the Vltava River, the **Malá Strana (Little Quarter)** dominated by the **Nicholas Church,** and the **Petřin Hill** with the Observatory. The Mánes Bridge leads to the Little Quarter, which you will visit another time. Note the **Rudolfinum** on the square. This nineteenth-century building houses the Academy of Music and the world-renowned Czech Philharmonic. Do return here some evening for a concert of classical music, for which Prague is justly famous.

With the square behind you, now follow Křižovnická ulice, then turn left on Platnéřská until you arrive at Dr V. Vacka Square. Wander over to the **Clementinum,** next to Prague Castle the largest complex of buildings in the city. Built between 1578 and 1730, it houses the State Library and the University Library, containing over three and a half million books and rare manuscripts. Especially noteworthy are the library on the first floor, the frescoes representing Science and Art, the rococo Mozart Room, and the Mirror Chapel, where concerts and exhibits are held. (Open daily, 10:00–5:00.)

Now take Husova Třida until you get to No. 20, one of Prague's most handsome baroque buildings, the **Clam-Gallas Palace.** J. B.

Fischer von Erlach designed this building in the early eighteenth century. The giant statues at both portals and the fountain with its sculpted triton are particularly attractive. Today the palace contains the Archives of the City of Prague (at this writing, not open to the public).

Continue along Husova until you reach Karlova, where you turn left to find **Malé náměsti (Small Square),** a delightfully intimate square. In its center stands a fountain enclosed by a Renaissance iron gate. At No. 3 is a particularly beautiful façade, "The Three White Roses," which has Roman ruins in its cellar. No. 11, consisting of two connecting Gothic houses, used to be the oldest pharmacy in Prague.

Leave the square via Železná ulice and continue until you reach No. 9, the **Carolinium,** part of the renowned Charles University. Its Gothic arches and chapel contrast strikingly with the baroque reconstruction. The Carolinium was the site of much Hussite activity under the leadership of rector Jan Hus. Right next to it, at No. 11, you'll see the **Estates Theater,** the oldest in Prague, where Mozart's *Don Giovanni* had its world premiere. Mozart operas are still performed here today. The theater was completely restored in 1991.

Continue along Železná ulice, and turn right on Rytiřská ulice until you arrive at Martinská ulice. Here you will notice an unusual church, **St. Martin-in-the-Wall.** Begun in the twelfth century, it was reconstructed in the Gothic style, then renovated in the early 1900s.

Continue along Na Perštýně on the right until you reach Betlémské náměsti (Bethlehem Square). Noteworthy here is the **Bethlehem Chapel,** a contemporary reconstruction of a fourteenth-century chapel built by Czech patriots who insisted on holding all sermons in Czech instead of Latin. The chapel's most celebrated preacher was Jan Hus; from this pulpit, he spread his revolutionary ideas and inaugurated one of the most dramatic chapters of Czech history (open daily, 10:00–5:00). Before leaving the square, stop at U Plebána, a wine cellar that serves *Znojmoer,* allegedly the wine of the Bohemian kings, and typical Czech food.

Now take Náprstkova until you get to the river, then turn right on the wide quay and enjoy another stunning view of the castle dominating the Vltava. Proceed to Novotného lávka and the recently renovated **Smetana Museum,** honoring the great Czech composer, best-known for his amusing opera, *The Bartered Bride.* Music lovers should not miss it. (Open daily except Tuesday, 10:00–5:00.)

Continue straight ahead and you will arrive at Křižovnické náměsti (Crusaders' Square) encircled by the Salvator Church, the St. Francis Church, and the Bridge Tower. It is worth dropping by **St. Francis** (open daily, 10:00–5:00), an imposing baroque structure built by the French architect Jean Matthey. Admire the priceless Gothic Madonna adorning the altar. The **Bridge Tower** (open daily, 10:00–5:00), entrance gate to the impressive Charles Bridge, was once part of the city gates. It's worth climbing all 138 steps of the tower; you will be rewarded with an incomparable view of the Charles Bridge, the Old Town behind you, and the far bank of the Vltava.

The **Charles Bridge** is to Prague what the Acropolis is to Athens or the Eiffel Tower to Paris—one of the great tourist attractions of the city. It was begun in 1357 under Charles IV's reign, and completed in the fifteenth century. The bridge, 517 meters long and ten meters wide, is closed to traffic. It's a favorite promenade for young couples and has recently become an open-air shopping bazaar. Artists present their paintings, designers of original costume jewelry show their wares—a Prague specialty—and you may wish to pick up a little ceramic bell, symbol of the Velvet Revolution. Thirty splendid baroque statues of saints line the bridge. Look behind you at the Old Town, glance down the stairway leading to Kampa Island, the idyllic "Venice of Prague," and savor the dramatic view of

Prague Castle, St. Vitus's Cathedral, and the white towers of St. George's Basilica.

Malá Strana

The Malá Strana, or "Little Quarter," is perhaps the most romantic neighborhood you will visit in Prague. Built in Charles IV's time, the quarter was heavily damaged by fire in the fifteenth and sixteenth centuries. Thereafter it was rebuilt in the baroque style, and became a residential area for the wealthy aristocracy and church notables. This historic quarter was spared the reconstruction that affects other parts of Prague; you will be struck by its authenticity as you wander through its still streets and rest awhile in its luscious gardens.

Begin your walk at Charles Bridge on the left bank of the Vltava. Passing the Bridge Tower, go to your right to the tiny square Dražickeho námĕsti. At No. 12 you'll find an interesting Renaissance house, **At the Three Ostriches.** Stop in for a bite in the restaurant, where you can admire authentic seventeenth-century beams. Here Prague's first café opened in 1714. Cross over to the Mostecká ulice (Bridge Street), which used to be part of "Coronation Way" leading to the castle. Admire some of its splendidly restored baroque houses, notably Nos. 1, 15, and 16. Now turn left on the Lázeňská ulice (Bath Street) and glance at No. 6, which used to be a famous hotel. Among its noted guests were Peter the Great and the French writer Chateaubriand. At No. 11 there's another former hotel, the Golden Unicorn, where Beethoven resided in 1796. Proceed to the striking church **Our Lady Below the Chain,** originally a Romanesque building but later rebuilt in the Gothic and baroque styles. It still retains its Gothic façade (open daily, 10:00–5:00).

Now continue to one of the picturesque little squares typical of the Little Quarter, **Maltézské náměsti (Malta Square).** Note the attractive group of statues depicting John the Baptist. After admiring the gracious façades (the Japanese and Dutch embassies are located here), head for the north end of the square where there's an old wine cellar, U Maliřů (Artist's Café), the best and one of the most expensive restaurants in Prague.

Proceed to your left to the **Velkopřevorské náměsti (Grand Prior's Square),** yet another quaint, peaceful spot in the heart of historic Prague. Magnificent baroque palaces line the square. Notice in particular No. 2, currently the site of the French Embassy.

Then take Hroznova ulice on the right to **Kampa Island,** separated from the Little Quarter by a branch of the Vltava, the Čertovka (Black Devil). Wander through this peaceful haven, a favorite of Sunday promenaders. Notice the rustic wooden Grand Prior's Mill, which once belonged to the Knights of Malta. It is the last of several mills on the Čertovka to survive and dates from the seventeenth century. As you stroll across the small island, you will notice some houses with amusing names, including the Golden Grape, the Golden Lions, and the White Boots, many sporting colorful house signs that illustrate the titles. From "The Venice of Prague" you can enjoy a striking view of the **Vltava River, Charles Bridge,** and the **Old Town.** At **Na Kampe,** No. 7, you'll find the smallest café in Prague, where you can enjoy a cool drink or a hot red wine laced with spices.

Walk south along the island until you reach Řični ulice, where you will notice a small Gothic church, **St. John's-at-the-Fishpond.** Now turn right into Karmelitská ulice, one of the oldest streets in the quarter, known for its elegant baroque palaces. (In the Little Quarter alone, there are over two hundred former palaces.) Stop to visit the **Maria de Victoria Church,** known primarily for the Spanish statue, the *Infant of Prague,* which is supposed to work miracles (open daily from 9:30–6:00). At No. 25, the **Vrtba Palace** has a remarkable terraced garden filled with interesting sculpture—it's considered the finest baroque garden in Europe. (At this writing, it is closed to the public for restoration.) Climb to the top of the palace for a dramatic view of **St. Nicholas Church,** with its belfry and turquoise cupola.

Continue along the Karmelitská until you arrive at Malostranské náměsti (Little Quarter Square), the heart of the Little Quarter. Dominated by St. Nicholas Church are a number of grandiose baroque palaces, notably the **Lichtenstein Palace** (No. 13), the **Smiřický residence** (No. 18), and the **Little Quarter Town Hall** (No. 21), with its late Renaissance façade and impressive door ornaments with the Prague coat of arms.

St. Nicholas Church (open daily, 9:00–4:30) is Prague's most stunning example of baroque art at its flowering. The huge ceiling fresco (among the largest in Europe) has been carefully restored. Notice particularly the golden statue of St. Nicholas on the altar. The church was constructed over a period of sixty years by the Jesuits, who wanted it to symbolize their rise to power and the supremacy of the Catholic Church. If you are ready for lunch, try U Mecenáše, a restaurant over four hundred years old. Its antique furniture, old weapons, and paintings create a romantic atmosphere.

Now take Tomášská ulice at the north of the square, stopping to admire yet another baroque house, **At the Golden Stag,** with a particularly lovely house sign. Then proceed to Valdštejnské náměsti (Waldstein Square).

Waldstein Palace, at No. 4, was built in honor of Gen. Albrecht von Waldstein (Wallenstein). He was a brilliant soldier who distinguished himself in the Thirty Years' War; ultimately, however, his unbridled ambition led him to betray the Emperor to Sweden.

Eventually, he was brutally assassinated by the Emperor's men. Late Renaissance touches mingle harmoniously with the overall baroque style. Dramatic ceiling frescoes depict Wallenstein as the God Mars. The nearby chapel is decorated with painting and sculpture representing St. Wenceslas, Czechoslovakia's patron saint. Today, it houses the Ministry of Culture.

Now go out into the garden where concerts and plays are given during the summer months. Sit down for a brief rest in this oasis of baroque greenery, punctuated with impressive statues—note in particular the Laocoön, the central figure in a group of bronze statues. Swedish soldiers took the original as war booty; these are twentieth-century copies. (Gardens open May–September, daily, 8:00–7:00.)

The other buildings on the square pale in comparison with the Waldstein Palace. You may, however, wish to stroll through the enchanting garden leading up to the Prague castle. Go to the **Kolovrat Palace,** at No. 10, where you'll find the entrance to the garden, landscaped in the Italian style and typical of the Little Quarter.

Return to Little Quarter Square via the Sněmovni ulice. Then turn right into Nerudova ulice, named after the nineteenth-century Czech poet Jan Neruda, who once lived at Nos. 44 and 47. At No. 46, drop in to admire the antiques. You may find a piece of jewelry to take home. This street is considered one of the finest in Prague, and is noted for its unusual house signs, some of which date back as far as the fourteenth century. They were chosen to reflect the owner's profession or character; among the more amusing ones are the Two Suns (No. 47) and the Three Violins (No. 12). Both houses have been turned into wine cellars. End your walk through the Little Quarter with a visit to one of these cozy establishments, where you can sip a glass of wine and enjoy a snack amid a friendly atmosphere and Old World charm.

To the Castle and Hradčany

The Pražský Hrad, or **Prague Castle,** a symbol of Czech history, dates back to the eleventh century, and has since undergone a number of reconstructions. Under Charles IV, the castle and its surroundings knew their most glorious hour, as the castle was transformed from a modest Romanesque villa to a royal palace. Damaged during the Hussite wars, it was rebuilt in the Gothic style in the late fifteenth century. The castle—vast, sprawling, awesome—towers over Prague and conveys a mystic, other-worldly quality. (Kafka captured its spirit perfectly in his classic novel *The Castle.*) Today it is the seat of the Czech government.

Take a taxi from the center of the city to the castle. It is worth an extended visit, and you would do well to take an English-language guided tour to help you find your way through the castle's mazes. You should spend some time in the **Art Gallery,** which contains remarkable paintings by Tintoretto, Titian, Veronese, and Rubens. Of course you'll want to linger in **St. Vitus's Cathedral,** an imposing Gothic construction and the largest church in Prague. Note especially **St. Wenceslas's Chapel,** decorated with jasper and amethyst, containing the tomb of the Czech patron saint. You may want to return to the cathedral one evening for a concert of religious music, then dine nearby at Vikárka, a famous restaurant immortalized in one of Jánaček's operas. Its Gothic cellar setting will delight you. (The castle is open May–October, daily except Monday, 9:00–6:00. The art gallery and cathedral are open daily except Monday, 9:00–4:00.)

Now you'll want to explore the Hradčany quarter. From the cathedral walk to Jiřske náměsti (George Square), past the George Basilica with its striking white towers. Next to the Basilica, take a moment to visit the remarkable St. George Gallery, specializing in primitive and Baroque Czech art (open daily except Monday, 10:00–5:00). Then take Jiřská ulice, and turn left on U Daliborky, which will lead you to one of the most charming streets in Prague, the Zlatá ulička, or Golden Lane. The intimate, cozy atmosphere contrasts strikingly with the austere castle looming above. Saunter along this winding, cobbled street and admire the toylike houses, painted in bright blue, green, and ocher. Flowers peek out from behind a pastel-painted gate; people stop to gossip in small groups. Legend has it that Golden Lane was once inhabited by alchemists, who tried to please the Emperor Rudolph II by promising to find the recipe for gold and, incidentally, the elixir of life.

Now cross over to the **Paradise Garden,** which overlooks the city. Walk through the garden until you reach Hradčanské náměsti, a square that has retained its medieval dimensions. Worth visiting is **Šternberk Palace,** at No. 15, housing Prague's **National Gallery,** where you may admire an impressive collection of Czech and European paintings (open daily except Monday, 9:00–5:00). Pause at No. 17, the **Archbishop's Palace,** known for its remarkable Gobelins tapestries. If you're interested in old weapons, you'll find a wealth of treasures at the **Schwarzenberg Palace,** at Nos. 1–2, which today is the **Military Historical Museum** (open daily except Monday, 9:00–5:00). Then why not pay a visit to a favorite Prague beer café, **U Labuti** (At the Swans') for a refreshing glass of Pilsen beer?

Now leave the square via the Kanovnickná ulice. Continue along Nový Svět (New World Street), which used to be the poor quarter of Prague. You'll enjoy wandering among the clusters of simple, rustic houses, now splendidly restored—most of them are owned by artists. Perhaps it's time to stop for lunch. Try a wine cellar patronized by natives, **U Zlaté hrušky (The Golden Pear)** at Nový Svět 3.

Return to the Hradčanské námĕsti and take the Loretánská ulice. At No. 1, stop to admire the Renaissance **Hradčin Town Hall,** which used to be the administrative center of the royal town Hradčany. Note the imperial coat of arms on its façade. You'll pass the **Hrzán Palace** at No. 9, a recently renovated baroque house, which today is used for official receptions.

Now you arrive at Loretánské námĕsti, one of the most beautiful, spacious squares you'll see in Prague. Particularly noteworthy is the **Černin Palace,** (today the **Ministry of Foreign Affairs**) at No. 3, which has a small but lovely garden in the back, open to tourists. Just opposite is the **Prague Loretto** (open daily, 9:00–5:30), a pearl of baroque architecture containing the Santa Casa, an exact replica of the chapel in the Italian town Loretto which, according to an old legend, was the home of the Virgin Mary. The Loretto is famous for its treasures—in particular the Diamond Monstrance, a late seventeenth-century Viennese work, studded with 6,222 diamonds. The Loretto carillon in the belfry plays hourly.

Now leave the square via Pohořelec ulice and continue until you reach the **Strahov Monastery.** Founded in 1140, it houses the **Museum of Czech Literature.** The Strahov Library collection is famous for its many rare illuminated manuscripts (open daily 9:00–5:00). Wander through the adjoining gardens and enjoy the panoramic view.

Then take a taxi to Václavské námĕsti (Wenceslas Square), the commercial center of modern Prague, where you'll find shops featuring fine Czech garnets and crystal. Try the jewelry shop at No. 53 or the boutique **Krystal** at No. 30. It is appropriate to end your visit to Prague on this historic square, which used to be a horse market. Under the former régime, annual demonstrations took place and the Velvet Revolution originated here.

15.
Budapest

THE PARIS OF CENTRAL EUROPE

In the Hills of Buda

Budapest has an exotic, almost oriental flavor all its own. It has been occupied by Celts, Huns, Romans, Mongols and Turks, Austrians, Germans, and until recently, Russians. Budapest is, today, both familiar and different. Its wide avenues and chic cafés justify its nickname, "the Paris of Central Europe."

When the Iron Curtain collapsed in 1989, Budapest began to flourish: literary cafés and rock groups abound; shops offer luxury wares worthy of Paris or Rome; and despite a still fragile economy, Budapest is a cheerful, romantic city.

During your first walk you will visit Matthew's Cathedral, the Royal Palace, and Mount Gellért. Your starting point is the Lánchíd (Bridge of Chains), the first of eight bridges linking Buda to Pest on the left bank of the Danube. Destroyed during World War II, it was reconstructed in 1948. When you arrive at Adam Clark tér, take the funicular at the left of the tunnel, then turn right to **Dísz tér.** (Open daily, 8:30 A.M.–9:00 P.M.) Turn right into Tárnok utca, where, at No. 18, you'll pass the **Pharmacy Museum** with its antique instruments dating from the Middle Ages. (Open daily except Monday, 10:00–6:00.) Take a peek at the tiny passageway Balta Köz and its enchanting old houses brightened by flowering window boxes.

Now you face Szentháromság tér, and on your right you will come to Matthew's Cathedral, one of the most beautiful in Central Europe. Named after King Matthew, it was transformed into a mosque during the Turkish occupation and was restored in the nineteenth century. On your left notice the eighteenth-century Béla Tower and on your right, the Gothic-style Matthew Bell. Be sure to visit the **Loretta Chapel** with its lovely black Madonna, the Trinity Chapel, and the crypt, today a museum of religious art. (Open April–September, daily, 8:30–8:30; October–March, 9:00–7:00.)

Behind the Cathedral, observe the Roman-style Fisherman's Fort, never intended to defend Buda, but to round off the square. Pause a moment to take in the breathtaking view of the Danube and the Pest rooftops.

A couple of steps from the Cathedral, on Hess András tér, is the controversial **Budapest Hilton,** parts of which are over five hundred years old. Completed in 1977, it incorporates the cloister and the nave of the medieval St. Nicholas Church. Next to the Hilton, in the eighteenth-century Nicholas Tower, is the charming **Halászbástya** restaurant offering spicy Hungarian dishes and traditional gypsy music.

On the corner of the square and Szentháromság utca, you'll pass the old **Town Hall,** built in the baroque style. The statue in the corner represents the goddess Athena, holding the Buda coat of arms. On the eastern wing of the chapel note the Bell Tower. Now you may be ready for a luscious Hungarian pastry. Try the cozy, Viennese-style tearoom **Ruszwurm,** at No. 7, Szentháromság utca.

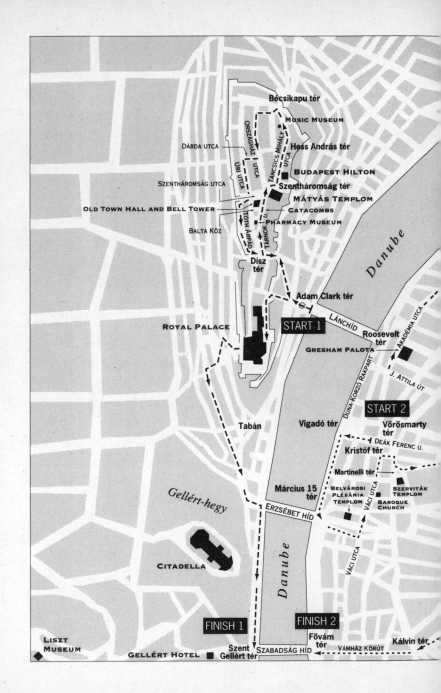

Bécsikapu tér

MUSIC MUSEUM

DÁRDA UTCA

ORSZÁGHÁZ UTCA

ÚRI UTCA

TÁNCSICS MIHÁLY UTCA

Hess András tér

BUDAPEST HILTON

SZENTHÁROMSÁG UTCA

Szentháromság tér

MÁTYÁS TEMPLOM

OLD TOWN HALL AND BELL TOWER

CATACOMBS

PHARMACY MUSEUM

TÓTH ÁRPÁD

TÁRNOK U.

BALTA KÖZ

Dísz tér

Ádám Clark tér

LÁNCHÍD

ROYAL PALACE

START 1

Roosevelt tér

GRESHAM PALOTA

AKADÉMIA UTCA

DUNA-KORZÓ RAKPART

J. ATTILA ÚT

START 2

Tabán

Vigadó tér

Vörösmarty tér

DEÁK FERENC U.

Kristóf tér

Martinelli tér

SZERVITÁK TEMPLOM

Március 15 tér

BELVÁROSI PLÉBÁNIA TEMPLOM

VÁCI UTCA

BAROQUE CHURCH

Gellért-hegy

ERZSÉBET HÍD

Danube

CITADELLA

VÁCI UTCA

FINISH 1

FINISH 2

LISZT MUSEUM

GELLÉRT HOTEL

Szent Gellért tér

SZABADSÁG HÍD

Fővám tér

VÁMHÁZ KÖRÚT

Kálvin tér

Danube

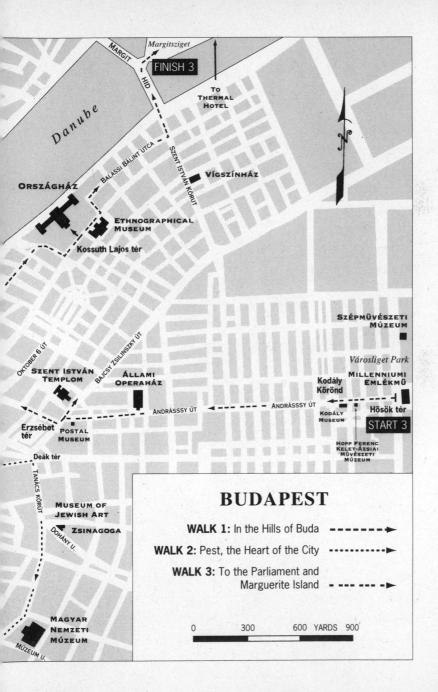

MARGIT

Margitsziget

FINISH 3

To
THERMAL
HOTEL

Danube

N

BALASSI BÁLINT UTCA

SZENT ISTVÁN KÖRÚT

VÍGSZÍNHÁZ

ORSZÁGHÁZ

ETHNOGRAPHICAL
MUSEUM

Kossuth Lajos tér

SZÉPMÜVÉSZETI
MÚZEUM

OKTÓBER 6 ÚT

SZENT ISTVÁN
TEMPLOM

BAJCSY ZSILINSZKY ÚT

ÁLLAMI
OPERAHÁZ

Városliget Park

Kodály
Körönd

MILLENNIUMI
EMLÉKMÜ

ANDRÁSSY ÚT

ANDRÁSSY ÚT

KODÁLY
MUSEUM

Hősök tér

START 3

Erzsébet
tér

POSTAL
MUSEUM

HOPP FERENC
KELET-ÁZSIAI
MÜVÉSZETI
MÚZEUM

Deák tér

TANÁCS KÖRÚT

MUSEUM OF
JEWISH ART

ZSINAGOGA

DOHÁNY U.

MAGYAR
NEMZETI
MÚZEUM

MÚZEUM U.

BUDAPEST

WALK 1: In the Hills of Buda ------▶

WALK 2: Pest, the Heart of the City ••••••••▶

WALK 3: To the Parliament and
Marguerite Island - --- --- -▶

0   300   600   YARDS   900

Proceed to Hess András tér, the square adjacent to Szenthárom-ság Square. At No. 3, stop to admire the three medieval houses grouped together in the eighteenth century, when it was an inn (the Vörös Sün Ételbár, or the Red Porcupine). For over two hundred years it was the Old Town's only inn, where balls, feasts, and the-atrical productions were held. Its windows are pure Gothic and the Gothic doors open to a room with four cross vaults. In 1810 it was reconstructed and acquired a neoclassic façade. You'll be amused by the red porcupine in relief on the parapet of the middle window. At No. 4 have a glass of Tokay wine in the Gothic cellar of the ele-gant **Fortuna** restaurant.

Cross the square and take the second street to your left, Táncsics Mihály utca, part of the former Jewish quarter. The Hungarian freedom fighter in the 1848 revolution, Kossuth, was once impris-oned in No. 9, and Beethoven resided at No. 7. Today, this baroque-style house is the **Music Museum.** It belongs to the Hun-garian Academy of Science, and music lovers will be fascinated by the old instruments, musical scores, and books in all languages on the history of music. In the basement, there's a splendid auditorium where concerts are given. (Open April–mid-November, Monday, 4:00–9:00; Wednesday–Sunday, 10:00–6:00; November–March, Monday, 3:00–6:00; Wednesday–Sunday, 10:00–5:00.)

Follow Táncsics Mihály utca until you reach Bécsikapu (the Vi-enna Gate). In medieval times this was the site of Buda's Saturday market. Behind the statue of Kazinczy, a famous nineteenth-century Hungarian poet, you will come upon a striking group of houses. Initially built in the Middle Ages, they were totally reconstructed in the eighteenth century. On the corner of the square is the Protes-tant Church, where you can attend evening concerts in the summer. From the Vienna Gate, the view of Buda is magnificent, especially at sunset. The garden below, on your right, called the European

Woods, is full of trees planted by the mayors of European capitals in honor of Budapest's centenary.

To the left of the Vienna Gate, pass the National Archives until you reach Országház utca, lined with beautiful medieval façades— notice in particular No. 20. Turn left, then take the Dárda utca until you turn left on Úri utca where baroque façades have replaced the original medieval ones, except for No. 31 with a miraculously preserved Gothic façade. At No. 33–35 you'll pass a fourteenth-century convent with Gothic windows.

From Úri utca, turn right on Szentháromság utca until you reach Tóth Árpád. For a pleasant stroll leading you back to Dísz tér, follow the ramparts on the western side of the hill until you reach the **Royal Palace** (open daily, except Monday, 10:00–6:00). Totally destroyed during the siege of 1686, it was reconstructed in 1770 in the baroque style and burned down at the end of World War II. Once again it was rebuilt in the postwar period to house museums, galleries, and the National Library.

The **Hungarian National Gallery** (open daily, except Monday, 10:00–6:00) hosts concerts every Sunday morning at 11:00. The Gallery looks out on the Danube and has an impressive art collection, notably of the Gothic period and of nineteenth-century Hungarian artists such as Mihály Munkácsy, Pal Szinyei Merse, and Károly Ferenczy. Stop to contemplate the dreamy landscapes of Tivadar Csontváry Kosztka, one of Hungary's most remarkable artists. Climb up to the cupola for a fine view of the river and Pest.

Now enter the palace's inner courtyard, via the Lion's Door, to reach the Library (open daily, except Monday, 10:00–6:00). Totally restored in 1970, it contains ancient manuscripts and over two million books. **The Museum of the History of Budapest** (open daily except Monday, 10:00–6:00), opposite the Lion's Door, has permanent exhibits on the history of the city. You will admire antique furniture, jewelry, and paintings as well as splendid Renaissance and Gothic rooms containing fragments of fourteenth- and fifteenth-century sculpture, including some superb heads discovered in the 1970s.

When you leave the Library, turn right until you reach the Ferdinand door near the Buzogány Tower, leading to Tabán, the southern side of the hill and a beautifully kept park. As you head for Elizabeth Bridge, you'll note on your right a restaurant, *The Golden Stag,* where gourmet Hungarians go for a luxury dinner. At the bottom of the hill, to the right of Elizabeth Bridge, are the delightful **Rudas baths,** typical of Turkish architecture, with its octagonal pool and glass-encrusted dome.

At Elizabeth Bridge, turn right on Szent Gellért tér and head for the **Gellért Hotel,** built in the Art Nouveau style. Its thermal baths are world-famous. You may want to end your first walk in Budapest with a well-deserved swim in the pool.

Pest, the Heart of the City

Start your second walk through the liveliest part of town at Vörösmarty tér. You may want to have breakfast at **Gerbeaud,** the famous 150-year-old tea shop with its elegant velvet-covered walls and marble tables. The pastries are a delight. At No. 1 of the square, stop by **Hungaroton,** where you can find inexpensive and excellent compact discs of Liszt, Bartók, and gypsy music.

Take the Deák Ferenc utca (to the right of Hungaroton) to Vigadó tér and the **Concert Hall,** where Liszt and Brahms used to perform. Destroyed during the last war and totally reconstructed, it reopened to the public in 1980. Try to attend a concert during your stay.

Walk south to the Quay Duna-Korzó, a favorite haunt of Hungarians. You pass the Marriott Hotel, then come to the **Catholic Church.** Built in the eighteenth century, its rococo façade was rebuilt a century later. (Services Saturday, 6:00 P.M.; Sunday, 10:00 A.M.) Continue south and follow the Danube until you reach **Március 15 tér.** On this square, which commemorates the 1848 revolution, you'll discover the ruins of a Roman fort. The Parish Church of the City, on the same square, was initially conceived in the Roman style. Subsequently, it was rebuilt in the Gothic manner, then changed into a mosque by the Turks. Destroyed by a fire in the eighteenth century, it was once again reconstructed, this time in the baroque style.

Cross the square and take the Váci utca on your left. This pedestrian island is famous for its elegance—and its high prices. At the **Folkart Centrum** (No. 14) you'll want to browse and perhaps purchase embroidered table linen or some colorful Hungarian pottery. Books are relatively inexpensive—try **Stúdium** at No. 22. The **Pest theater** at No. 9 used to be an inn. Note the interesting façade of No. 11. The **Hotel Taverna** has become a meeting place for "in" young people. But you haven't come to culinary-conscious Budapest for fast food!

Turn right on Kristóf tér to **Martinelli tér,** which formerly was an open market and today is one of the busiest squares in Pest. Take a moment to visit the **Szerviták Church** with its unusual baroque interior. Then keep to your right until you arrive at Tanács Boulevard. Turn right again until you arrive at the corner of Dohány utca and the **Budapest Synagogue,** one of the largest in Europe. Built in the nineteenth century by the Viennese architect Ludwig Forster, its two towers, 140 feet high, will remind you of Moorish minarets. To the left of the main entrance is the splendid **Museum of Jewish Art** (open April–October, Monday and Thursday, 2:00–6:00; Tuesday and Friday, 10:00–1:00). One of the rooms is devoted to honoring the memory of Holocaust victims.

When you leave the Synagogue return to Tanács Boulevard, which becomes the Múzeum Boulevard. At No. 13 wander into Budapest's oldest bookshop, **Központi,** offering antiquarian books from all over Europe. Take a peek at the courtyards of Nos. 17 and 21, where you can admire some remarkable remains of the medieval wall that used to surround Pest. Soon you'll arrive at the **Hungarian National Museum,** a large neoclassic building (open daily, except Monday, 10:00–6:00). The prehistoric and Roman periods are well represented; particularly impressive are the crown jewels, notably St. Stephen's crown, which disappeared during the Nazi occupation and was relocated in Germany by American scholars. The United States returned this national symbol to Hungary in 1978.

Cross Kálvin tér and then take Vámház Boulevard to Fövám tér, near Liberty Bridge and the Budapest market. This amazing covered market with its nineteenth-century metallic structure, reminiscent of the old Paris "Les Halles," displays a colorful variety of vegetables, fish, and famous Hungarian spices. Why not purchase some authentic Hungarian paprika to take home?

To the Parliament and Marguerite Island

Begin your walk at Hösök tér, or Hero's Square, in front of the **Városliget Park.** You'll want to return there some evening for dinner at the **Gundel,** the Maxim's of Budapest in a bucolic setting.

The huge square, site of political demonstrations and Labor Day parades, with its Millennium Column commemorating the arrival of the Magyars in Hungary, honors national heroes from Saint

Stephen to Kossuth. To the left is the **Fine Arts Museum,** one of the most interesting in Central Europe (open daily, except Monday, 10:00–6:00). You should not miss the exquisite collection of Italian art, including works by Titian, Raphael, and Tiepolo. The Flemish school is also well represented by Rubens, Rembrandt, and van Dyck. Don't miss the exceptional Grecos and Goyas, the finest outside Spain. The gallery of modern art emphasizes the Impressionist school. When you leave the Museum take the vast tree-lined Andrássy ut, connecting Hero Square to the center of Pest. You will pass several majestic embassies and at No. 103 the **Far East Museum.** (Open daily, except Monday, 10:00–6:00.) Its collection of vases, jewelry, and artifacts from China and Japan were donated to the Hungarian state by the private collector Ferenc Hopp. At Nos. 87–89 Andrássy ut do not miss the **Kodály Zoltan Museum and Archives.** Kodály was a major twentieth-century composer and a contemporary of Bartók. The Museum includes his apartment, furnished as it was when he lived there, with the grand piano on which he composed and played for friends and famous visitors such as Casals, Menuhin, and Stokowski. There is also a concert hall where you may wish to listen to Hungarian music. (Open daily, except Monday, 10:00–6:00.)

Cross Kodály Körönd and continue along this elegant avenue to admire the Italian-style palaces. Now you will be ready for a Hungarian pastry and coffee, served with old-world charm at **Lukács,** whose Art Nouveau setting will enchant you. Continue along the avenue until you reach the **Liszt Museum and Concert Hall** (the entrance is on the corner of the Boulevard and Vörösmarty 35). Renovated a few years ago, the Liszt Museum offers a permanent exhibit of Liszt's furniture, instruments, and musical scores. Formerly the Conservatory of Music, which Liszt founded, he taught here at the end of the last century. Today, concerts are given regularly, emphasizing the music of Hungary's most celebrated composer. (Open daily, except Monday, 10:00–6:00.) Continue until you reach **the Opera** at No. 22. Similar to the Vienna Opera, it was entirely refurbished in 1984 and has a repertory of nearly ninety operas. You can almost always get seats for a performance the same evening.

You'll want to visit the **Postal Museum** at No. 3, interesting primarily because it's in a private nineteenth-century apartment house, allowing you to imagine what the romantic atmosphere of historic Budapest must have been like. (Open daily, except Monday, 10:00–6:00.)

Continue along Andrássy út, then turn right until you reach the wide Bajcsy Zsilinszky út, named after a Resistance leader executed during the last war, and lined with impressive nineteenth-century villas. On your left you come to **St. Stephen's Basilica,** the largest in Budapest, which has a curiously doomed history. Begun in the mid-nineteenth century, its construction by the Hungarian architect Hild was interrupted when the cupola collapsed. After Hild's death another architect took over, but he did not survive to complete the construction. The third architect to tackle this task, Josef Kanser, finally finished the Basilica in 1906! The central dome, 315 feet high with two towers, has quite an overwhelming effect. The interior is sumptuously decorated with ornate sculptures of Hungarian saints. The cupola's mosaics originally came from Venice.

When you leave the Basilica, retrace your steps on Bajcsy Zsilinszky út until you get to J. Attila út, leading you to Erzsébet tér, a square that used to be a cemetery in the Middle Ages. On the corner of J. Attila út and Oktober 6 út, notice the well-preserved nineteenth-century house. Look at the courtyard with its ancient well and wrought-iron staircase.

Continue on J. Attila út until Roosevelt tér, near Chain Bridge.

Opposite the bridge is the Gresham palace, a striking example of early twentieth-century architecture. The Renaissance-style **Academy of Science** dominates the square.

To the right of the Academy, take the Akadémia utca until you reach **Kossuth Lajos tér,** easily one of the most impressive squares in Budapest. It measures 700 square feet and in the middle of the square is a flagpole raising the Hungarian flag on national holidays. At No. 12 you'll discover the **Ethnographical Museum,** with its permanent exhibit of daily life in Hungary from the late eighteenth century to the end of World War I. Its thirteen galleries contain artifacts, folk costumes, and tools reflecting the varied landscapes, as well as the ethnic, religious, and social diversity of the Hungarian people. Particularly interesting are the reconstructed houses from southwestern Hungary showing what medieval life was like, and a complete bride's trousseau from the middle of the last century. (Open daily, except Monday, 10:00–6:00.)

Facing the Danube is the **Hungarian Parliament;** Byzantine, Roman, and oriental styles mingle harmoniously in this imposing building, which took twenty years to construct. Depending on the angle, it will remind you of Notre Dame in Paris or of the British Parliament. Its twenty-seven doors, twenty-nine staircases, and ten courtyards all contribute to the impression of grandeur. When Parliament is in session, it is closed to the public. At other times, only groups are allowed inside. You should contact a Hungarian tourist agency or your hotel concierge for more information.

When leaving Parliament, take Balassi Bálint utca on your right, parallel to the Danube, until you reach Szent Istvan Körut. Notice the nineteenth-century Vigszinház Theater, which has recently been carefully restored.

Here you can take Tram No. 4 or No. 6 going to **Marguerite Island.** Over a mile long and closed to traffic, this haven of peace can best be explored on foot. Wander through the rose gardens or sunbathe on the beach to enjoy this spacious park in the middle of Budapest. You'll want to visit the **Thermal Hotel** with its view of the park and the Danube. Here you can play a game of tennis or "take the baths" as the Hungarians do for their aches and pains.

The island is named after Saint Margit, the heroic daughter of Béla IV, who chose to spend most of her brief, sad life in a convent—the ruins still exist today. Particularly in summer, Marguerite Island is a delightful mini-paradise where you can attend open-air concerts or simply relax over a glass of *Barack* (apricot brandy) in a fairytale setting.

To conclude your visit to Budapest, have dinner on one of the boats touring the Danube, and admire the illuminated bridges, palaces, and churches you have visited on your walks. For information and reservations, contact Tourinform, Budapest 5, Sütö utca 2 (near the Deák Square metro station).

16.
Munich

ART, MUSIC, AND BEER

Within the Sound of the Glockenspiel

Munich, more than any other German city, will impress you as one of Europe's leading centers of art and culture. As you walk through this city of more than 1.3 million people, you will be struck by its beautifully laid out, spacious streets and squares, its attractively landscaped parks and gardens, and its classic atmosphere. Despite tremendous war destruction and subsequent rebuilding, Munich has preserved its prewar, old-world elegance and kept its appeal for those who love painting, music, and learning. Its cultural reputation is maintained by its renowned **university** with more than sixty thousand students and its magnificent **art galleries** and **museums.** And, on the lighter side, its open-air **beer gardens** are unmatched in their ability to spread a sense of relaxation and good fellowship, especially on warm summer evenings.

Your first walk in Munich should be in the **older section.** Start in the morning at **Max-Joseph-Platz** and walk past the **National Theater,** the home of the Bavarian State Opera, and a block or so along

Maximilian Strasse until you reach Am Kosttor on the right. Turn down here about a hundred yards and you will come to a little square known as the **Platzl.** On your left is the typically nineteenth-century building of the famous **Hofbräuhaus** or court brewery, owned by the State of Bavaria. You will want to return here in the evening for a stein or two of *Helles* or *Dunkels* either in the great banquet hall upstairs, where you will be entertained by a lively brass band, or in the more plebeian beer hall on the ground floor. Over four million people visit the Hofbräuhaus every year and consume about forty thousand pints a day of the famous beer.

Just across the street is the **Platzl.** This is a lively restaurant featuring typical Bavarian singing and dancing—an exciting spot for an evening's entertainment. Continue along Orlando Strasse past the Hofbräuhaus one block to Lederer Strasse, where you turn right, cross Sparkassen Strasse, and go through an archway. Now wander into the **Alter Hof,** the ancient residence of the dukes of Bavaria, which dates from the thirteenth and fifteenth centuries. Its old-fashioned courtyard, with the only surviving towered Gothic building, still retains its historic atmosphere, and has recently been restored.

From the Alter Hof saunter along **Burg Strasse,** one of Munich's most ancient streets. In a moment you will come to Munich's oldest house in **No. 5.** Inside the Gothic entrance you will find the **Weinstadl,** a charming wine inn, where huge wine casks add color to the tavern's original furnishings. Another interesting house is **No. 11,** where the great rococo architect François de Cuvilliès lived. Burg Strasse, probably more than any street you will see in Munich, conveys the flavor of the city's early history.

Turn right at the end into **Marienplatz,** named after the Virgin Mary, in whose honor Maximilian I erected the red marble statue in the center of the square. In the heart of Munich this busy square boasts an underground shopping center. You'll see that it's a favorite meeting place because of its lively cafés and restaurants. If you started your stroll in the morning, you should reach the new (1867–1908) City Hall in time to see the entertaining performance of its **musical clock,** a famed Munich attraction, which children particularly find a great treat. At 11:00, after the hour strikes, colorful figures appear: knights jousting as in a tournament and dancers performing to melodious chimes. Every day, crowds of people congregate in the square to enjoy this spectacle. Take a moment to visit the **Prunkhof,** a beautifully decorated courtyard with an impressive staircase. In the summer, the **Ratskeller** restaurant installs a terrace café here.

From this point stroll beyond the square into **Kaufinger Strasse,** one of Munich's most popular shopping streets, now a pedestrian zone. At the second block turn right a few yards to get to the **Frauenkirche,** the city's most famous and popular church, built in the Late Gothic style some five hundred years ago. The massive twin red-brick steeples (328 feet high), topped by copper "onion-bulbs," have been for centuries a Munich landmark, just as they were a symbol of the wealth of the burghers who built them in the fifteenth century. Although the church's interior seems somewhat bare today as the result of heavy war damage, you will be impressed by the vastness of the nave and the height of the roof. An elevator in the south tower will carry you to the top, where in clear weather you can see the Alps. (Open April–October, except Sunday and holidays, 10:00–5:00.)

Returning to Kaufinger Strasse, walk along a little farther to **St. Michael's Church,** an excellent example of German Renaissance architecture and a symbol of the influence of the Jesuits in the late sixteenth century (open May–October, Monday–Friday, 10:00–1:00; closed Sunday and holidays). Cross the street and do a bit of window-shopping on your way back to Marienplatz. Then take a sharp right in the Rosen Strasse, continue in the narrow Pettenbeck

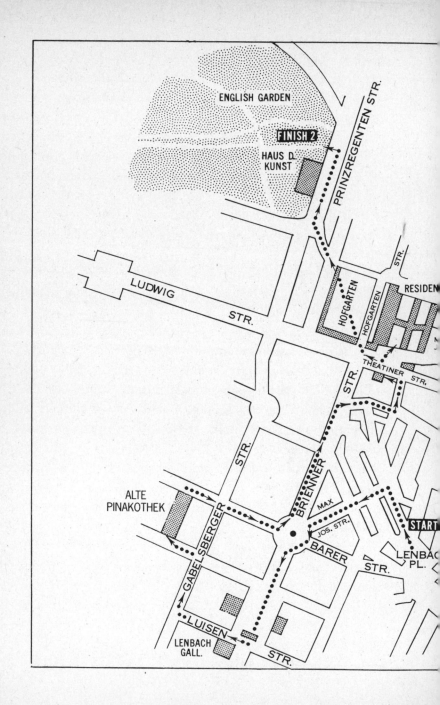

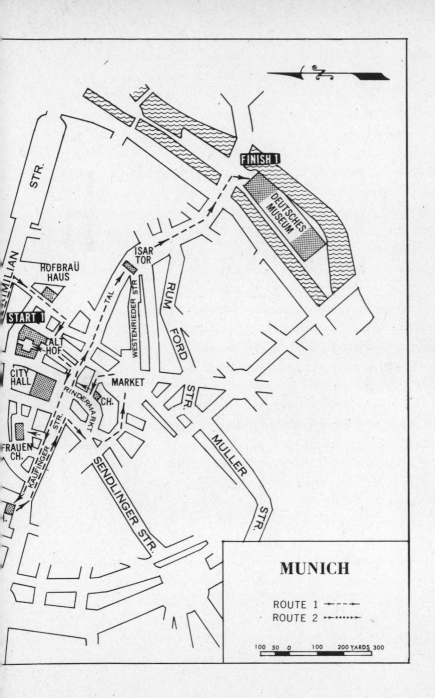

STR.

FINISH 1

DEUTSCHES
MUSEUM

MAXIMILIAN STR.

HOFBRAÜ
HAUS

ISAR
TOR

START 1

TAL

WESTENRIEDER STR.

RUM
FORD

ALT
HOF

CITY
HALL

RINDERMARKT

MARKET

CH.

STR.

STR.

MULLER

FRAUEN
CH.

KAUFINGER

SENDLINGER STR.

STR.

MUNICH

ROUTE 1 •—•—•—•→
ROUTE 2 •••••••••→

100 50 0   100   200 YARDS 300

Strasse, and make a left turn into Rosental. This will bring you into the Viktualienmarkt or **food market**—a most interesting and colorful sight. Here you will find dozens of open stalls displaying all kinds of provisions. In one corner of the square is the fish market, with live fish swimming about in huge tanks of water. Prices for trout, eels, and so forth are chalked up on a blackboard. Not far away is the vegetable section ("Munich's quality vegetables fresh daily"), where potatoes are separated according to size and quality. Across the road you will find the egg and fruit markets. Each stand is fascinating not only for the variety of products but for the attractive manner in which they are presented for sale. There is a real country touch in the market. And, indeed, many of the vendors are farmers. Nearby you will find a great variety of flowers, and just opposite there are stands selling all kinds of dried fruits, cheese, nuts, and bottled jams. Great tubs are full of different sorts of pickles and raw sauerkraut. At the **Bratwurstglöckl** you can try a *weisswurst,* a favorite sausage among Müncheners.

The three monuments in the form of a fountain were erected in 1953, in honor of three Munich musicians, and are kept covered with flowers by the people of Munich.

Just a block away you will see the cupola of **Peterskirche,** the oldest parish church, which dates from the middle of the eleventh century (1050) and was reconstructed after World War II. Climb the tower, called *Alte Peter,* (Old Peter) for a breathtaking view of the city. (Open Monday–Friday, 9:00–6:00; Saturday, 8:30–6:00; Sunday, 10:00–6:00.) A few steps beyond the church will bring you back to Marienplatz. Now turn right, and on the far left side of the square you will see the surviving part of the Old Town Hall, the **Alte Rathaus.** The building stands astride the main street. Completely restored, in the Gothic style, its tower houses the **Toy Museum** (open Monday–Saturday, 10:00–5:30; Sunday and holidays,

10:00–6:00). You can admire wooden figurines, locomotives, doll-houses, castles, and carousels, as well as the most sophisticated electronic games. Traffic moves from Marienplatz to the Tal under vaulted archways. Walk down the Tal and in a block or two turn around for a fine view of the towers of the Frauenkirche. Shortly you will come to the **Isartor,** the only old gate to the city whose main towers are still standing. Although built in 1314, it was reno-vated and a fresco was added early in the nineteenth century.

You continue through the **Isar Tor Platz** and along Zweibrücken Strasse to the **Isar River.** Cross the first bridge (Ludwigsbrücke), and on your right is the **Deutsches Museum,** one of the greatest sci-entific museums in the world, specializing in the development of technology in industry. For the layman the great attraction of this museum is the remarkable way in which the exhibits demonstrate the operations of modern industry. For example, you visit a coal mine perfectly reproduced in life size. Not far away you stand on the bridge of a ship facing a scene in Hamburg Harbor. Scale mod-els of power stations and steel mills show exactly how they func-tion. Many of the experimental models can be operated by pushing a button. In addition, the museum contains one of the greatest col-lections anywhere of original scientific apparati and technical ma-chinery. No visitor to Munich should fail to spend a considerable time in the Deutsches Museum, and for children it is an eye-opening educational experience. (Open 9:00–5:00; closed holi-days.) You can have lunch in the excellent Museum restaurant.

Alte Pinakothek and the English Garden

The second walk through Munich covers mainly the newer and more spacious section of the city, whose planning was largely influenced by King Ludwig I of Bavaria (1825–48), a devotee of the classic tradition. As you walk around this well-laid-out part of Munich, you will encounter a world-famous art gallery, the Alte Pinakothek, as well as the delightful English garden.

Begin at the **Lenbach Platz,** one of Munich's most attractive squares. At the far end, the decorative **Wittelsbach Fountain** (named for Bavaria's oldest ruling family), with its terraced design, creates a splendid effect. The adjoining square, **Maximilians Platz,** has such a quiet appealing air, with its trees and gardens, that you should walk through it before turning left on Max Joseph Strasse to **Karolinen Platz.** The tall obelisk in the center is a memorial to the Bavarian soldiers who died in the Russian campaign of 1812. **Amerika Haus,** the American Cultural Center, including a large library, stands on the left.

A block ahead along **Brienner Strasse** you come into the broad **Königs Platz,** a monument to King Ludwig I's passion for Hellenistic art. Here he tried to recreate the spirit of the Grecian period by constructing a neoclassic marble gateway based on the Propylaea in Athens. The **Glyptothek,** also in the Greek style, is on your right. It was restored in 1971, and currently houses the collection of the Gallery of Ancient Sculpture. Go past the Propylaea and on the corner of Luisen Strasse, on your right, you will come to the lovely **Villa Lenbach,** originally the home of the nineteenth-century German painter Franz von Lenbach. Now it houses the excellent **Municipal Modern Art Gallery** (open daily, except Monday and holidays, 10:00–6:00). The **Kandinsky collection** is outstanding, but you should also look around the other rooms in this rather intimate gallery. Outside the ocher-colored building there is an attractive garden with statuary and a fountain.

As you leave the Villa Lenbach, turn left on Luisen Strasse, walk one block and then turn right on Gabelsberger Strasse past the

Technische Hochschule, Munich's technical university, to the **Alte Pinakothek** (open daily except Monday, 9:00–4:30; Tuesday and Thursday, 7:00–9:00 P.M.). It is set back from the street facing a large lawn.

This magnificent **art collection,** the finest in Munich, is another of the great European galleries. It comprises all the leading schools of European art but is particularly distinguished for its masterpieces by Raphael, Titian, Dürer, Rembrandt, and Rubens. If you are an art lover, you will want to spend considerable time here, either now or later, viewing these wonderful paintings.

On leaving the Alte Pinakothek, take Barer Strasse for one block to return to Brienner Strasse at Karolinen Platz.

As you saunter along this street, you will pass many attractive and fashionable shops. In two blocks you will come to an open square, the end of Maximilians Platz. Now cross Brienner Strasse and take the street on the right that leads to Salvator Platz. On the other side of this small square you will be in **Kardinal Faulhaber Strasse.** Stop at No. 7 to view the ornate façade of the **archbishop's residence,** one of the most elegant private houses still standing in the city.

Next, retrace your steps a few yards and make your way through the arcades of one of Munich's typical postwar buildings to Theatiner Strasse. The use of arcades and passageways with stores on the inside as well as on the street is a hallmark of the architectural design of much of the city's recent business and shopping construction.

On **Theatiner Strasse** there are many luxury shops and delightful cafés. On your left in the next block toward Brienner Strasse you will come to the grand **Theatinerkirche,** the most imposing baroque church in the city. This huge yellow seventeenth-century edifice with the twin towers set the style for many of the baroque churches throughout Bavaria. Its white rococo interior, splendid ornamentation, and fine paintings create an impressive effect. When you stand in front of the church, you will see the **Feldherrnhalle** just to the right facing the large **Odeons Platz.** This is another creation of King Ludwig I and is copied from the Loggia dei Lanzi in Florence.

Now cross the square and enter the **Residenz,** before World War II the most luxurious group of buildings in Munich. It used to be the residence of the dukes (later kings) of Bavaria. Again, Ludwig I was responsible for much of this lavish palace, largely destroyed by air attacks during the war. Most of the rooms have been restored, and you can see many of the movable objects that were saved. Perhaps the most interesting museum is the **Treasure Room,** or Schatzkammer, which you enter from Max-Joseph Platz. (Open Tuesday–Sunday, 10:00–4:30; closed Monday.) Here is an unusual **collection of jewelry and silver,** including royal crowns, **gold work** from Charlemagne's period, Late Gothic and Early Renaissance **precious stones,** and a lovely **statuette of Saint George.**

The other exceptional building in the Residenz is the exquisitely restored **Cuvilliès Theater.** Today, it is a concert hall, where ballet and opera are also performed.

Return to Residenz Strasse, and at No. 1 you will find the theater's entrance, off a large oblong interior courtyard whose entire façade has been rebuilt in a baroque design. The theater's interior is one of the most enchanting examples of elaborate rococo style to be seen anywhere.

From the Residenz stroll along Odeons Platz for a hundred yards and turn right, opposite Brienner Strasse, into the pleasant **Hofgarten.** There are several cafés here where you can enjoy a drink by the flower gardens. While crossing to the far end of the Hofgarten, you should turn around for an interesting view of the towers of the

Theatinerkirche. The arcades surrounding the garden have been rebuilt. Here you can visit an art gallery or enjoy a drink at one of the several outdoor cafés. The large bombed-out building ahead of you, a block or so away, is the former **Army Museum.** When you emerge from the gardens, walk a short distance and make a half right onto Prinzregenten Strasse. At No. 3, you will find the **National Bavarian Museum** (open daily, except Monday, 9:30–5:00). Just across this broad street you will see the **Haus der Kunst,** or House of Art. The part of the building before you contains the permanent collection of the **Neue Pinakothek** and the **Neue Staatsgalerie,** with art from the nineteenth and twentieth centuries. The Neue Staatsgalerie is today one of Germany's major twentieth-century museums, and has been totally restored in 1991–1992. Among the artists exhibited are Picasso, Klee, Hartung, and Motherwell. Also represented are major artistic movements such as Fauvism, Expressionism, and the famous German "Blue Rider" school. (Open 9:00–4:30; Thursday, 7:00–9:00 P.M.; closed Monday and holidays.)

Just beyond the House of Art you can enter the **English Garden,** one of the most attractive and natural parks in any European city. The middle path along the canal is one of the pleasantest. The combination of fine trees, meandering walks, open meadows, waterfalls, and a lake, as well as a Chinese pagoda, makes this extensive park unusually appealing. At the **Chinese pagoda** you will find a café and restaurant. This park is just the place to wander or simply sit in a pleasant nook at the end of your day's walk.

17.
Geneva

The Old Town
Vistas and Courtyards

Geneva has been one of the crossroads of the world ever since Julius Caesar passed through it during his campaign against the Gauls in 58 B.C. Today, the city maintains this status, drawing diplomats to the **United Nations** and **International Labor Organization,** as well as international businesspeople and just ordinary tourists. For the visitor, Geneva has a special allure—it occupies a beautiful position at the end of Lake Geneva, it has a truly cosmopolitan air, and it has the attraction of a French-speaking community. On clear days, snow-covered **Mont Blanc** rises majestically in the distance, providing an exciting sight from the lakefront promenade.

Walking is by far the best way to see Geneva. It's not a large place; the population is only about 168,000. As you walk about the city, you sense its intimacy and small-town atmosphere. The **main shopping district** comprises only a few blocks on both sides of the river. The **promenade and parks** along the lakefront are most invit-

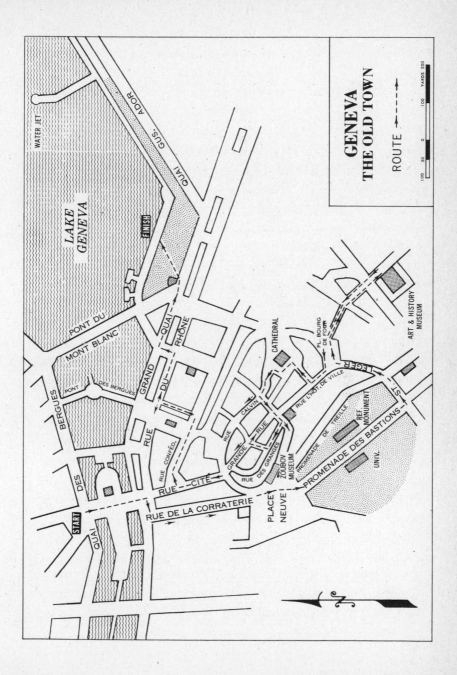

GENEVA
THE OLD TOWN

ROUTE

YARDS 200   100   0   50   100

WATER JET

LAKE
GENEVA

QUAI GUS ADOR

FINISH

PONT DU

MONT BLANC

PONT DES BERGUES

QUAI DU RHÔNE

GRAND RUE

CATHEDRAL

PL. BOURG
DE FOUR

ART & HISTORY
MUSEUM

BERGUES

RUE DES BERGUES

RUE CONFÉD.

RUE CALVIN

RUE

RUE L'HÔT-DE-VILLE

LÉGER ST.

RUE DES

RUE CITÉ

GRANDE RUE

RUE DES GRANGES

ZOUBOV
MUSEUM

PROMENADE DE TREILLE

REF.
MONUMENT

PROMENADE DES BASTIONS

UNIV.

START

QUAI

RUE DE LA CORRATERIE

PLACE
NEUVE

N

ing. In particular, the small, **old town** on the heights—the most appealing part of Geneva—just cannot be seen properly except on foot.

This is the section to visit first, so let us start in the morning at the **Place St. Gervais** and cross the bridge over the **Rhône,** which divides the city, to Rousseau Island in the middle. It is believed that this is the site of the first bridge over the Rhône, built even before the time of Caesar. There used to be a thirteenth-century castle here (later a prison), but all that remains is the tower with the clock—the **Tour del l'Île.** This is a historic spot for the liberty-loving Swiss, because here in 1519 Philibert Berthelier was beheaded for his defense of freedom. Wander around the little island with its attractive houses.

Cross to the other side of the stream, turn right into the Place Bel Air, and at its far side take the wide **Rue de la Corraterie.** After a few blocks along this busy thoroughfare you will reach the **Place Neuve,** Geneva's finest square. The **Musée Rath** on your right holds temporary art exhibits. (Open daily except Monday, 10:00–5:00; Wednesday, 7:00–9:00 P.M.) Just beyond it is the **Grand Théâtre,** a smaller edition of the Paris Opera.

On the opposite side of the square you come into a pleasant park, the **Promenade des Bastions,** with broad walks. Here, on your left, is the impressive **Reformation Monument,** separated from the gardens by a small moat and a fountain. The monument is actually built into the old wall, which the Reformers under John Calvin constructed as a defense of the city. The 100-yard-long memorial, dedicated in 1917, commemorates the great leaders of the Reformation. Larger-than-life statues of the four great Reformers, including Calvin and Knox, occupy the center of the monument. **Bas-reliefs** show the major events in this religious revolution that occurred in different countries. Americans will be interested in the **inscription from the Mayflower Compact,** carved in stone, and the scene depicting the **Pilgrim Fathers,** whose leader is clasping the Geneva Bible.

The buildings of the **University of Geneva** and its library stand back in the park on the opposite side from the Reformation Monument. The library exhibits ancient manuscripts and books on the Reformation, with a special section devoted to Jean-Jacques Rousseau. (Open daily except Saturday afternoon, Sunday, and holidays, 10:00–12:00 and 2:00–5:00.)

Leave the gardens at the gate beyond the monument, and turn left on **Rue St. Léger.** After passing below an archway, you will start to climb the hill to the old town. On either side of the winding street you will pass interesting old houses. Don't miss the decorative doorway at **No. 35.** You are now coming into the lower level of the **Place du Bourg-de-Four,** Geneva's most enchanting square. There is a tiny shaded garden just ahead below the wall that supports the upper part of the square. Many interesting shops line the street. Above them you will notice the signs of old inns that formerly stood here. The street veers to the left, circling the park, and leads you into the main square, with its eighteenth-century fountain. Pause for a few minutes and just look around. Five streets meet in this unspoiled **center of old Geneva,** which still preserves so much of the spirit of an earlier age. This was a crossroads in Roman days. The gray buildings, with their gables, uneven roofs, and chimney pots, will remind you of a corner of Paris. The antique shops and art galleries, many bursting from open cellars under acacia trees, add a Bohemian flavor to the spot. At No. 38 is an attractive bookshop, appropriately called "La Joie de Lire." Why not stop at the delightful café La Clémence on the corner facing the square and watch the life go by? There's an attractive clock on the wall just overhead, and it may indicate that it is late morning, just the time for an apéritif at an outdoor table behind the grillwork. You will probably find lots of students, artists, and local residents here, basking in the sun. Overhead, huge elms shade a side of the square. Before you leave this spot, teeming with local color, browse about the shops a bit. The bakery, pharmacy, hairdresser, and butcher all contribute to the animated scene.

From the square turn right into the Rue des Chaudronniers. In a block or so you will come to a large building on your right, the **Musée d'Art et d'Histoire** (open daily except Sunday and holidays, 10:00–5:00). Although the gallery includes ancient sculpture and decorative arts, you should concentrate on its painting collection on the first floor to see a good selection of Impressionists, as well as works by Corot and artists of the Italian and Dutch schools.

Return to the Place du Bourg-de-Four, and on the far side take the **Rue de l'Hôtel-de-Ville.** In a few yards turn right into the **Rue de la Taconnerie.** You will pass some attractive houses (note the heads in relief over the store at **No. 6**) before reaching the lovely little **Place de la Taconnerie** in the shade of a huge elm. At the left of the square, up a few steps, you will find a **statue of Jeremiah.**

The **Cathedral of St. Peter,** which dominates the square, was built between the tenth and thirteenth centuries on the site of a **Roman temple** and became a **Protestant church** in 1536 (open daily, except Monday, 10:00–1:00 and 2:00–6:00. In the summer you can attend a free organ concert every Saturday at 6 P.M.). The interior is rather simple, but one interesting relic is the chair said to have been used by John Calvin. If you feel so inclined, you can climb to the top of the tower for a wonderful panorama of Geneva, the lake, and the Alps. In any case, be sure to walk behind the cathedral to a terrace where you have quite a good view over the city. Opposite the front of the cathedral, and in the small square to the right, there are some beautiful **patrician houses.** The large one with masks on the façade was built in the style of Louis XIV by one of the architects responsible for Versailles. Follow the short Rue Otto Barblan away from the cathedral, then turn right at a little fountain, one of the oldest in Geneva and decorated with geranium pots, and immediately left into the **Rue Calvin.** There are several stately houses in this block—one of the most noted is **No. 9** where Madame de Staël lived. **Calvin's house,** at No. 11, was rebuilt early in the eighteenth century. Just pull open its wooden door to see the typical courtyard and façade of this fine building.

Now return to the entrance of the Rue Calvin and turn right on **Rue du Puits St. Pierre.** On your right, at No. 6, you pass the fifteenth-century **Maison Tavel** with its circular tower. This, the oldest building in Geneva, has been tastefully restored. Particularly worth seeing are the antiques and silverware on the second floor. (Open daily, except Monday, 10:00–5:00.) Just ahead at the next corner stands the ancient **Arsenal** with a few old cannon. It is the arcaded building with a wooden beam roof directly opposite Geneva's **Hôtel de Ville,** or Town Hall. Aside from a delightful courtyard, the most interesting feature of the Town Hall is the sixteenth-century inclined ramp with stone vaulting that leads to the upper floors. You can ask the doorkeeper to show you the **Alabama Room** where the first Red Cross convention was signed in 1864.

Continue beyond the Town Hall along the Rue Henri Fazy past the Tour Baudet—dating from 1455, where the **Geneva Council of State** meets—to the **Promenade de la Treille,** the oldest terrace in Geneva. This broad terrace, shaded by chestnut trees, commands a fine view of the mountains. Retrace your steps a few yards and turn left into the **Rue des Granges** for a glance at several of the magnificent mansions that overlook the Promenade de la Treille and the Place Neuve below. At No. 10 go through the alley and on to the terrace above the old city wall. The courtyard at No. 6 is also quite impressive. At No. 2, take a moment to visit the **Zoubov Collection,** in the Countess Zoubov's former apartment. Many objects come from China or Russia. In particular, note the splendid eighteenth-century French furniture and the sumptuous oriental rugs. (Guided tours Thursday at 6:00, and Saturday at 2:30 and 3:30.)

Take the Rue du Cheval Blanc from the Rue des Granges into the **Grande Rue,** probably the finest of these old streets. Jean Jacques Rousseau was born on June 28, 1712, at **No. 40,** which has since been rebuilt. You will get an idea of the hidden attractions of these houses if you enter Nos. 29–31 and go along the passage to an iron grilled gate, and then climb a few steps. Through a window you see a most picturesque courtyard in front of an ivy-covered Spanish-style house with a tile roof and balcony. The wooden stairs from the cobblestoned court, the gay flower boxes in the windows, and the statues in the flower beds make an unusually striking scene. At. No. 11, the **house of the French Resident,** Napoleon gave audiences when passing through the city in 1800. Today the Swiss Alpine Club has its headquarters here.

In the adjoining square, the **Place du Grand Mézel,** there is a charming fountain. From here continue down the hill into the Rue de la Cité, then turn right into the busy Rue de la Confédération. Just beyond the large church in the **Place de la Fusterie** you should turn left into an arcade, a lively **shopping center** with an enticing food shop and other tempting stores. Geneva's most up-to-date café and restaurant, **Mövenpick,** is in the Place de la Fusterie. It's an excellent place to enjoy anything from a *pâtisserie* or salad plate to a full-course meal at moderate prices. After leaving Mövenpick you turn right along the **Rue du Rhône,** a main shopping street. In a couple of blocks you will reach another of Geneva's old towers, in the **Place du Molard.** Walk a short block to the **Grand Quai** along the lake and cross over to the gardens. Here is Geneva's decorative

floral clock. As you end your stroll along the lakefront in this delightful park, you will see the **Jet d'Eau,** which from May to September hurls a stream of water nearly five hundred feet into the air. It is reputedly the world's highest fountain—a dramatic finish to this walk in old Geneva.

The Lakeshore
To the UN

The European headquarters of the **United Nations** is one of the principal sights in Geneva and well worth visiting. One way to get there is a delightful walk, mostly through parks along the lake, from the center of town, which should not take much more than an hour and a half.

If you take this walk to the UN immediately following the first walk, which ends at the lakefront promenade, you will enjoy crossing in one of the little launches that goes from the nearby quay to **Pâquis.** After landing, turn right along the broad walk along the **Quai du Mont Blanc.** On a clear day you have a magnificent view, through a soft bluish haze, of snow-covered Mont Blanc about one hundred miles away. Excursion boats leave the wharf for tours along the lake.

This stroll along the flower-bordered promenade, with the lake on your right, the hills of **Cologny** beyond, and the **Alps** in the distance, is probably the most dramatic in Geneva. The sailboats and small craft in the anchorage on the lakeshore add a scenic touch.

At the end of the Quai du Mont Blanc you veer to the left into the **Quai Woodrow Wilson** and soon pass the original building of the **League of Nations,** where a tablet commemorates President Wilson.

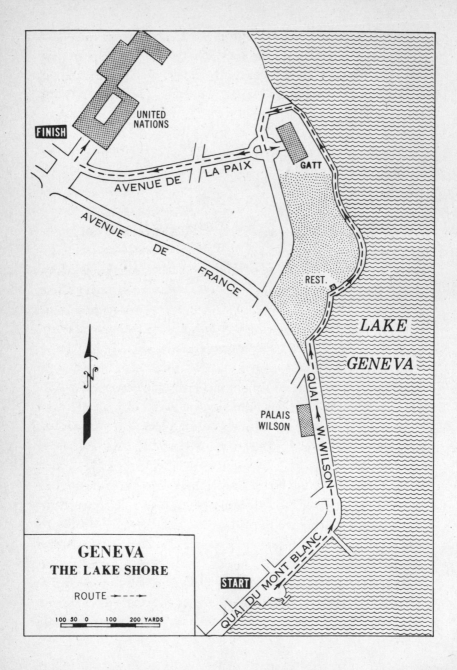

FINISH

UNITED
NATIONS

GATT

AVENUE DE LA PAIX

AVENUE DE FRANCE

REST.

LAKE

GENEVA

N

QUAI W. WILSON

PALAIS
WILSON

START

QUAI DU MONT BLANC

GENEVA
THE LAKE SHORE

ROUTE - - - ➤

100 50 0   100   200 YARDS

In a few minutes you will come to the large and beautifully kept park, **Mon Repos,** that runs along the lakefront. The **Perle du Lac** restaurant, a short distance farther on, is one of Geneva's best. It occupies a superb position overlooking the water to distant Mont Blanc. Keep on the path that skirts the lake and, after you pass a promontory from where you have a fine view, you will come to the building that used to house the **International Labor Office** before it moved, in 1973, to an ultramodern building on the Route des Morillons, where the International Bureau of Education also has its headquarters (open weekdays, 9:00–12:00 and 2:00–6:00). Today, this palace houses the General Agreement on Tariffs and Trade, **(GATT),** a special branch of the UN.

Cross the square in front of GATT into the interestingly land-scaped **Botanical Gardens,** and then take the **Avenue de la Paix** to the entrance of the **UN building** (open summer, 9:00–12:00; the rest of the year, 10:00–12:00 and 2:00–4:00; closed on weekends in winter). It is worthwhile to take the guided tour through this fine building, constructed in 1937 for the League of Nations, to see, in particular, the impressive **Political Council Room,** where major international conferences are held. The **terrace and gardens** overlooking the lake are especially attractive. Stroll down to the **bronze globe** decorated with the Signs of the Zodiac, an artistic **memorial to Woodrow Wilson.** Just opposite the UN building is the **Ariana Porcelain Museum,** where you can admire magnificent samples of Meissen, Sèvres, Delft, and Chinese porcelain, as well as contemporary works. (Open daily, except Tuesday, 10:00–5:00.)

You have now experienced the scope of Geneva—a scope that spans the centuries and encompasses the varying atmospheres of the old town on the heights and the UN on the lake, the pulpit of John Calvin, and the international forum inspired by Woodrow Wilson.

18.
Barcelona

BARRIO GÓTICO

Mons Taber to Picasso

The popularity of Spain's **Costa Brava** in recent years has brought many more tourists to **Barcelona,** the capital of Catalonia. The more discerning have discovered that Barcelona is full of historic and artistic interest. It is a city to visit, not just to pass through.

One of the largest port cities on the entire Mediterranean shoreline, Barcelona is a dynamic metropolis—the chief industrial and commercial city of Spain. Barcelona's history goes back more than two thousand years to the time when the Phoenicians from Asia Minor settled here. The Romans, after capturing Barcelona from the Carthaginians, made it an important center of Roman Spain. You will see many remains of the Roman period.

There are really two cities in Barcelona—the old and the new. The new city, just as impressive as Madrid, boasts broad, stately avenues like the **Paseo de Gracia** and the **Avenida Diagonal,** crowded with imposing modern office and residential buildings.

But it is old Barcelona—a small area near the port called the

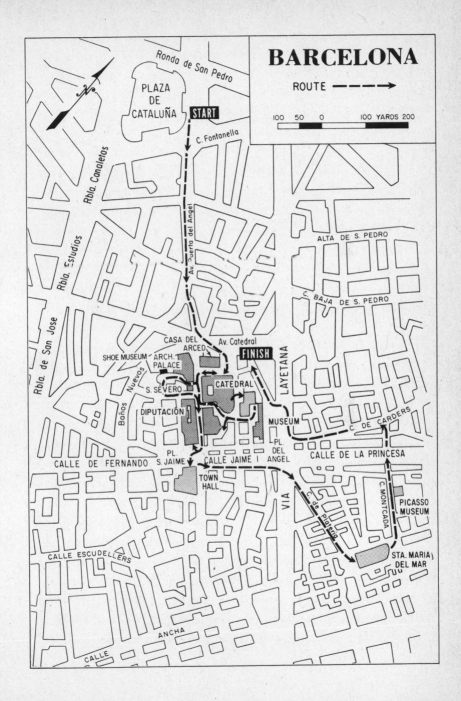

"Barrio Gótico"—that will attract you the most. Full of character and crammed with interesting places, this section can be covered easily on foot in half a day. Few cities offer the tourist such a wealth and variety of sight-seeing within a few hundred yards as you can find in the quarter around the **Cathedral.**

Let's start this walk through old Barcelona at the city's main square, the **Plaza de Cataluña.** Stroll from this wide esplanade, with its handsome fountains surrounded by flower beds, into the **Avenida Puerta del Angel,** now closed to traffic. A noisy street fair with music blasting from loudspeakers may be under way. The Puerta del Angel narrows just beyond a large department store on the right. Take the left fork for a hundred yards or so. You will pass on your left a fine modern building with huge glass windows and an unusual stone façade—quite a contrast to the ancient Cathedral across the Plaça Nova, where an antique market takes place on Thursday.

Located on a site that dates from the early Christian era, Barcelona's distinguished Gothic cathedral was built mainly during the fourteenth century. The Cathedral can be visited from 7:30 to 1:30 and 4:00 to 7:30. You will be struck by its high vaulted arches and particularly by the shafts of light that brighten the otherwise dark, mysterious air of its interior. After looking around the many chapels and beautifully carved choir stalls, go out through the door near the high altar into the narrow Calle de los Condes de Barcelona.

Immediately on the left you enter the **Museo Federico Marés** (open Tuesday–Sunday and holidays, 9:00–1:45 and 4:00–7:00; closed Monday) located in the sixteenth-century **Viceregal Palace.** You may care to inspect the Marés collection of medieval religious art but far more interesting are the Roman remains in the **Museum of the History of the City of Barcelona** (open 9:00–8:00; Sunday and holidays, 9:00–1:30), which you reach by descending to the **underground excavations.** Here you will see the ruins of a second-century Roman forum, the remains of a fourth-century Christian basilica, and the foundations of a Roman palace and homes. It's fascinating to wander around these subterranean excavations—all extremely well lit and marked. Some are directly under the Cathedral itself. At the far end you will find a model that shows the relation of the Roman ruins to the later buildings.

After climbing the steps marked *Salida* (Exit), you should ask the guard to show you the **chapel of St. Agatha,** a fourteenth-century Gothic church that belonged to the kings of Catalonia. Just beyond is the huge **Salon del Tinell,** the reception hall of the Royal Palace, with its original stone arches and wooden roof beams. Ferdinand and Isabella received Christopher Columbus in this hall in 1493 on his return from his first voyage to America.

You can leave the Barcelona Historical Museum by descending a stone stairway in the courtyard into the Calle del Veguer. A few feet to your right and you will be in the impressive **Plaza del Rey.** Pause for a few minutes to admire the ancient walls surrounding the small square, the wide staircase, and the lofty lookout **tower of King Martin** with its five tiers of round arches. This is one of the most impressive corners in old Barcelona.

Wander into the courtyard next to the Plaza del Rey. Here is a quiet, peaceful spot in the midst of a metropolis—a beautiful stone staircase, an arched cloister, and a bubbling fountain in the center of the court.

Go out the far side of the court to the rear of the Cathedral, then stroll to the left for a couple of minutes along the Calle de la Freneria. From here you have an unusual view of the Cathedral's tower rising above the old houses with their iron-grille balconies.

. Returning to the Cathedral, you now take the narrow street directly behind the apse to the left, the **Calle del Paradis.** Just before it turns right a few yards ahead, go left into the courtyard of a medieval house and you will see an arrow that points to the four Corinthian columns of a Roman temple. They mark the summit of **Mons Taber,** the highest point in Roman Barcelona. Note the old millstone embedded in the street just before you cross the threshold. In all these little streets around the Cathedral you'll find many antique shops; why not have a break from sight-seeing and enjoy a look around?

On leaving the medieval house, turn right, then left into the Calle de la Piedad, which brings you to the Cathedral's **cloisters.** The high Gothic vaulting of the arches and the various guild chapels are two outstanding features of these delightful cloisters that surround a garden patio planted with palms and magnolias. Don't miss the flock of geese, traditionally associated with Barcelona, that live in the gardens. Pause for a moment while walking around the cloisters for a view through the arches or the palm leaves of the Cathedral's bell tower and Gothic spire.

Go out on the **Plaza de A. Garriga Bachs** and then a few steps to the right. On your left you'll see the delightful patio of the Romanesque **Archbishop's Palace.** Opposite a magnificent stone staircase, a fountain stands beneath a terrace and arched galleries. This is one of the most artistic patios in Barcelona.

Another attractive little patio is the adjacent **Casa del Arcediano** on the left of the Calle de Santa Lucia and opposite the Cathedral. A moss-covered fountain plays in the patio, which is colorfully decorated with old blue-and-yellow tiles.

Returning to the Plaza de Garriga, turn right along the Calle Mont Juich del Obispo. This leads to a small square, the **Plaza de San Felip Neri,** with a fountain in the center. The house on the left displays a coat of arms (1740) of shoes, boots, and shoelaces over the beautiful wrought-iron grille balcony because it used to belong to the Guild of the Shoemakers. Today it houses the Shoe Museum, where you can admire a collection of Renaissance shoes as well as contemporary foot gear once owned by celebrities. (Open Tuesday–Saturday, 11:00–2:00.) At this point wander off to your right. After turning left along the Calle Felipe de Neri, you will see on the Calle San Severo some old houses with attractive balconies and narrow cobblestone streets. Don't miss the little shrine with an inscription on colorful tile that is built right into the façade of a house. Returning in the direction of the Cathedral, along the Calle San Severo, you see on your left the entrance to the **Church of San Severo.** Have a look at its baroque interior.

A right turn from the **Plaza de Garriga** will take you along the Calle del Obispo Irurita. Straight ahead you will see a modern **Gothic bridge,** between two buildings. The façade of the building on the left (Diputación or Provincial Council) changes its style from baroque to Renaissance to Gothic.

In a moment or two you will be in the large **Plaza de San Jaime,** Barcelona's historical and administrative center. A sharp right turn will bring you into the **courtyard of the Diputación** (generally closed to the public, although special permission may be obtained by calling 402 46 18). As you ascend the broad staircase, don't miss the pointed Gothic arches supported by delicately carved slim stone columns. At the top of the stone staircase the wooden beams of the gallery's ceiling are beautifully painted and decorated with inlaid wood in Moorish style. Opposite the staircase is the door to the **Chapel San Jorge,** which is decorated with Flemish tapestries and a beautiful altarpiece. Go through an arch from the gallery into a large enchanting patio planted with orange trees and dominated by a pinnacled tower. On the left of the patio, the State Council of Catalonia meets in an ornate council chamber with gilded ceiling, huge Venetian glass chandelier, and fifteenth-century tapestry on the wall. (The concierge at the entrance to the building will take you to visit the Chapel and Council Chamber.)

On your return to the Plaza de San Jaime, you may feel like taking a turn on the **Calle Fernando** to your right. This is old Barcelona's main shopping street and continues for a few blocks to the **Ramblas.** Before you leave Barcelona you should walk along the colorful Ramblas—the traditional promenade—from the Plaza de Cataluña to the **statue of Columbus** opposite the docks. Along the Ramblas and on the streets just off it, you'll see everything from sailors' cafés to the covered **markets of San José,** a small edition of what used to be Les Halles in Paris.

The **Town Hall** (closed to the public; special permission can be obtained by calling 402 73 62) is the imposing neoclassic building directly opposite the Diputación. Go to the concierge's office in the beautiful courtyard and ask for a *macero* (guard) to show you the elaborate salons. The **Salon de Ciento,** named for the municipal councillors' meeting place, dates from 1373 and is distinguished for its Gothic arches, Renaissance doorway, and highly decorative Mudejar ceiling. You should also see the **Salon de Sert** where the great Catalonian artist José Maria Sert depicted the history of Catalonia in spectacular murals and ceiling frescoes.

Turn right from the Town Hall in the Calle de Jaime I. As you pass the second street crossing, look left for views of the Cathedral tower rising above the old buildings in this part of the city.

In a few moments you will be in the **Plaza del Angel.** Cross the square and after turning right into the Via Layetana, bear left along the **Calle de Plateria.** As you walk along this street (named for the silversmiths whose shops used to line it), you will pass little alleys and narrow passageways, the heart of medieval Barcelona. Wander into one of these if you feel like exploring what lies beneath the wrought-iron balconies and ancient doorways with their coats of arms. Washing is stretched across the tiny alleys from house to house in this slum area.

Shortly you will reach the recently restored fourteenth-century **Church of Santa Maria del Mar,** old Barcelona's finest Gothic church after the Cathedral. Despite the fire of 1936, you will see several interesting chapels and fine fifteenth-century stained glass. (Open daily, 9:00–12:30 and 5:00–8:00; closed Saturday and Sunday.) The door at the back of the church opens on to the **Paseo del Borne,** a lively and amusing marketplace with flower stalls and food shops.

A few yards beyond the rear of the church turn sharply to the left into the narrow **Calle de Montcada**—a fascinating old street with many fine mansions. Their huge doorways, iron-grille balconies, overhanging roofs, and gargoyles recall the days when Spanish nobility and wealthy merchants made these palaces and fine homes centers of cultural and ostentatious living. You will want to wander in and out of these ancient doorways, admire lovely flower-filled patios, and stroll past old-style lampposts that protrude over the narrow street. Stop at No. 20 on the left, the **Palacio de Dalmases,** to see the elaborately sculptured stone balustrade and fine arches. Or look into the recently renovated patio at **No. 18.** At **No. 19** there is an imposing staircase with iron railing and attractive palms in the patio. At No. 12, you will find the **Palacio Lió,** which houses the **Clothes Museum** (open Tuesday–Saturday, 10:00–5:00; Sunday, 10:00–2:00; closed Monday and holidays), and at No. 25, the contemporary art gallery **Maeght.**

No. 15, on the right, is the wonderful **Picasso Museum** (open daily, 10:00–8:00; closed Monday and holidays), formerly the fourteenth-century Aguilar palace. This exhibit of Picasso's paintings and drawings is an extensive and intensely interesting collection of his early and blue periods as well as his later works, including his ceramics. The old palace has been excellently restored. You will admire the fine stone stairways, Gothic arches, and roof beams in the patio as well as the modern lighting of the salons. Take the elevator to the top floor of this magnificent Gothic building. Here you look out over the tiled roofs of the old quarter, or look down from the little cloistered walk into the attractive patio. Visit the exhibitions rooms as you descend to the ground floor. The great Spanish artist left much of his personal collection to the city where his artistic genius first flowered.

From the Calle Montcada you cross the busy Calle de la Princesa and in fifty yards you will come to the little Romanesque **Chapel of Marcus** in the tiny square of the same name. Turn left along the Calle de Carders and then through the **Plaza de la Lana,** where the wool traders used to be located. A few minutes more along the Calle de la Boria and you will be back on the Calle Layetana. Turn right to the nearby Plaza de Berenguer el Grande. Just across the square are the Roman walls—only minutes along the Calle de la Tapineria from the Cathedral.

Since taxis in Spain are quite reasonable, you may want to drive to the edge of the city to see the fantastic *Art Nouveau* Güell Park, containing a gingerbreadlike construction by the Spanish architect, Gaudí. Also don't miss the Sagrada Familia church, following Gaudí's original design. In 1981 eight towers and one façade were finished, but construction is far from being completed.

19.
Madrid

The Old Town
Plaza Mayor to Rastro

Old Madrid is the most interesting and fascinating part of Spain's capital city, a metropolis of four million people. Most of the city is modern and reflects the great expansion that took place first in the late nineteenth century and again after the civil war in 1936. Although you will include the world-renowned Prado art gallery and the Royal Palace in another walk around Madrid, you will get a better feel of the city by starting in the old section. Here you will sense Madrid's historical background. While wandering in these narrow streets and artistic squares, you will be carried back to earlier times—especially the glorious days of seventeenth-century Spain. If you are only visiting Madrid and will not have the chance to tour other cities that are more typical of pre-industrial Spain, the old part of Madrid will at least give you some of the romantic flavor of those days.

Old Madrid is very accessible—right in the center of the city.

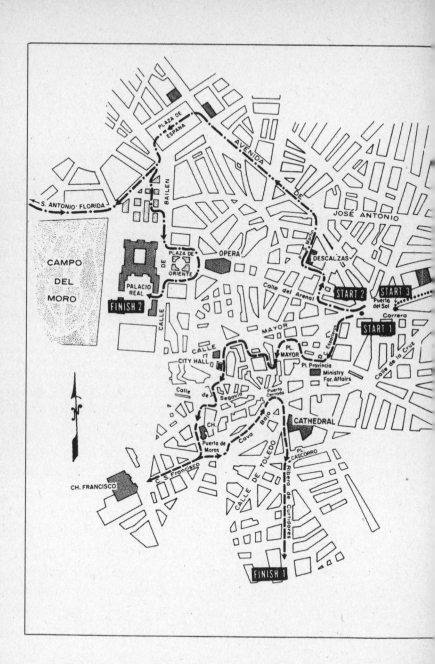

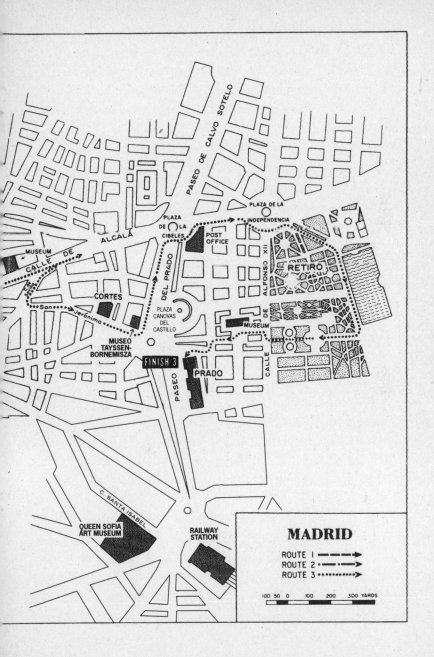

PASEO DE CALVO SOTELO

PLAZA DE LA
INDEPENDENCIA

PLAZA
DE LA
CIBELES

ALCALÁ

POST
OFFICE

MUSEUM

CALLE DE

CORTES

DEL PRADO

RETIRO

CALLE DE ALFONSO XII

San

Jerónimo

PLAZA
CANOVAS
DEL
CASTILLO

MUSEUM

MUSEO
TAYSSEN-
BORNEMISZA

CALLE DE

FINISH 3

PASEO

PRADO

C. SANTA ISABEL

QUEEN SOFIA
ART MUSEUM

RAILWAY
STATION

MADRID

ROUTE 1 ----→
ROUTE 2 -·-·-→
ROUTE 3 ······→

100 50 0   100   200   300 YARDS

You'll find that it is concentrated, does not cover a large area, and is quite an easy walk. In fact, you can see it properly only on foot. There are many little turnings, passageways, and patios off the narrow streets that you would miss in a car. When you are strolling, you have time to look more carefully at the details of the buildings and churches that you pass.

Start at the **Puerta del Sol**—the historic heart of Madrid and still the center of the city's life. It is only a few yards away from the old section. Nine streets meet in this bustling, traffic-crowded, commercial square. Its name, Puerta del Sol, comes from the fact that a sun was painted over the door of a chapel that used to stand here by an ancient gate in the city wall.

The large building in the French style facing the square is the **Ministry of the Interior.** Both time and distance in Spain are set at this spot. The clock in the tower is the country's official timepiece, and the marker on the pavement is the measuring point to major cities throughout the country.

If you are facing the Ministry, walk a few yards to the right and you will be in the Calle Mayor. Almost at once bear left along the Calle de Esparteros and in a couple of minutes you will come to the **Plaza de Santa Cruz.** Directly in front of you across the square stands the elegant red-brick seventeenth-century building of the **Ministry of Foreign Affairs.** The slated square towers, typical of this part of Spain, reflect the Austrian influence of the Hapsburgs.

Turn right from the Plaza de Santa Cruz on the Calle de Gerona and go under a lofty arch to enter the splendid **Plaza Mayor,** built by Philip III in 1617. His bronze statue dominates the square. This was the center of life under the Hapsburg monarchs. Here fiestas, religious plays, autos-da-fé during the Inquisition, political and criminal executions, bullfights, and public festivals took place. The famous Spanish riding school also performed in this square. On the north side you will see the twin towers of the **Panandería.** The king presided over these public occasions from the center balcony. Stop to visit the **San Ginés Church,** and admire a superb El Greco painting (open 7:45–1:00 and 7:00–8:00 P.M.).

Arcades run beneath the five-storied brown stucco buildings with their iron-grille balconies, French windows, and decoratively painted façades. Pause for a few moments in the center near one of the four lampposts, similar to those in the Place Vendôme in Paris, and glance around the square. As you face the baroque Panadería, you can imagine a seventeenth-century scene when the Plaza Mayor was the brilliant center of Madrid life—the king in his royal box, thousands of citizens leaning out of the balconies and windows in the three upper stories, and the square jammed with people.

Now stroll casually around the arcades, stopping at the little shops that sell a great variety of goods. On Sundays vendors put up stands under the arcades for the sale and exchange of stamps and coins. Just to the right of the Arch of Gerona (where you came in), you will see several shops displaying old silverware in the Calle de Zaragoza. Continuing around the square counterclockwise, you can go in the **Casa de la Panadería** just under the center balcony with the crest above it. The bakery originally was on the ground floor. Upstairs you will see a tiled room with tapestries just off the royal balcony.

At the far left-hand corner of the square from the Arch of Gerona, you will reach a flight of steps. Just on the right there is the popular restaurant **El Pulpito,** named for a pulpitlike stair landing. When you pass, you may see the chefs preparing seafood, which is their specialty. Just ahead go through one of the Plaza's great archways—the **Arco de Cuchilleros**—and down the steps to the street below. This is a popular corner of the old town, often the subject of song and verse. Just at the foot of the steps there's an old bar and wine cellar, **Las Cuevas de Luis Candelas,** built in the cellars below the Plaza. Just ahead a few yards on the left, on the **Calle de Cuchilleros,** is a night club, **Arco de Cuchilleros,** where you can enjoy Flamenco dancing from 10:30 P.M.–3:30 A.M. A few yards farther will bring you to the **Restaurant Sobrino de Botín,** an attractive old inn. It is fun to watch the chef roast suckling pig in a huge oven decorated with colorful tiles. University students, dressed in medieval costumes, often serenade the diners.

Return to the foot of the steps and keep to the left along the **Cava de San Miguel** beside the high walls of the buildings that face the Plaza Mayor. There were prisons and dungeons in the cellars of these buildings during the time of the Inquisition.

The **market** of San Miguel is just ahead on the left. In this hectic place you will be jostled by the people of the neighborhood doing their daily shopping. Stands display meats, chickens, eggs, Spanish sardines, other fish, and great bowls with all kinds and varieties of olives. Young boys dash about with cuts of beef slung over their shoulders. Outside on the street are more stalls with fresh vegetables and fruits.

From the market walk a few yards to the nearest main street, the **Calle Mayor,** then go left. In about fifty yards on your left, you will reach the **Plaza de la Villa.** The red-brick and stone building with twin towers across the square is Madrid's **City Hall,** the **Casa de la Villa** or Casa Ayuntamiento. On the left of the square is the **Torre de los Lujanes.** Note the fine Late Gothic doorway just beyond the tower built in Mudejar style (a mixture of Moorish and Christian), where Francis I was kept prisoner in 1525. This palace, which you enter at No. 3, belongs to the Royal Academy of Moral and Political Science. Go inside and you will find a delightful enclosed patio with a grape arbor and potted palms. Up the late fifteenth-century stairway is the reading room of the Hemeroteca Municipal, an outstanding **newspaper library** (open 10:00–1:00 and 5:00–7:00, except Saturday afternoon and Sunday.) Connected to the City Hall by an arch is the **Casa de Cisneros,** which has a picturesque façade and an attractive courtyard, noted for its beautiful Flemish tapestries.

At the end of the short Calle del Cordón you will reach the small and charming **Plazuela del Cordón.** Pause for a moment at the corner of the Calle Sacramento before crossing to the plaza. Glance up at the iron-grille balconies on the stone building (the Casa Cisneros) at the corner. There are some attractive ocher-colored houses opposite you along the street. Notice at your right the baroque St. Michael's Basilica.

After descending a flight of steps from the plaza, turn right on the Calle del Conde. Here is the **Mesón de San Janvier,** an old-style Madrid restaurant. Continue down the cobblestoned Calle del Cordón to the Calle de Segovia. A few yards on the right is a famous inn—the **Hosteria Carlos III**—over 450 years old. You'll enjoy poking around its ancient wine cellars.

On the other side of the Calle de Segovia stands the ancient **Church of San Pedro** and its tower. Turn right, just opposite the church, along the Calle del Principe Anglona and continue for a couple of minutes to the medieval Plaza de la Paja. At the end of the square on the left, at No. 5, you will discover the stone stairway and entrance to the sixteenth-century **Capilla del Obispo.** This is a Renaissance church with the most beautiful altar in Madrid. Highly ornamental, its carved wooden panels are covered with gold.

Now go around the church to the left to the Plaza de los Carros, then bear to the right and walk down the hill on the Carrera de San Francisco for a few minutes to the large **Church of San Francisco el Grande** (open daily, except Sunday and Monday, 11:00–1:00 and 5:00–8:00, summer; 4:00–7:00, winter). Its exterior resembles the Pantheon in Rome. Its circular interior, erected in the eighteenth century, has a cupola whose diameter is greater than that of St.

Paul's Cathedral in London. Be sure to see the richly carved choir stalls from El Paular near La Granja, as well as an extremely fine Goya in the chapel to the left of the altar.

Retrace your steps up the Carrera de San Francisco, then cross the large square, Puerta de Moros. Now take the street to the left that is on a lower level—the **Cava Baja** or Low Ditch, so-called because it used to carry water. This is one of the most interesting streets in the old city. It is lined with posadas, or old posting-house inns and charming bars. Try the **Palacios,** at No. 10. Don't fail to read the inscriptions over the entrance doors. Wander along this street and stop on the left about one hundred yards along at a typical Madrid restaurant, **Viejo Madrid.** Notice how the old colored tiles decorate the doorway. At No. 30, the **Mesón del Segoviano,** you will find old beams and an amusing painting of a donkey drawing a carriage just inside the entrance. Above the old courtyard there is an iron-grille balcony from which one enters the bedrooms.

At the end of the Cava Baja you are at the **Puerta Cerrada**—the intersection of five streets—where in the Middle Ages the country people waited in the morning for the city gates to open. If you happen to reach here at about 2:00 or 2:30 P.M., why not cross over to the Calle Cuchilleros and lunch at the **Casa Botín** only a few yards along on the right?

Otherwise turn right from the Cava Baja in the Puerta Cerrada, where you will see a stone cross, and after a few yards, turn right again into the Calle de Toledo. On the left is the baroque **Cathedral of San Isidro.** Bear left at the fork into the Calle de los Estudios. In about one hundred yards the street opens up and you will see ahead a large square usually filled with parked cars. This is the **Plaza de Cascorro.**

On the far side of this elongated square you enter the **"Rastro,"** on the Ribera de Curtidores, often called Madrid's **flea market.** It's particularly busy on Sunday mornings. Vendors at outdoor stalls shout their wares—clothing, house furnishings, leather saddles, watches, copper, and brass. As you descend the wide street, you'll feel like joining the prospective customers who are examining the goods.

In addition to the outdoor stalls, well-patronized antique dealers and curiosity shops are located in courtyards off the street.

Go into **No. 12** on the right. This interesting stone courtyard with a little fountain in the center is crowded with antique shops in both the lower level and the gallery above. Colored tiles and potted plants decorate the patio. Wander into some of the shops. You will find old furniture, marble statues, copper and brass, as well as religious relics and figures. There are stone tubs for garden plants and old brass carriage lamps. One shop may specialize in old maps and guns, another in oriental chandeliers, a third in old furniture.

Another group of antique shops on the opposite side of the street farther down is also worth visiting—the **Galerias Piquer.** The shops in these galleries usually are open until 2:00 and again at 5:00. Here you can also browse for pottery, silver, and Chinese pieces.

This is a leisurely place to end this walk through old Madrid. To return to the center of town, you can pick up a taxi in the **Plaza de Cascorro.**

The Modern City
Puerta del Sol to Royal Palace

Promenading is a national custom in Spain and a particular pleasure in such an attractive city as Madrid. Visitors to Madrid often compare it to Paris, perhaps because of its wide tree-lined boulevards and many buildings erected in the early part of this century. But Madrid is a much newer city than Paris and is much more compact. The main places you will want to visit, like the **Royal Palace,** the **Prado,** and **Retiro Gardens,** are located in the same central part of the city.

If you have walked through old Madrid to get a feeling of the city's history and tradition, you'll now be keen to stroll along the busy thoroughfares and visit the most interesting sights in modern Madrid. So that you won't try to do too much at one time, two walks are suggested. Neither is long and each includes fascinating places you will want to see. In fact, these two walks and the one in old Madrid cover nearly all the major points of interest in the city.

Both of these walks also start at Madrid's "Times Square," the **Puerta del Sol.** On your right as you face the clock tower, you'll find the **Calle del Arenal** at the end of the square. Stroll along this crowded street for about two hundred yards, then turn right into the Plaza del Celenque. This leads you to the Calle del Maestro Victoria. In a few yards go left on the **Calle de la Misericordia,** and on your right you'll see the large stone and brick building of the **Museo de las Descalzas Reales.** (Guided tours, Tuesday, Wednesday, Thursday, and Saturday, 10:30–12:30 and 4:00–5:30; Friday, 10:30–12:30; Sunday, 11:00–1:30; closed Monday and holidays.)

This is one of the most unusual museums in Madrid and has been open to the public only in recent years. It is part of a convent founded for royal nuns by Juana, daughter of Charles V, in 1559. Used by nuns today, it still has an air of seclusion and quiet, though right in the center of the city. You are not likely to visit any other museums in Madrid with rooms and furnishings of the period of Emperor Charles V that are so well preserved. An English-speaking guide will take you on an hour's tour of the fourteenth-century building and its many works of art. The convent was in effect a part of the royal palace because so many ladies of royal blood took the veil there. As a result, it acquired not only lavish religious treasures such as vestments, jeweled monstrances, and magnificent altars, but also an extraordinary collection of paintings. In addition to excellent examples of Flemish primitives, including a Brueghel, there are portraits by Titian and Rubens as wall as Zurbarán's fine portrait of St. Francis. Be sure to see the delightful **cloister** with its wooden beam roof that looks out on a large flower and vegetable garden right beneath the back wall of one of Madrid's big department stores, the **Galerias Preciados.**

On leaving the convent, turn right into the square and along the Postigo de San Martin, which narrows into the **Plaza del Callao.** The tall modern building on the right is the Galerias Preciados.

At this point you might like to do a little window shopping along the **Avenida de José Antonio,** known as the **Gran Vía,** one of Madrid's finest shopping streets (opened in 1918), specializing in jewelry shops and fashion boutiques. Then cross the broad avenue and turn left along it down the hill past popular restaurants and movie theaters. In a few minutes you will come to a large square, the **Plaza de España.** Rising above it are Madrid's skyscrapers, two of the tallest buildings in Europe. One is a thirty-four-floor apartment house and office building, the **Torre de Madrid,** and the other, the **Edificio España,** contains the Plaza Hotel.

Cross over to the little park, planted with sycamore trees. After looking at the monument to Cervantes, have an apéritif at the refreshment bar in the park. From the far side of the square you can get a good view of the Torre and its attractive balconies overlooking the city.

If you have time, you can take a diversion from the park that will lead you in about twenty minutes to the **Chapel of San Antonio de la Florida.** Here is the tomb of Goya but, more important, some of his greatest art. He painted a magnificent series of frescoes on the ceiling that many consider the most striking example of Goya's genius. The individual figures, so realistically portrayed, have an extraordinary dramatic quality. To reach the charming eighteenth-century chapel, you take the Paseo de Onésimo Redondo downhill at the far corner of the Plaza de España, then continue past the Estación del Norte, and keep right on the Paseo de la Florida to the little church on the right (open Monday, Tuesday, Thursday, and Friday, 11:00–1:30 and 3:00–6:30; closed Wednesday, Sunday, and holidays). If you don't feel like taking this detour now, make a point of going later to see these remarkable frescoes.

From the Plaza de España, cross the street and go into the **Jardines Sabatini**—the gardens opposite on the Calle de Bailén. Trimmed boxwood and tall cypress trees line the path before you descend to the lower gardens where statues are grouped around the fountains. In summer this is the locale for the *Son et Lumière* performances. From the terrace you have a fine view of the **Casa de Campo Park** on the far side of the river that flows below the palace.

A couple of minutes farther along the other side of the Calle Bailén will bring you to the **Plaza de Oriente.** The equestrian statue of Philip IV is surrounded in the formal gardens by numerous others of Spanish kings and queens. The large building on the left facing the park is the **Gran Teatro** or Madrid's Opera House, where symphony concerts are given. At No. 2 of the square, enjoy a hot chocolate at the elegant **Café de Oriente.**

Now cross the Calle Bailén to visit the **Palacio Real,** or **Royal Palace** (open in summer daily, 9:00–6:15; in winter, 9:00–5:15; Sunday and holidays, 9:00–2:00). You may wish to return for your visit to the palace. There is so much of interest that you will need an hour or more to see it.

The Royal Palace, certainly one of the finest in Europe and one of the best maintained, includes an exceptional collection of Flemish tapestries, beautiful paintings, and clocks, as well as the private apartments of the last royal family to rule Spain prior to the civil war.

You enter the palace on the far right of the large courtyard. English-speaking guides are available to take you through. Be sure to buy the full ticket in order to visit the art gallery.

Located on the site of the old Alcázar, the present palace was begun in 1738 and took twenty-six years to construct. As you go through the palace, you will be particularly impressed by the following: the magnificent main stairway of marble, the Tiepolo ceilings in the Hall of the Guards and the Throne room, the rococo Gasperini room decorated with Chinese enamel flowers, fruit, and birds, the large ornate chapel, the illuminated glass chandelier, a replica of Columbus's *Santa Maria,* and the royal library with its exquisitely bound books. It's quite an experience to be in the clock collection when all seventy clocks of every conceivable design chime the hour simultaneously.

After touring the palace, walk to the far end of the large courtyard overlooking the park (the Campo del Moro) to visit the **Royal Armory,** one of Europe's finest collections of armor, especially of the medieval period. It was started by Charles V. (Open daily in summer, 9:00–6:15; in winter, 9:00–5:15; Sunday and holidays, 9:00–2:00.) You may also wish to see the museum of old carriages just below the palace before leaving the grounds.

To the Prado

This walk through modern Madrid will take you to the delightful Retiro Gardens, the city's wooded park, and to the world-famous Prado art gallery.

From the Puerta del Sol, go left as you face the clock into the

Calle de Alcalá, a fine broad avenue and main shopping street. A few steps to the left will bring you to the **Royal Academy of Fine Arts** (open daily, 10:00–1:30 and 4:00–6:30; Sunday and holidays, 10:00–1:30). This outstanding collection of paintings includes, in addition to Flemish and Italian works, excellent examples of Goya and Zurbarán.

Stroll a block or so farther along the Alcalá, which for years was the glamorous center of Madrid life and a magnet for provincial visitors until most of its famous cafés disappeared. Then imposing banks and office buildings replaced them. But it still has much of its old-world dignity and atmosphere. There's a fine vista down the Alcalá at the junction of the Gran Vía. From **Dolar's café** at this corner you look down the hill to the artistic **fountain of the Cibeles.**

Cross over from Dolar's and walk back a block or so on the opposite side of the Alcalá to the Calle de Sevilla where you turn left for a hundred yards or so to reach another of Madrid's fashionable shopping streets, the **Calle de San Jerónimo.** Turn left down this street to the **Palacio de las Cortes,** a classic building with two bronze lions flanking the steps. This is the seat of the **Cortes Españolas,** which meets from time to time to enact legislation approved by the government. The American Express office is one block farther on the left.

Continue two blocks to the large square, the Plaza Cánovas del Castillo, then stroll to the left along the wide tree-lined Paseo del Prado, past the Plaza de la Lealtad, to the **Plaza de la Cibeles.** This eighteenth-century fountain, a goddess driving a chariot drawn by lions, should also be seen at night under floodlights.

If you want to enjoy strolling along Madrid's spacious **Paseo** planted with trees and flowers, you can continue straight ahead for quite a distance. But perhaps you'd rather save this promenade for late in the day or the early evening.

To the right of the square stands the extraordinary and bizarre **Post Office** building. Its cathedral-like size and 230-foot tower have given it the popular nickname of "Nuestra Señora de las Comunicaciones" (Our Lady of Communications).

A couple of blocks past the Post Office building on the Alcalá will bring you to the **Plaza de la Independencia,** a large square dominated by the Puerta de Alcalá, a late eighteenth-century arch.

You now enter, on your right, the **Retiro,** Madrid's finest park. One of the most beautiful and largest city parks in Europe, the Retiro includes a lake, zoo, rose garden (lovely in spring and summer), as well as informal paths through shrubbery and wooded groves—the remains of a forest that used to surround Madrid. If you happen to be visiting Madrid in summer, this stroll through the cool shaded Retiro will be a welcome change from the sunny streets. In many ways the formal and informal landscaping of the Retiro will remind you of the Luxembourg gardens in Paris. Also, you'll find many baroque statues in odd places. Although the park dates from the fifteenth century, when it was a forest park attached to Philip II's palace, it was replanted about a hundred years ago.

If you walk along the Avenida de Mexico through the gate from the Plaza de la Independencia, you will soon come to the large artificial lake surmounted by a huge, ornate monument to Alfonso XII. You can turn right at the far end of the lake and leave the Retiro by the Puerta de Felipe IV.

After crossing the **Calle de Alfonso XII,** which runs along the Retiro, you will be in the Calle Felipe IV. In a moment you will see on your right a red-brick building, the **Army Museum,** built on the remains of the old royal palace of Buen Retiro. Now it houses a vast military collection of guns, models of forts, and weapons from the fifteenth century to the Spanish Civil War. The museum is open

10:00 to 5:00, daily except Monday. Almost opposite the entrance, and facing the broader part of the Calle de Felipe IV, stands the **Casón de Felipe Cuatro,** a classic building with stone pillars, the last remaining part of the old Retiro Palace and now used for special exhibits.

One block along the Calle de Felipe IV and another to the left will bring you to the Gothic **Church of San Jerónimo el Real,** where heirs to the Spanish throne took the oath of allegiance.

From the Prado, rest your weary feet and treat yourself to the excellent ice cream sold in front of the Museum. Then take a taxi south to Via Santa Isabel, opposite the railway station, to the **Queen Sofia Art Center.** The former San Carlos Hospital (open daily, 10:00–9:00; closed Monday and holidays) was completely rebuilt and modernized in 1986 and is a major European modern art museum, with splendid paintings by Miro, Picasso, Dali, and Magritte. Temporary exhibits are of interest and you must not miss Madrid's "Beaubourg" under any circumstances.

From the front of this church it's only a short block to the main entrance of the **Prado,** Spain's national collection of painting and sculpture and one of the world's greatest art museums. (Open Tuesday–Saturday, 9:00–7:00; Sunday, 9:00–2:00; closed Monday and holidays.) You should allow at least a couple of hours to view the superb works of art exhibited here. Although the museum specializes in the great Spanish masters, with an unrivaled collection of Goya, Velasquez, and El Greco, you will also want to see the unusual selection of Flemish and Italian paintings as well as the famous Greco-Iberian statue, the *Dama de Elche.* The Prado is so vast that you should organize your tour according to the artists and schools you most want to see.

Cross the square Canovas del Castillo to the early-nineteenth-century **palace, Villhermosa,** which houses one of the most fabulous private art collections in Europe, belonging to the Baron Thyssen-Borhemisza. Containing roughly eight-hundred paintings—ranging from Hals, Holbein, Rubens, and the Spanish school to the Impressionists and contemporary artists—the museum is a must-see when you visit Madrid. Its opening in 1992 was a major artistic event in Spain. (Open daily, except Monday and holidays, 9:30–7:30.)

20.
Toledo

THE SPIRIT OF EL GRECO

From Cathedral to Alcázar

Toledo is so much the essence of Spain that the entire city has been declared a National Monument. The most characteristic of all Spanish cities, Toledo embodies the country's turbulent and varied past. From the days when it was a Roman settlement, Toletum, at the beginning of the Christian era to the siege of the Alcázar in the Spanish Civil War, Toledo has figured prominently in the great movements of Spanish history. Christian and Arabic cultures are intermingled because Toledo was Moorish for three hundred years. It is a city of art treasures and was the home of El Greco for most of his life. The largest collection of the artist's works, including perhaps his finest masterpieces, are on exhibit here.

Dramatically perched on a rocky bluff, Toledo is encircled on three sides by the deep gorge of the Tagus River. It is a walled city with ancient stone gateways or *puertas*. There is a mysterious air of the past in its tiny, tortuous streets that wind like deep ravines beneath high buildings and walls.

Most visitors make Toledo a one-day trip by car from Madrid—a distance of forty-three miles. You should start early so you can stop en route at **Illescas** (halfway) to see the five superb El Grecos (especially the painting of St. Ildefonso) in the sixteenth-century chapel of the **Caridad Hospital.** To reach the hospital, leave the main road bearing right to the largest building in the village. Go into the patio and pull the bell at the door on the left next to an entry. A nun will be glad to open the iron-grille screen so that you can get close to the paintings.

Toledo is ideal for the walker. In fact it's the only way to explore the city. Many of the cobblestone streets are too narrow for wheeled traffic. If time permits, you should spend the night. Then you will have enough time just to wander around the old streets and poke about the squares and courtyards as well as other interesting corners that cannot be included in a one-day visit. (You can tour Toledo's outstanding historic and artistic monuments in a single day.)

In typical Moorish fashion, delightful patios are hidden behind huge wooden doors and high walls. Often the door is open so you can look inside, but the towering houses above the canyonlike streets do obstruct prominent landmarks and make it harder to find your way.

Start your tour in the **Plaza del Ayuntamiento** in front of the magnificent **Cathedral.** It contains such a wealth of treasures that you should go there while you are fresh for at least a preliminary visit. You can return in the late afternoon to see the stained-glass windows at their best. The seat of the Primate of Spain, the Cathedral dominates the city architecturally and artistically. It is certainly one of the finest in Spain and ranks among the great cathedrals of Europe. It was finished in 1493—one year after the discovery of America—is French-Gothic, and took more than 250 years to build.

Before entering the Cathedral, you should walk to the far side of

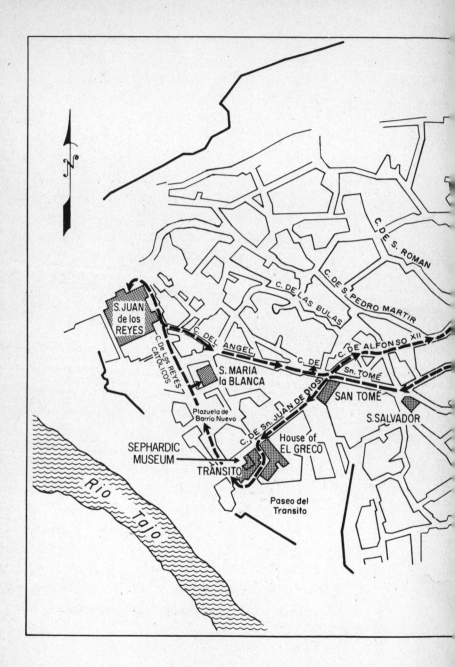

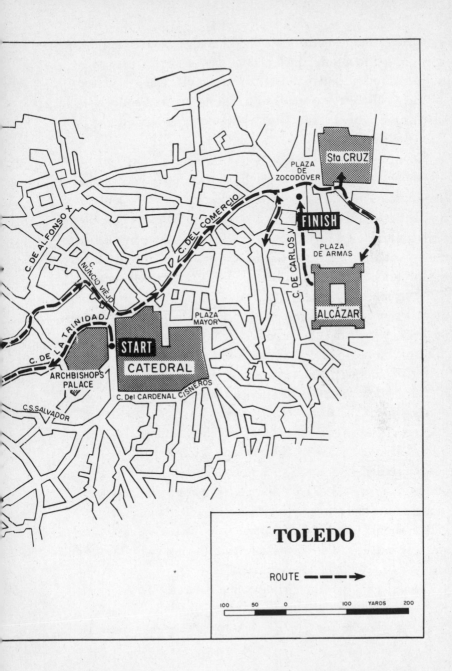

PLAZA DE ZOCODOVER

Sta CRUZ

FINISH

PLAZA DE ARMAS

C. DEL COMERCIO

C. DE ALFONSO X

C. NUNCIO VIEJO

C. DE CARLOS V

ALCÁZAR

C. DE LA TRINIDAD

PLAZA MAYOR

START

CATEDRAL

C. DE LA TRINIDAD

ARCHBISHOPS PALACE

C.S.SALVADOR

C. Del CARDENAL CISNEROS

TOLEDO

ROUTE - - - ➤

100   50   0   100   YARDS   200

the plaza, where you can view the decorative exterior and the impressive 295-foot tower, built in three main sections.

Then stroll around to the south side (on the right as you face the building) to see the **portal of the Puerta de los Leones** with its sixteenth-century bronze doors, elaborate stone carving, and ornamental sculpture.

Enter the **Cathedral** (open 10:30–1:00 year-round and 3:30–7:00 in summer; 3:30–6:00 in winter) through the Puerta del Mollete at the foot of the tower. The vast interior is filled with an unusual number of artistic and religious treasures in the many chapels and throughout the cathedral. You will be struck at once by the beautiful iron-grille screen of the **Capilla Mayor.** Behind this, the massive Gothic gilded altarpiece of larch wood rises to a height of ninety feet. On either side are two Plateresque pulpits. The carved-walnut double choir stalls opposite the main altar are considered the finest in Spain. Behind the Capilla Mayor, light shines through a specially constructed rose window in the roof on a fantastic ornamental screen of baroque sculptures—known as the **Transparente.**

The sacristy possesses an unusual collection of paintings by El Greco—including *Christ Being Stripped of His Garments,* one of the artist's greatest works in Toledo. See the beautifully illuminated, French thirteenth-century Bibles in the vestry next to the sacristy. The **Custodia,** a 7-foot, 500-pound gilded silver monstrance of the sixteenth century with highly ornamented diamonds and precious stones, is the most elaborate piece in the Cathedral's Treasure.

You should linger for a few minutes in the two-story cloister on the way out. It is a delightful courtyard planted with flowers and trees.

From the cloister turn right past the **Palace of the Archbishop,** across from the Cathedral, and then go left along the Calle de la Trinidad following the signs pointing to the **Casa del Greco.** There is a convent to the right on the way up the hill. Along the narrow street are faded red-brick buildings and a high bell tower, a frequent sight in Toledo.

At the end of the street stands the **Salvador Church.** Here you can see remains of the days when the Visigoths occupied the city. Visigothic sculpture on the marble columns next to the altar dates from the sixth century.

After visiting this church, bear right and follow the signs along the **Calle de Santo Tomé.** On the left is an interesting old house with glass bay windows. Farther down on the left you will see the Mudejar bell tower of the **Church of Santo Tomé** (open 10:00–1:45 and 3:30–5:45; 6:45 in summer). (Mudejar style is an architectural mixture of Christian and Moorish.) Inside the church is a masterpiece by El Greco, *The Burial of the Count of Orgaz,* which hangs above the Count's tomb. The artist himself is included among the group of Toledans in this painting—another of El Greco's greatest works.

Just nearby, at **No. 6,** you can look around a typical Toledan patio by entering an old wooden door embellished with huge nail heads—characteristically Moorish. The shops opposite the Church of Santo Tomé have interesting collections of Toledan metalwork on display. You will be interested to watch the craftspeople at work.

Straight ahead along the street leading to El Greco's house, you should stop in at **No. 20** to glance at the patio of a modern house. Just to the right you can glimpse the spires of the Church of San Juan de los Reyes.

A left turn (as indicated by the marked route) leads into the **Calle de Samuel Levi.** Immediately on the left is the building known as the **house of El Greco.** Although the artist never lived here, he probably resided nearby. It was built in the fourteenth century by Samuel Levi, Pedro the Cruel's Jewish treasurer and chief landowner of this Jewish quarter. The house (open 10:00–2:00 and 4:00–6:00; Sunday 10:00–2:00; closed Monday) has been restored as a sixteenth-century Toledan residence and contains an interesting collection of paintings by El Greco and other Spanish masters, as well as furniture of the period. For example, you can see the original writing table shown in El Greco's painting of San Ildefonso at Illescas. The wooden gallery, sixteenth-century kitchen with a large fireplace surrounded by cooking utensils and colorful pottery, as well as the fine linenfold paneling, make the house well worth visiting. Stroll around the delightful garden from which there is a striking view of terra-cotta-colored roofs, ocher bell towers, and several nearby *cigaralles,* country houses that look out over the Tagus.

Adjoining the house is a small museum with many unusually fine paintings. Also, you should visit the chapel inside the museum decorated with ancient Moorish tiles and frieze below an artesonado ceiling (constructed of little pieces of wood artistically fitted together).

Go down the alley just a few yards from the House of El Greco to the **ancient synagogue** of the Jewish aristocracy, **El Tránsito.** Built in 1366 for Samuel Levi, and later converted into a Christian church after the expulsion of the Jews from Spain in 1492, its interior is richly decorated. Oddly enough, the Hebraic inscriptions as originally carved on the frieze remain, as do some old tombs. The row of Moorish arches above the frieze and all around the building is a fine example of the ornamental Andalusian style. The original larch-wood ceiling inlaid with ivory in geometric designs and the elaborately decorated front wall help to make the interior one of the most beautiful in Toledo. Take a moment to visit the impressive **Sephardic Museum,** dedicated to Jewish art, costumes, and books. (Open 10:00–2:00 and 4:00–7:00; 6:00 in winter.)

Turn right outside the synagogue and follow the sign marked **Church of San Juan de los Reyes** on the street of the same name. Shortly after crossing a large square you will see the entrance to **Santa Maria la Blanca** beyond a small garden of cedars and locusts. Before being converted into a church this was the oldest **synagogue in Toledo** and was founded in 1180 (open 10:00–2:00 and 3:00–7:00). Note the lovely Moorish horseshoe arches and the carving on the stone capitals of the pillars, which has recently been restored.

Just a short distance farther along the **Calle de los Reyes Católicos,** you will find on the right an interesting antique shop with an ancient cellar.

The **Church of San Juan de los Reyes** (open 10:00–1:45 and 3:30–7:00, summer; 10:00–1:45 and 3:30–6:00, winter) on the left is, except for the Cathedral, Toledo's most elaborate church. It was originally planned by Ferdinand and Isabella as their last resting place. However, after conquering Granada, they chose to be buried there. Just before entering the church, you should notice on the outside of the apse the chains of Christians captured by the Moors and released by Ferdinand. The interior, unusually bright for a Spanish church, contains much elaborately carved stonework. But it is the double cloister that makes this church so remarkable. In florid Gothic design, its exquisitely carved stone arches, doorways, and pillars make it one of the finest in Spain. Go up to the second story and look out over this wonderful cloister and the tall cypresses in the garden courtyard.

After visiting the church, pause on the terrace to enjoy the fine view over the old city wall, the river below, and the Tagus valley beyond. The stone gateway with twin towers on the right is the **Puerta de Cambrón.**

Retrace your steps to the entrance of the church. A few steps beyond, make a left turn up the hill on the **Calle del Angel.** The street goes up a slope and beneath an archway. Don't miss the overhanging tiled roofs. Just ahead is the **Tower of Santo Tomé.** About twenty yards before reaching the tower, look carefully on the left for a tiny alleyway, the **Callejón de la Soledad.** This is one of those fascinating corners of Toledo that make wandering around it so delightful. Here is an old house with iron grillwork, which has that mysterious air of the past, so prevalent in old Toledo.

Opposite the Tower of Santo Tomé follow the narrow cobblestone street, Calle de la Campaña. Have a look at some of the tiled patios on either side. At the top bear right, then left on Calle Alfonso XII. On the right side of the tree-planted square facing the **Church of San Ildefonso** take a narrow street—**Callejón del Nuncio Viejo**—down a slope. At some places this street is only three or four feet wide. After about fifty yards turn right, and shortly you will come out on the Cathedral square.

It is only about a ten-minute walk from the Cathedral to Toledo's main square, the **Plaza de la Zocodover,** where you can find hotels and restaurants for a late lunch following Spanish custom.

From the Cathedral turn right beyond the cloister into the narrow **Calle del Hombre de Palo.** Have a look at the alleys on the right and left. Just ahead several little streets meet in a small square, the Plaza de las Cuatro Calles. Straight ahead is Toledo's main shopping street, the **Calle del Comercio.** A few yards farther along it, on the left beyond the little Plaza del Solarejo, you will see a strange building in nineteenth-century style. Five stories high, its long glass windows seem out of place in Toledo.

Note the decorative street sign on the left at the next little square—**Calle Toledo de Ohio**—in honor of the long connection between the two cities.

The three-cornered Plaza de Zocodover just ahead is the center of Toledan life and was the scene of bullfights, autos-da-fé, and other events in past centuries. Iron-grille balconies decorate the buildings around the square. It is amusing to wander down the two arcades and stop in at one of the crowded cafés.

If you want to lunch in one of Toledo's best hotels, take the **Calle Barrio del Rey** almost opposite the clock tower and bear left past a church tower for about twenty-five yards to the **Hotel Carlos V** on the right.

After lunch, you can complete the short remainder of this walk. On returning to the Plaza de Zocodover, stop on the left at the **Plaza del Corral de Don Diego.** In the courtyard, outdoor dramatic performances took place in the seventeenth century.

Leaving the main square, go through the high archway beneath the clock—the **Arco de la Sangre**—of Moorish design. The home of Cervantes, the great Spanish novelist, used to stand a few yards from the bottom of the steps below the arch before its destruction during the Spanish Civil War.

The **Museum of Santa Cruz** on the left is Toledo's most interesting museum and art gallery (open daily, 10:00–6:00). Founded as a hospital at the end of the fifteenth century and built in the form of a Greek cross, it is considered one of Spain's finest Renaissance buildings. The entrance façade is particularly elegant. In addition to an archaeological section in its spacious and richly decorated halls, there is, on the second floor, a wing of fine paintings by El Greco.

After visiting the museum, you will be enchanted by the magnificent two-story Plateresque cloister, which is adjacent, and its ornamental marble stairway. Stand for a moment in an archway and admire the tall cypress in the patio silhouetted against the terracotta roof.

Climb the flight of steps opposite the hospital, pass through a gate, and continue up the hill to the **Alcázar,** Toledo's historic citadel. There is a wonderful view over the Tagus and the surrounding countryside from the terrace.

The Alcázar (open 9:30–7:00, in summer; 9:30–6:00, in winter) located on the highest point in the city—at one time the site of a Roman camp—is perhaps the most famous fortress in Spain. Ever since the days of Ferdinand the Great and Charles V, the Alcázar has been the scene of battle. Burned three times, its last great siege was during the Spanish Civil War in 1936. Stop at the impressive monument just below the terrace in memory of those who died here in the civil war.

From the Alcázar it takes only a few minutes down the **Cuesta del Alcázar** to return to the Plaza de Zocodover.

Before returning to Madrid, you should be sure to see the dramatic views of Toledo from overlooks on the road that circles the hillside on the opposite side of the river. Cross the Tagus on the new bridge below the Alcázar, and return to the Madrid road by the thirteenth-century bridge of San Martín.

21.
Segovia

A WHIFF OF MEDIEVAL SPAIN

From Alcázar to Aqueduct

An excursion to **Segovia** will take you back several centuries to the days of medieval Spain. Only an hour and a half by car from Madrid, Segovia can be visited in a one-day trip.

The fairyland quality of the turrets and towers of Segovia's **Alcázar** expresses the romantic, enchanting mood that pervades Segovia.

It is a quiet town—not crowded with tourists like Toledo. Aside from the Alcázar, there isn't too much intensive sight-seeing to do. Rather it's the kind of place where you feel transported into the past. As you wander around the crowded, narrow streets and into the little squares, where so often you will discover a magnificent Romanesque church and quaint houses, you will sense the atmosphere of the Spanish Middle Ages. You feel little has changed in Segovia for its seems still relatively untouched by modern civilization.

Perched on a long, narrow, rocky eminence, Segovia is sur-

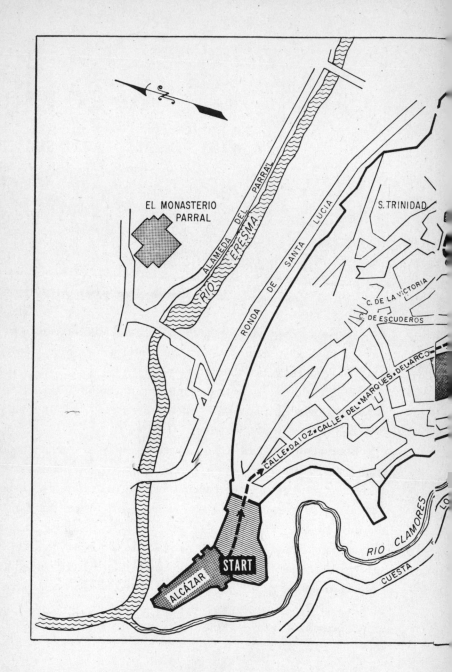

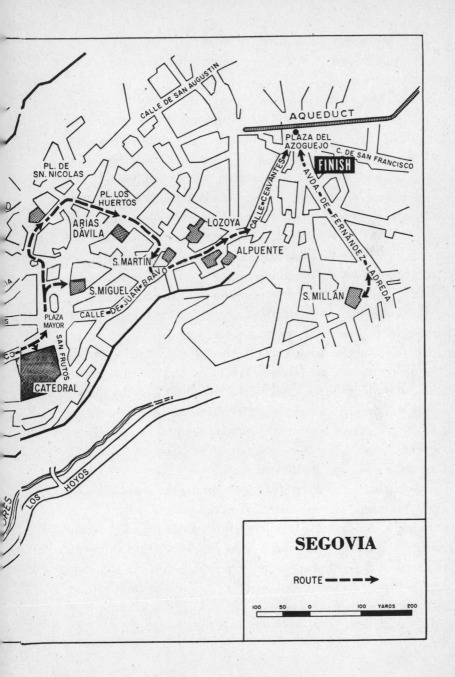

CALLE DE SAN AUGUSTIN

AQUEDUCT

PLAZA DEL
AZOGUEJO

C. DE SAN FRANCISCO

PL. DE
SN. NICOLAS

PL. LOS
HUERTOS

FINISH

CALLE CERVANTES

ARIAS
DÁVILA

LOZOYA

ALPUENTE

AVDA. DE FERNÁNDEZ LADREDA

S. MARTÍN

CALLE DE JUAN BRAVO

S. MIGUEL

S. MILLÁN

PLAZA
MAYOR

SAN FRUTOS

CATEDRAL

LOS HOYOS

RES

SEGOVIA

ROUTE ---→

100   50   0   100   YARDS   200

rounded by ancient walls dating from Roman times. At various points there are striking vistas over the countryside and the valley beneath the town.

You will find walking delightful in Segovia. At every turn you encounter an artistic scene. There is little motor traffic to disturb you; many of the streets are too narrow for cars, and the city is quite small and compact. The soft and clear light, for which Segovia is noted, casts a special aura over the ocher-colored buildings.

Begin your stroll through Segovia at the **Alcázar**—its most dramatic building architecturally and most interesting historically. Before you cross the drawbridge over the moat, walk along the curving terrace, the Paseo de Ronda, to get a full view of the castle. From here you will see the round turrets and their steeply sloping slate roofs and the battlemented central tower rising above.

The **Alcázar** (open 10:30–7:30 daily; to 6:00 in winter, guided tours only) is one of the most famous fortress-castles in Spain. Founded in the eleventh century, the present building dates mostly from the fourteenth and fifteenth centuries. You will notice both Gothic and Moorish influences in the great halls and magnificent chambers. Lovely Romanesque arches, elaborate gold-leaf ceilings, and Mudejar friezes in plaster are among the Alcázar's artistic attractions. Columbus made his will here in 1505, six months before his death, and his king, Ferdinand, acted as a witness.

Walk out on the battlemented terrace both to look up at the Alcázar's towers and for a wonderful panorama of the valley, with, at the far right, the sprawling fifteenth-century monastery of El Parral. Before you leave Segovia, for the finest view of the castle, drive to the bridge at the confluence of the two streams you see below the rocky buttress. From this point the rocky promontory on which the castle stands appears like a prow of a ship. Here you will sense that fairylike quality that is so characteristic of the Alcázar.

In the small **armory** you will find a collection of medieval artillery, including one of the first cannons in Spain—a fourteenth-century piece. On your way out pause for a few minutes in Clock Court—a charming patio.

After leaving the Plaza del Alcázar, you should bear to the right along the narrow **Calle de Daoiz.** Segovians call it the Canonjia de Velarde because the tiny houses with iron grillwork and tile roofs belonged to the canons of the Cathedral. Stop in on the left at the patio of **No. 32** to look at the flowers, plants, and trees on the terrace. Note the crests carved in stone over the Romanesque doorways. In a moment you will pass the arch of the Puerta de la Claustra—once the gateway to the canons' quarters.

Just beyond the Plaza de la Merced you will be in the **Calle del Marqués Arco.** At **No. 6,** on the left, you should step inside to see the attractive patio belonging to the palace of the Marqués del Arco.

The **Cathedral** (open 9:00–1:00 and 3:00–6:00 in winter; 9:00–7:00 in summer; Sunday and holidays, 9:00–7:00) is a fine example of sixteenth-century Castilian Gothic architecture. You will be impressed by a feeling of light and space in its beautifully proportioned interior, which is further distinguished by graceful vaulting and fine stained-glass windows. The baroque wrought-iron gates of the chapels and the carved choir stalls are examples of most artistic workmanship. Before leaving, stroll around the Gothic cloisters, and visit the museum.

The **Plaza Mayor,** Segovia's main square, faces the Cathedral. Wander under the colonnades to the **Church of San Miguel** on the far side. On the way you will pass some interesting old streets that radiate off the square. From the church's steps you can see the towers, buttresses, and pinnacles of the Cathedral.

Now take the Plaza del 4 de Agosto at the same end of the

square. Bear to the left for about ten yards, then right on the Calle de Valdelaguila, and there is the Calle de la Trinidad beneath a high wall. In a few moments you will come to the Romanesque **church of Santa Trinidad.** The graceful arches of its porch, its bell tower, and beautifully restored interior make it among the most beautiful churches in Segovia.

As you continue along the Calle de la Trinidad, you will pass attractive gardens and tall cedar trees. In the **Plaza de Guevara** there is, on the left, a fine building with massive wooden doors. If you go into the patio, you will come upon a fountain and an iron-grille gate.

Now follow the Calle de Doctor Laguna just opposite, into the Plaza del Doctor Laguna. On the far side of the little park you will see the battlemented tower of the **Arias-Dávila palace**—the finest of its kind in Segovia.

After passing the tower, two streets farther and down some steps will bring you to the **Church of San Martín.** Here is Segovia's finest Romanesque church. Its exterior galleries, portal, and porch are quite exceptional. You should study this magnificent church from different angles. The outer porticos, which distinguish so many of Segovia's Romanesque churches, are a regional characteristic. They offer protection from the sun in summer and on cold, clear winter days are often warmer than the church's interior. (Open summer only, 9:00–12:00; all year during Sunday Mass.)

Just below the church is the little square of Plaza de San Martín. The high, square-topped tower rising behind the **statue of Juan Bravo,** leader of the revolt against Charles V, is the fifteenth-century **Casa de Lozoya,** one of the finest residences in Segovia.

At this point you should stroll along the **Calle Real** (officially, the Calle Juan Bravo) for a few moments toward the Plaza Mayor. Just before you reach the square you will pass on the left the **Convent of**

Corpus Christi (open 10:00–1:00 and 3:00–6:00). Before 1410 this was the leading synagogue of Segovia's important Jewish community.

Retrace your steps to the Plaza de San Martín. On the right you will find several interesting and fine Segovian residences. One, the **Casa del Siglo XV,** a charming fifteenth-century house with a balcony, is now a tastefully restored gift shop. Another, the Gothic palace of the **Conde Alpuente,** is located a few yards down a little lane. The third one you should notice is the **Casa de Tordesillas** at No. 40 on the Calle J. Bravo—a house with a decorative façade and graceful arches above the portal.

A little farther on the left, you will come to the fortresslike façade of the **Casa de los Picos.** It was built about 1500, but a hundred years earlier had been a fortified mansion to defend this gate of the city.

From here continue down the main street, and shortly you will see ahead the majestic arches of the great **Aqueduct.** Dating from the days of Trajan, this remarkable construction is one of the best-preserved Roman aqueducts in Europe. It is hard to realize that these tremendous blocks of granite have stood for two thousand years without any mortar to hold them together. As you look up at the highest of its arches (93 feet), you will be impressed by the well-proportioned tapering pillars that give an extraordinary effect of lightness and slenderness to the entire structure. The conduit above the double tier of arches is about a half mile long and still carries water to the city.

When you reach the **Plaza del Azoguejo,** walk under the arches for a short distance in order to see the Aqueduct from beneath, and from a different angle on the other side. It is particularly effective to stand on the side away from the sun to see the design created by the light and shade.

By now you are probably ready for a late lunch. The **Mesón del Candido** in the Plaza del Azoguejo, an attractive medieval house full of Castilian atmosphere, is the best restaurant in Segovia, but if you are in tourist attire, you are better off going to one of the less formal eating places on the Plaza Mayor; or try the **Casa Armado** at No. 9, **Avenida de Fernández Ladreda,** which is on your right as you face the Mesón del Candido. After lunch, stroll right at the fork and walk under the arcades on the right-hand side of the street for a short distance to the **Church of San Millán.** The exterior of this pure Romanesque church is particularly beautiful, especially the arcaded gallery, portal, and apse. Go inside to see the Mudejar carved roof and carved columns of the nave.

Before going to the **bridge below the Alcázar,** as suggested earlier, stroll back to the Aqueduct. These two monuments, each so extraordinarily dramatic and thrilling and yet so completely different, provide the two poles for a delightful and interesting walk through medieval Segovia.

INDEX

Numbers in *italics* refer to maps.